THE WORK OF WRITING

THE WORK
OF WRITING

Literature and Social Change in Britain, 1700–1830

CLIFFORD SISKIN

The Johns Hopkins University Press
Baltimore and London

07 06 05 04 03 02 01 00 99 98   5 4 3 2 1

The Johns Hopkins University Press
2715 North Charles Street
Baltimore, Maryland 21218-4319
The Johns Hopkins Press Ltd., London

Library of Congress Cataloging-in-Publication Data
will be found at the end of this book.
A catalog record for this book is available from the British Library.

ISBN 0-8018-5696-5

Part of Chapter 2 appeared in earlier form as "Gender, Sublimity, Culture: Re-theorizing Disciplinary Desire," *Eighteenth-Century Studies* 28, no. 1 (Fall 1994): 37–50. Parts of Chapter 4 appeared in earlier form as "Working *The Prelude*," in *The Prelude: Theory and Practice,* ed. Nigel Wood (Buckingham, England: Open University Press, 1993) 98–124, and as "Wordsworth's Prescriptions: Romanticism and Professional Power," copyright © 1990 by Clifford Siskin, from *The Romantics and Us: Essays on Literature and Culture,* ed. Gene W. Ruoff, copyright © 1990 by Rutgers, The State University. Reprinted by permission of Rutgers University Press. Part of Chapter 5 appeared in earlier form as "The Lyric Mix: Romanticism, Genre, and the Fate of Literature," *The Wordsworth Circle* XXV, no. 1 (Winter 1994): 7–10. Part of Chapter 6 appeared in earlier form as "Eighteenth-Century Periodicals and the Romantic Rise of the Novel," *Studies in the Novel* 26 (Spring/Summer 1994). Copyright by the University of North Texas in 1994. Reprinted by permission of the publisher. Part of Chapter 7 appeared in earlier form as "The Rise of Novelism," in *Cultural Institutions of the Novel,* ed. Deidre Lynch and William B. Warner (Durham, N.C.: Duke University Press, 1996) 423–40. All rights reserved. Part of Chapter 8 appeared in earlier form as "Austen and the Engendering of Disciplinarity," copyright © Devoney Looser from *Jane Austen and the Discourses of Feminism* by Devoney Looser (1995). Reprinted with permission of St. Martin's Press, Incorporated, and Macmillan Press Ltd.

To Johanna, Nathaniel, Corin, and Leslie

CONTENTS

ACKNOWLEDGMENTS

The work of writing this book has fallen on more shoulders than my own—the closer to me, the heavier the burden. That means acknowledging family first, a generic twist to open a book that traces the twists and turns of genres. Johanna as the youngest has had to bear up at home with me the longest, Nathaniel (after leaving for college) lost his bedroom to books, and Corin has, at every gift-giving occasion, worked to figure out what someone who writes on writing really wants to read. Leslie Santee Siskin read—and read again—all I wrote while somehow writing two books of her own. I thank my parents, Roy and Dorothy Siskin, who keep spaces on their shelf for all of our efforts, and Marlene and Marshall Miller for providing an outlet, and their company, in Delaware.

During a two-year stay in Palo Alto, I came to know as colleagues Herbert Lindenberger and John Bender. This book is in large part a product of their friendship and professionalism. It has also been shaped by the ongoing companionship and ideas of Anne Mellor and Philip Martin. Conversations with—and the support of—Marilyn Butler and William Warner have been invaluable. I am grateful as well to Nancy Armstrong, Marshall Brown, Stuart Curran, Len Findlay, Robert Folkenflik, J. Paul Hunter, Elizabeth MacArthur, Michael McKeon, Douglas Patey, Mary Poovey, John Richetti, Len Tennenhouse, James Thompson, and Martha Woodmansee.

Here at Stony Brook, I have enjoyed the support of Michael Sprinker, Helen Cooper, Lou Deutsch, Ann Kaplan, Ira Livingston, and Adrienne Munich. Repeated visits to the United Kingdom have introduced me to an additional pool of colleagues, including (in addition to those cited above and below) Stephen Copley, Robert Cummings, Josie Dixon, Tom Furniss, Vivien Jones, Dorothy Porter MacMillan, David Norbrook, Stephen Prickett, David Punter, Nicholas Roe, Nicola Trott, John Whale, and Duncan Wu.

The institutional support for this project has been significant. I thank Wayne State University for starting me off with a very generous Career Development Chair and the English Department at Stanford University for hosting me as a Visiting Scholar. My next base was the Stanford Humanities Center; I am particularly grateful for the material and intellectual support of its director, Bliss Carnochan. Since my arrival at the State University of New York at Stony Brook, the Dean's Office and the English Department have provided funds for travel and equipment. I thank, as well, the United University Professions for three travel grants.

During 1995 and 1996, I completed this book with the help of an Honorary Senior Research Fellowship from the University of Glasgow and a Visiting Fellowship from Magdalen College, Oxford University; Magdalen also appointed me the Waynflete Lecturer. I am deeply grateful to President Smith and the members of Magdalen's Senior Common Room for an extraordinarily pleasurable and profitable stay in Oxford. To J. Drummond Bone and Richard Cronin I owe thanks for a remarkable series of visits to Glasgow—remarkable both for the library resources I found and for the collective collegiality of the English Department.

In addition to the very helpful reference personnel at the Glasgow Library, I wish to thank the library staffs at Stanford University (particularly Mary Sevilla), SUNY Stony Brook, SUNY Buffalo (particularly Gayle Hardy), Magdalen College, and the Bodleian. Thanks as well to the consistently first-rate students in my graduate seminars at Stony Brook, some of whom will find themselves cited in the Notes. Finally, I am grateful for the straightforward advice of Willis Regier, Director of the Johns Hopkins University Press, and for the care his staff has taken with this book.

The Argument

WRITING AS A NEW TECHNOLOGY

§● The written word, it seems, has lost its power to undermine the morals of an individual. But video, and now the Internet—for many technophobes a synonym for pornography—have yielded profitable scare stories in even the most respectable newspapers. —Robert Potts, *The Guardian*, 1996

Present and Past

This book is about the changes—sudden and violent as well as slow and impalpable—that haunt the advent of new technologies. I write this on a morning—November 27, 1995—that New York City is haunted by the image of Harry Kaufman, set afire by two men who squirted flammable liquid into his subway token booth.[1] There was no immediate precedent; seven years had passed since the last such attack. However, a film called *The Money Train* opened the same weekend—a film that depicts two nearly identical incidents. This "strong coincidence," as the police commissioner put it, adds to the confusion we now face in coming to terms with new forms of representation and communication. From similar "coincidences," such as teenagers being run over while imitating characters from a movie, to concerns over the effect of television on attention spans, to efforts to censor the Internet—as well as more positive claims for the transformative powers of global communication and of virtual reality—we seem to be asking not just "What do we do with these technologies?" but "What are these technologies doing to us?"

My purpose here is not to answer such questions by predicting a future, but to clarify the stakes by recovering their past. Echoes of their mix of promise and threat, anticipation and dread, resound in the writings of the eighteenth and early nineteenth centuries in Britain—a time and a place when the newly disturbing technology was writing itself. This book is about that earlier technological shift. It argues that the proliferation of writing—in print and through silent reading—worked to induce and shape substantial change; in fact, even the thought that it might or could do so was often self-fulfilling. What changed—strikingly and fundamentally—were that society's ways of knowing and of working; the eighteenth and early nineteenth centuries in Britain saw the simultaneous advent of modern disciplinarity, on the one hand, and modern professionalism, on the other.

I focus on these new divisions of knowledge and of labor, and on the engendering, at their intersection, of the discipline that took writing as its professional work: Literature. By *engendering*, I mean to call attention both to the historicity of Literature as a newly restricted arena for the work of writing and to the ways those restrictions followed and produced faultlines of gender, excluding women writers in startlingly systematic ways. The result of all of these changes, I conclude, was that a technology that haunted its users early in the eighteenth century was largely domesticated a century later—writing became, that is, a powerful part of the everyday life of a nation.

Having lived so comfortably and so long with this now mundane technology, we must work to reconstruct the shock that accompanied its initial spread in Britain. Writing proliferated then as something new through, in large part, writing about writing—that is, writers throughout the eighteenth century were so astonished by the sheer volume of writing they began to encounter that they wrote about it—and thereby astonished themselves.[2] The engine here was not the oft-cited growth of the reading public or rise in the literacy rate. To use *writing* as shorthand for the entire configuration of writing, print, and silent reading[3] is to cast its proliferation as not simply a matter of when and how many learned a skill, but of skills interacting in practice.

In fact, as J. Paul Hunter has pointed out, the most reliable studies suggest that, since the primary literacy boom occurred during the first three quarters not of the eighteenth but of the seventeenth century, it is not at all certain that a child in 1775 was more likely to learn to read than a child in 1675.[4] Thus the proportion of literates may not have increased during the first eight decades of the eighteenth century, but what did grow was the amount of writing—a rise in both kinds and quantity in print and in situations calling for that practice. The combined circulation of newspapers, for example, increased eight-fold in only forty-five years, between 1712 and 1757.[5] That surge in print provoked Pope in *The Dunciad* and then alarmed Johnson, who, in writing up his age as the Age of Authors, also linked the power of writing to a sense of being overpowered: the province of writing was being invaded by the busy part of mankind.[6] New forms of busi-ness—particularly, as I argue in Chapters 4 and 5, the advent of modern professionalism—helped to fuel this increase in the practice of writing, whether the result was a novel, an account book, a contract, or an exam. More people had more occasions to write more. And, even if their contact with writing was limited to reading, or to hearing it read aloud, "everyone," concludes Henri-Jean Martin, "felt surrounded by written culture."[7]

A recurring topic of concern was the probable effects of this activity. As with the speculations I cited earlier regarding the influence of today's technologies on attention spans, family values, and even scholarly productivity, so, back then, the new technology of writing gazed self-reflexively on its own unknown potential: a large part of what people wrote and how they wrote had to do with often discomforting expectations regarding the productive power of writing. Thus to classify the innumerable warnings against young women reading novels as simply a manifestation of Augustan conservatism is to miss the historical point—the particular attitude toward change was secondary to a primary issue: writing's capacity to produce that change.

The history of writing[8] I am trying to recover is thus—remember Harry Kaufman—a tale of high stakes: what changed and who paid the price. I realize that each of the changing classifications I examine—disciplinarity, professionalism, and Literature, as well as gender—merits its own book, and thus this one risks criticism for what it leaves out in trying to engage them all. But I hope my readers will be convinced that the gaps are worth it, for this project is not about any one of the separate categories but about how—as I observed earlier regarding the skills of reading and writing—they interrelated in practice. Given, for example, the historical sequence I have described above—the rise in writing occurring after the rise in the literacy rate—one fundamental form of practical, interactive change was the transformation of reader into writer. To grasp its impact, we need again to juxtapose past and present technologies. The current heightened concern with the behavioral consequences of electronic media is occurring—not surprisingly—at the moment at which more people are becoming more behaviorally invested in them. As they appear on stages, in the audiences, and on the telephones of talk shows, and as they star in, shoot, mail in, and display videos on network programs and local cable channels, formerly passive viewers become participants in, and partial producers of, what they consume.

The middle decades of the eighteenth century saw parallel forms of investment in writing, particularly in the form that was proliferating most substantially at that time: periodicals. As I discuss in detail in Chapter 6, increasing numbers of readers became writers, their flow of contributions inducing the flow of capital, for this was the appropriation of surplus value in its purest form: almost all of this material was provided (and could be reprinted) for free. New periodicals could thus be launched and sustained with very little capital, making them a primary engine for the take-off in overall publication levels in the latter part of the century. Writing induced a fundamental change in readers—leading them to behave as writers—which, in turn, induced more writing. Writing's capacity to produce change, in other words, was, in this basic way, historically crucial to what I have been calling its *proliferation*—the production of more writing.

For those experiencing these specific historical changes—both the initial proliferation of writing and their innovatively transformative roles within it—a central concern became who and what else would be changed and in what ways. That concern was at issue in every act of writing in the eighteenth century, such as taking the newly instituted exams that could change your occupation, and in every kind, such as the tracts of political economy which, in David McNally's words, constituted "an attempt to theorize the inner dynamics of changes [toward capitalism] *in order to shape and direct them*" (emphasis mine).[9] This same imperative of change informed Priestley's strategy of writing a history of electricity to *induce* scientific progress[10] and Hume's efforts to wreak "havoc" on libraries by writing philosophy.[11]

The Power of Writing

Engaging the problem of the constitutive power of writing is thus a crucial historical and theoretical step in this book. I argue in Chapter 4 that writing was one kind of work—among the eighteenth century's growing multiplicity of kinds—and that, in representing itself as a type of labor, writing played a critical role in valorizing and hierarchizing other kinds. It was during the eighteenth century that knowledge crucial to those kinds was first classified and written down within the subject-specific boundary lines that now configure the universities and the culture they help to articulate.[12] It was during the latter half of that same century that those lines were institutionalized through such acts as the founding of the Sunday schools and systems of credentialing, including written examinations.[13] And, it was also then that the ranks of the literate—whatever their precise rate of growth—became filled with those who would take the tests.

This issue of whether those who possess skills are willing to practice them arises at both chronological ends of what Raymond Williams has called "the history of writing"—the tale of how, after only two hundred years,[14] the "standard" ways of using writing, print, and silent reading are already undergoing change. If, at our end of that history, the technological shift from the written word to electronic media is furthering what sociologists are now calling *aliteracy*—being able to read and write but choosing not to—then we need to explore, at the other end, how the choice *to* use those skills was first made. Unprecedented numbers of people learned both the skills *and*—that crucial component of modern literacy—the belief in their transformative power[15]: that writing was work that worked on an individual level and on a national one, producing cultured individuals privileged in sharing a national culture.

I speak of *writing* rather than *Literature* as a way of acknowledging that only *as a result of this very process* did the latter term come into its present meaning. *Literary,* which had been synonymous with *literate* in the sense of being well-read, was not, until the eighteenth century, identified with the practice and profession of writing. And, only then were it, and *literature,* even more specifically written up—hierarchically up—as referring solely to special kinds of deeply imaginative writing.[16] Thus in the same century that writing first classified itself within the everyday world of work—Defoe actually described it as a "very considerable branch of English commerce"[17]—writing's work was to rewrite that world, including itself, in terms we now find familiar: hierarchical specialization—a dividing up of knowledge and of tasks (and thus of the individuals who know and work)—figured and valorized as depth.

My argument thus links disciplinarity, professionalism, and Literature together as *historical* categories—categories constituted through acts of classification—acts that select hierarchically, and thus empower, particular kinds of knowledge, particular kinds of work, and particular kinds of writing. That empowerment has, in turn, entailed the naturalizing of those hierarchies, such that disciplinarity became the proper path to truth, professionalism became an unavoidable product of economic development, and the selection we know as Literature became the transcendent output of the human imagination—simply the best.

My point is not that these formations were or are "wrong" but that they are bound to a particular historical moment and to a particular technology—the classifying, hierarchizing, and naturalizing largely transpire *in* writing. The first two sections of this book map out some of the generic locations for this work of writing. The final two focus on Literature as the location where writing's role was both more intense—it is the end as well as the means—and more constrained—by imperatives of beauty and pleasure as well as by standards of disciplinary truth and professional expertise.

As such, I argue, Literature assumed a key role in the new organizations of knowledge and of labor as a specialization, but one that all of the others had in common—the prerequisite for entering them as autonomous professional fields. "Men are men before they are lawyers," wrote Mill,[18] who found humanity in Literature (through Wordsworth) rather than Latin. Literature's power as well as the sense that it is powerlessly detached from the real world lie in this classificatory ambiguity, for that ambiguity was not, historically, a falling away from already defined alternatives—professional/amateur, discipline/avocation, real/made up—but a means of generating and empowering them.

In recovering that history—in putting Literature into a history of writing—I join literary and social historians, sociologists, and others in the tasks of denaturalizing those still familiar formations. What I try to recover and index with terms such as *discomfort* and *domesticate* is just how that familiarity was achieved. "Comfort" levels point not to deep psychological truths, but to this rewriting of writing—its transformation from a threatening prescriptive technology into the transcendent but more cipherlike—and, as I argue in Chapter 8, "safe"—tool of Literature. In tracing that transformation, I try to pinpoint the price of such comfort, particularly for the women writers erased, until recently, from the memory of that discipline.

Today, as new technologies disrupt the norms of print culture, discomfort is on the rise, and new prices are being negotiated. But writing and writers are still very much at the negotiating table; in the quotation that heads this chapter, writing in the form of the newspaper works now to warn against the latest technological threats. New technologies, in other words, do not simply replace the old; they tend, in fact, to provide their predecessors with new contexts and uses. This book, by recovering the work that writing has performed, points to what it still can do—and what is at stake in doing it.

Current Crises

For those of us now working professionally in the disciplinary home of writing, for example, an alternative vocabulary for where we are and what we do is a place to start. As part of bringing the past to bear upon the present, I turn repeatedly to Wordsworth's term for his work, the "experiment" of Literature. Playing upon the ambiguity that *experiment*[19] still carried at that time opens, conceptually, some possibilities in ours: back then, it could have meant *experience*, and thus something that changes us, or, the now more common, *controlled trial*, and thus something that we can change—which, in fact, we are supposed to change. While still entertaining the former possibility, we can—without submitting ourselves and our departments to the divisive trauma of birth and death metaphors—act on the latter, assessing Literature's results and rethinking its hypotheses, ingredients, and procedures. In that way the disciplinary and professional work of writing may lead to some newly compelling forms of knowledge and of labor.

This gesture toward the "new" is not simply Romantic habit; although the advent of new electronic technologies has not, as I have been emphasizing, made the writing-based organizations of knowledge and labor obsolete, we certainly do experience them as older. All three of my central categories—disciplinarity, professionalism, and Literature—are currently meeting this fate; in fact, that is why I have arranged my argument around them. They are disturbed and disturbing; somehow, staying within one's discipline, being a professional, and knowing and working—or trying to get work—within an English department have become newly unsettling undertakings. The Death-of-Literature debate is that experience of change in particularly melodramatic form, but it also assumes more hopeful guises—interdisciplinarity as the cure for disciplinary limits—and more befuddling ones—professionalism as both excessively powerful *and* imminently threatened by an omnivorous service sector. In every case, what worked before does not seem to work in quite the same way anymore.

That means, quite simply, that we cannot work in quite the

same ways. If we do, we will find ourselves in the same binds I have just described: committing departmental suicide over an inorganic matter, seeking salvation from disciplinary limits by taking on more discipline, and feeling disempowered by the very status we have strived to attain. Even more self-defeating are the standard cause-and-effect scenarios that attempt to link these categories, such as blaming the current problems of Literature on professionalization, as if the latter stalked an originally pure (amateur?) version of the former.

To construct a diachronic narrative about any of these categories—to describe how they have changed and are changing—we need to address their synchronic interrelations—how they connect to each other at particular historical moments. When we do, scenarios such as the above can be reconstructed—as I do in more detail later in this book—in less dead-end terms. Literature, as I have just suggested, can be reengaged as experimental rather than mortal and thus renewable and—possibly—refundable. Interdisciplinarity—an activity that leaves the unit of knowledge intact even as it allows multiple units to interact—can be reconceived as only a transitional effect of what I call *dedisciplinarity*—the historical movement *from* increasingly unworkable forms of specialization. And, the currently ambiguous status of professionalism can be clarified—once we recognize that its capacity to empower any particular occupation is indexed to the historical viability of the technology informing that occupation. Literature has not been "ruined" by professionalization[20]—they did and do articulate each other; what is putting it in jeopardy is the difficulty of renegotiating its reliance on the now older technology of writing.

Chronology: 1700–1830

Age, in this case, is not a sign of inevitable obsolescence but an opportunity to innovate. I am working, of course, *in* writing, and in a traditional form of writing: the *book,* consisting of essaylike chapters that are intended to cohere as a whole. But in what I am trying to make cohere, and in how, lies a consistent—or at least persistent—effort to innovate through the mixing of inherited features. The chronological range of the book, for example—a crucial feature in matching works of literary history and criticism to an audience—is a deliberate mix of standard periods: the eighteenth century and Romanticism.

Putting dates of any kind into the subtitle is, first of all, a signal that what lies within is not an absolute theory of how writing works—in any time and in any place; rather, it is a description of some of the work that writing did do at that time in Britain. By specifying those dates as 1700 to 1830, I am deliberately trying to call into question the way that literary history has traditionally divided that span of time. As one of the very few conference-goers who attends both Romantic association meetings and those held for eighteenth-century studies, I am all too aware of the power of that division to constrain, in frequently frustrating fashion, the questions and answers posed by both groups.

This is particularly true in regard to the questions I want to pose about the history of writing. On the one hand, leaving off the years we call Romantic would prevent me from seeing and describing how, with the surge of print at the close of the century, concerns about writing consolidated into the pleasurable familiarity of Literature. On the other hand, skipping over the eighteenth century to start with Wordsworth's experimental turn to "pleasure" in 1798 would be similarly debilitating, for I would then be at a loss to explain why such experimentation was necessary.

Widening the chronological scope to well over a century can help to minimize such losses, but with an accompanying proviso: since covering every twist and turn of writing for that length of time exceeds the feasible, and useful, scope of any single book, my dates are offered as a range within which I can productively range, both identifying large-scale changes and accumulating key evidence for them. At first glance it may seem that this span should fall simply under the increasingly popular rubric of the *long eighteenth century,* or even the counterpart that Philip Martin and I have suggested to Romanticists fearful of the scholarly imperialism of their eighteenth-century neighbors: *long Romanticism.*[21] My purpose in mixing periods, however, is not to insist on dissolving standard boundaries but to test them under new conditions—within, that is, the larger spread.

The year 1700 is the marker for a cluster of turn-of-the-century events which helped to accelerate Britain's transformation into a print culture. With the lapsing of the Print Act during the parliamentary session of 1694–95, censorship through official licensing came to an end, and the political and legal maneuvering that led, after three quarters of a century, to the modern system of copyright (see Chapter 4) began. The stage was also set for the entry of the printers and booksellers of Ireland and Scotland into a print world that had been dominated by London; print both proliferated and performed a new role in nation building.[22]

An important part of that proliferation was writing by women, and 1694 also saw the publication of Part 1 of Mary Astell's *A Serious Proposal to the Ladies,* an exemplary event in the spread of print. Not only did it lead to Part 2 and numerous editions, but it also elicited an ongoing response: "Redeem the coming age!" wrote Elizabeth Thomas in a poem to Astell in 1722, "and set us free / From the false brand of incapacity."[23] Paralleling the growth of this discourse of gender difference was the emergence of innovative work on the nature of work roused, in part, by Dryden's translation of Virgil's *Georgics* published in 1697. Add in the late seventeenth-century spread of newspapers and the early eighteenth-century advent of the periodical project, and one has a strong case for using the roundness of 1700 to highlight the onset of significant change in the form, content, and contexts of writing.

The year 1830 may appear to be an obvious candidate for the endpoint, since it matches roughly the conventional close of British Romanticism, but it arises from this book for different reasons. A combination of technological and economic change points to the third decade of the nineteenth century as a kind of watershed: beyond that point lies the modern—in Williams's terms, fully "naturalized"—world of print.

- In that world, the basic printing processes, from papermaking to typesetting to the press itself, are fully mechanized—a point reached by roughly 1830 after decades of largely British innovations that were then followed, with the start of the railroads during that same decade, by the mechanization of the distribution network.[24]

- In that world, the products of those processes are priced for, and thus help create, a mass market—by 1830, following the early lead of tract and bible societies, major publishers began to issue low-cost books in paperbound and serial format aimed at a wide range of readers, with particularly precipitous price drops occasioned by the economic crises of the late 1820s.[25]

- In that world, this mass market is configured hierarchically into different levels of "culture" through procedures of reprinting, anthologizing, and illustration—by 1830, almost all publishers refused to publish the generic marker of High Romanticism— standalone volumes of poetry—as sales shifted suddenly to new mixed forms, particularly multivolume "libraries," illustrated literary annuals, and gift-book anthologies.[26]

- And, crucially, in that world, as I hope this book helps to demonstrate, the flow of writing itself, from production through consumption, is regulated and rationalized within hierarchical organizations of knowledge and of work—by the 1830s, both disciplinarity and professionalism were being instituted in their now familiar forms.[27]

Courses in English Literature, for example, were being taught in English universities,[28] and a section of school could, in Ian Michael's words, "be known as the English Department."[29] Departmentalization of newly forming disciplines brought new links between new educational institutions, such as London University, and the professions.[30] The latter were, at the same time, proliferating and thriving—as a result both of the professionalization of more occupations, such as engineering, and of the transformation of the traditional professions into their modern guises. Medicine, already engaged in an ongoing process of reform highlighted by the Apothecaries Act of 1815, saw, in the early 1830s, both new forms of empowerment—with legal access to bodies thanks to the Anatomy Act of 1833—and of regulation. The new controls were sometimes self-imposed, as with the association formed in Worcester in

1832, which evolved into the British Medical Association; others, however, were imposed from without, such as the 1834 Select Committee of the House of Commons investigating medical education.

The law also saw new professional associations, such as the one that later became the Law Society after being founded in 1825 and granted a royal charter in 1831.[31] Until then, professional training had been an almost exclusively oral affair—barristers, for example, chose between listening to lectures or eating a certain number of dinners at the Inns of Court.[32] Association and regulation, however, required another form of communication. The late eighteenth-century turn toward examinations, both inside and outside the universities, led those institutions, by 1830, to the technology of writing: the Oxford University Commission, reporting at mid century, noted that by 1825 examinations were already conducted "more and more on paper," leading three years later to a plan to print the questions. A foreign visitor "put his finger," to borrow A. M. Carr-Saunders and P. A. Wilson's words, upon the new system's "novel feature when he described the tests as consisting of 'extemporaneous *writing*'" (emphasis mine).[33]

The year 1830, then, emerges across my categories, halting my argument at roughly the time that the deployment of writing in Britain can be said to have largely assumed its most familiar forms. That time also saw, appropriately enough, the debut of the *next* new technology—one with which we are just now becoming familiar: in 1832, Charles Babbage demonstrated in London a version of his "Difference Engine," the first automatic computing device.[34] The fact that this date—in fact, 1832 in particular as the date of the Reform Bill[35]—also marks the traditional terminus for Romanticism is a significant outcome of my mixing of periods— especially in conjunction with the new weight my argument gives to the years that period is usually understood to start. I point to the 1780s and 1790s as the time that both population and print took off, that both lyricization and the boom-and-bust cycles endemic to industrialization began in earnest (see Chapter 5), that the genre of the novel rose quantitatively into a newly forming two-tier market (see Chapters 6 and 7), and that the working lives of women—literary and otherwise—were radically reshaped, as sharp (but Romantically brief) increases in the gross reproductive rate and in poor relief coincided with newly constricted options in both agriculture and authorship (see Chapter 9).

This combination of familiar dates and not-so-familiar changes is an important benefit of the mixing of periods in this book, for such mixing is not simply a gesture to dissolve boundaries, but a procedure to help us to rethink where they might be placed and to what ends. I discovered that a period with Romantic dimensions[36] — 1780 to 1830 — curiously re-formed within my narratives. But it did so not as the standard stretch of "imaginative" writing celebrated within histories of Literature; it appeared, instead, as the time span in which Literature itself — thanks to changes such as those I have named above — was consolidated as a newly narrowed category in the history of writing.

Methodology: Literature in the History of Writing

Realigning writing, Romanticism, and Literature in this manner is a crucial task of this book for it helps us to negotiate a central paradox posed by the last decade of historicist work on Romanticism: how to write about Romanticism without being Romantic. Whether seen as a feature of the Romantic ideology or as the ongoing addiction I centered in *The Historicity of Romantic Discourse*,[37] that form of repetition is our critical fate *if* we leave Romanticism inside Literature as only one its periods; this book intervenes by putting Literature within a re-formed Romanticism. The reason, in other words, that Romantic discourse so thoroughly penetrates the study of Literature is that Literature emerged in its presently narrowed — but thus deep and disciplinary — form during that period and thus *in* that discourse. To access the period, and thus Literature, in a less repetitive way, we need to step into a frame that can contain both.

Once we step into a history of writing, features found historically in Romantic discourse — spontaneity, intensity, depth — are less likely to be sublimed habitually into timeless markers of "great" Literature; they can be read, instead, as evidence of how writing was naturalized at that time by confounding textual effects[38] with authorial behavior—what writers did instead of what writing could do. It was not that issues regarding writing, language, and textuality were ignored, but that the mode of attention was systematically psychologized; in the large-scale terms of my argument, concern shifted from the potentially disruptive power of the technology of writing to the supposedly disrupted personalities of people who wrote. The literary landscape of the late eighteenth and early nineteenth centuries began to be portrayed as increasingly littered by newly fixed types: authors who were—like many of their characters—strange, mad, addicted, or suicidal.

I historicize Wordsworth's version, as found in "Resolution and Independence," in Chapter 1. Figures such as his disturbed poet can, like the periods they inhabit, tell different stories when no longer habitually subsumed within histories of Literature.[39] Genres, I maintain, can be similarly articulate. The standard generic stories told from that habit tend, like those told of authors, to focus on individual states of health: isolated from each other—often by period as well as by kind—each genre is made to measure up to Literature's standards. Thus the novel rises in the eighteenth century, and then the lyric blossoms into Romanticism. Mixing genres as it does periods, this book is structured to provide an alternative to such tales of aesthetic development, recovering the interrelations of genres with each other and with contemporaneous categories of knowledge and of labor. Threads regarding disciplinarity, professionalism, and Literature run over and under chapter threads on genres; all are sequenced to highlight both the overarching comparison between past and present technological changes and the key role of gender in those changes.

This weave results, I believe, not only in a different design, but in a different fabric than most other literary histories. By that I mean its primary content—what it produces knowledge about—is not *individual* authors, texts, themes, periods, or genres; as I have been stressing, my procedure is relentlessly combinatory, mixing categories in ways that turn even the categories themselves into objects of historical knowledge. Thus, in addition to re-forming periods, such as Romanticism, I analyze, as well, the critical role of the Author in the formation of Literature (see Chapter 6). This decision to "zoom out," as Steven Johnson puts the turn, from individuality to "system" may "alarm many critics trained in close readings."

I was so trained, and I do read texts closely, but in this book "close reading" itself falls—like the Author—under historical scrutiny, appearing as a particular kind of work tied to a particular kind of knowledge. The professional function of close reading in the discipline of Literature is to extract meaning, and possibly intention, from individual texts; the aesthetic value generated by the Author is supposed to be transformed expertly, by the critic's labor, into pleasurable knowledge for the reader. That transformation is what I would call *the work of Literature.* My turn to the *work of writing* is, in comparison, a turn from reading individual texts as the creations of individual Authors to placing them within the proliferation of a newly dominant technology, from ranking them within an aesthetic field that tends toward the absolute to grouping them within forms that mix hierarchically, but in historically specific ways. In doing so, however, I am not surrendering close-ness, or, I hope, pleasure; there is more than one way to be close—in reconstruing the object of knowledge, I am also reworking how to gain proximity to it.

Zooming out, in other words, can also be a way of zooming in. Although Johnson uses the notion of "zooming" to describe what happens when "chaos theory" mixes with literary criticism, he centers the same objects of knowledge which I do:

> Successful genres, for instance, function much like basins of attraction, luring the entire literary system toward their repeated patterns. Imagine a turbulent soup of different genres jockeying for attention within the culture at large, with no single attractor in sight—until a phase transition kicks in and the entire system organizes itself around a dominant genre in a matter of years. The story of the novel follows this pattern precisely.

To write such stories with authority, however, is not an easy disciplinary task. A literary criticism with "historical interests" in reorganization, Johnson observes, would have to arrive at an "understanding" of genres and a means of "classifying" their "formal devices."[40]

It is as part of that effort, I would maintain, that close-ness and its object need to be redefined. In Chapter 5, for example, I do read individual lyrics to provide evidence for my argument, but the focus of that argument is on the lyric as a kind of writing. This generic emphasis steers my gaze in two directions. On the one hand, as Ralph Cohen argues, "a genre does not exist independently; it arises to compete or to contrast with other genres . . . so that its aims and purposes at a particular time are defined by its interrelation with and differentiation from others."[41] Thus, when I look closely at the lyric during the time span of this book, I see how it mixes with another kind of writing, the critical. On the other hand, a genre is also, in Charles Bazerman's words, "a social construct that regularizes communication, interaction, and relations."[42] As such, we can close the distance to the lyric even further by examining its interrelations with another social construct of the time: those changes in the division of labor which we now associate with modern professionalism.

Organization: Disciplinarity, Professionalism, and Literature

This book proceeds throughout in similar fashion: identifying generic change and linking it to the three central categories: disciplinarity, professionalism, and Literature. All three categories, of course, are contested, but what may appear to be simply incompatible claims as to their meanings and functions may be seen more productively as interdisciplinary debate: different deployments by different disciplines for different purposes—purposes that may or may not call each other into question. Disciplinarity has surfaced within sociology, for example, as a system of knowledge-based sites for the distribution of institutional resources.[43] The emphases on the materiality of the sites as physical locations and on the politics of managing resources lend themselves to analyses of organizational behavior and institutional change.

Disciplinarity, as I use it as a literary historian, materializes in the technology of writing. Thus I can share with the historical sociologist an interest in how writing up a course as "English Literature" rather than "Rhetoric" helps to initiate disciplinary change, positioning the writer in relation to other teachers, and their courses, and into competition for students and institutional space. But that act, and others like it in Britain, were nineteenth-century acts largely outside of my time frame. I focus, instead, on the writing that helped to make those acts possible—on how they were prescribed by, in Bazerman's words, newly enabling constructs of communication, interaction, and relation. By *pre-scribed* I mean that the later, more visible changes were *written before*—written during the eighteenth-century proliferation, in quantity and in kind, of writing itself.

I emphasize *kind* because generic analysis provides us with a way of understanding and articulating how behaving in writing connects to other sorts of social behaviors.[44] "Texts are events and make history," as J. G. A. Pocock puts it, for "as they perform they inform."[45] What makes genre a particularly powerful analytic tool is that it not only provides us with ways of classifying the performances; the acts of classification themselves become performative events. Like individual texts, "stories of genre" are not, in the words of Kevin Sharpe and Stephen Zwicker, "merely evidence of cultural and political change" but "are themselves part of that history."[46] As I show in Chapter 7, for example, the different tales told about the novel in the eighteenth century functioned in very specific ways to configure the fate of that genre.

In telling this generic tale about genre itself, I hope, in similar fashion, to help to reshape it—to turn it into a tool for making historical sense out of different kinds of change. Ralph Cohen, for instance, can argue that

> an individual instance of a genre—*Oedipus Rex*—can reveal its individuality [not] only by comparison with other tragedies within the genre and within the oeuvre of Sophocles, but also by comparison with older oral genres. The conceptual change brought about by literacy permits us to identify a historical process of change. This

process includes the absorption of elements from nontragic forms to tragedy and in particular to Sophoclean tragedy. If, in other words, we wish to study literature as an interrelated system of texts and society, generic distinctions offer us a procedure to accomplish this.[47]

This example links social and technological (oral/written) change to generic change by emphasizing what I have been calling the combinatory nature of the latter—that genres exist only in their interrelations with other genres. Thus Sophoclean tragedy, emerging out of a particular historical relationship between the oral and the written, includes features from nontragic forms in a mix that, to borrow Pocock's phrasing, "inform[s]" the society that performs it.

The proliferation of new mixtures in eighteenth- and early nineteenth-century Britain should thus alert us to both the technological changes that fueled such innovation—the advent of print culture—and the ways those mixtures prescribed innovative activity of other kinds. I relate the kind of knowledge production and consumption which we now call *disciplinarity* to a number of specific generic combinations. Those include political economy's mix of the historical and empirical within philosophical prose, the aforementioned cocooning of the lyric within the critical, and the multiplicity of fiction-ing devices within periodicals. Together they helped to naturalize *truth* as the goal of different forms of knowledge even as they regrouped those forms according to different modes of accessing that truth: the strategic commingling of description and data in the social sciences, the hermeneutic interplay of the creative and the critical in the humanities, and the hypothesizing of what is not yet known in the natural sciences.

In the opening section of this book I emphasize the logic that shapes these enterprises and thus unites them—a logic that makes historical sense only in relationship to the proliferation of writing. The increase not only in the quantity of writing but also in the number of new generic combinations it assumed threatened eighteenth-century Britain, conceptually and materially, with what even the writers themselves saw as a *Dunciad*-like excess of knowledge(s).

But the solution, for a nation working its way into the accelerated forms of production and consumption we call capitalism, was not to curb production but to control it—in fact, to control it in such a way that productivity was actually enhanced. What worked, that is, was more writing. The work that writing performed was to constitute new classification systems that could provide *discipline* in what I argue is its distinctly modern sense: control for the sake of growth.[48]

David Hume, for example, sought to identify newly "proper subjects" by wreaking what he called philosophical "havoc" on the existing libraries. His havoc, however, was a carefully construed new order that insisted, skeptically, on narrowness and limitation—not as caps to, but as the enabling conditions of, productivity. Subjects made narrow could become deep according to this new logic of specialization. In Chapter 1 I show how the depth that logic valorized became an index to productivity in different forms of human endeavor. The result was a shift in the ways of knowing from the older organization, in which every kind was a *branch* of philosophy, into our present system: narrow but deep disciplines divided between humanities and sciences.

In arguing for this distinctively modern sense of *discipline*, I am agreeing with David Shumway and Ellen Messer-Davidow that the very "persistence" of the term since classical times has "masked the historical specificity of the organization and production of knowledge." As they put it, "the branches of knowledge themselves, as well as what 'a branch of knowledge' even means, have changed radically."[49] Joseph Priestley's words of 1768—"all knowledge will be subdivided and extended"[50]—both describe this change into modern disciplinarity and enact it, for it is in and through the technology of writing that barriers are raised and depth achieved. In looking for the faultlines in the old field of moral philosophy which this new breakup into fields followed, I focus particularly, in Chapter 2, on divisions of gender and, in Chapter 3, on specific geographical locations and institutional practices.

Understanding disciplinarity in these historical terms clarifies its mutually constitutive relationship with professionalism. "The division of labour," observes sociologist Robert Dingwall, "is also

a division of knowledge," and "that knowledge is, moreover, a social product, reproducing and constituting a particular order."[51]
Since writing was an important technology of reproduction in both
of these reorderings, seeing it at work can help us to understand
how they interrelate: the shift from philosophical branching to
modern disciplinarity paralleled the transformation of the established liberal professions into modern professionalism. In both
cases, innovative behaviors were at least partially prescribed by new
combinations of genres which redefined work from an earlier
ideal—that which a true gentleman does not have to do—to the
primary activity informing adult identity. Even the very word
professional—as an adjective describing a specific set of behaviors—
first appeared at the turn into the nineteenth century, a moment
also marked lexically by the debut of terms of difference such as
amateur.

Chapters 4 and 5 focus on combinations featuring the georgic
and the lyric, showing how those genres helped both to prescribe
these specific changes in the nature of work and to establish the
terms by which those changes would appear natural. Whereas the
georgic prescribed under the rubric of *description,* valorizing representation itself as a new kind of work, the coupling of the lyric
to personal, subjective feeling—the *I* expressing itself—naturalized
what I call its "experimental" role: lyrics functioned as "data" in
innovative efforts to know the present by linking it developmentally to the past. I connect this new work of writing, such as the deployment of developmental narratives, to specific changes in Britain's larger world of work, including the shifts from apprenticeship
to education, from by-employments to occupation, and from
combinations to trade unions, as well as the accompanying valorization of mental over physical labor. As with disciplinarity, the
reorganization these changes effected was engendered. Professionalization, I emphasize, newly marginalized women as effectively as
the advent of Literature—signaled by Wordsworth's "experiment"
of *Lyrical Ballads*—reclaimed the lyric: saving it, as one critic put it,
from "fall[ing] into the hands of women and children, ploughmen
and mad folk."[52]

The place of Literature in these shifting organizations of

knowledge and work is my subject in the next four chapters. I do not, however, tell tales of discipline and professionalization which feature Literature as a rather passive and pristine undertaking, one that was somehow overtaken by less palatable processes. Although valuable, recent histories of the study of Literature in departments of English—by Gossman, Eagleton, Graff, and others[53]—begin chronologically at the nineteenth-century moment that this one ends: the institutionalization of a newly naturalized and narrowed category of writing into a curricular core. I work, instead, on the prescribing of that core—that is, on the naturalizing and the narrowing; I treat them as experimental procedures, in both of the eighteenth-century senses of the word *experiment* which I mentioned earlier. On the one hand, when naturalized, writing came to seem like *experience;* on the other, the hierarchical narrowing of literary experience was rationalized—as in Wordsworth's "quantity of pleasure" hypothesis—as simply accurate evaluation based on *controlled trial.* To be *in* Literature thus became the experience of attempting to be systematically selective, and therefore deeply truthful, about writing.

I examine naturalization by turning, in Chapters 6 and 7, to the novel, or, more precisely, the cluster of generic innovations I term *novelism;* focusing next on narrowing, I analyze exclusion by gender in Chapters 8 and 9, using as touchstones the canonical inclusion of Jane Austen and current communication theory. In these ways, Literature—as a selective category of knowledge, as a site for professional activity, and as a subset of the technology (writing) that helped to prescribe such change—presides historically and conceptually over the last two sections. But because it does so not as a given, explanatory category, but as that which must be explained, both genre and gender get to do some explaining of their own, telling unfamiliar tales about themselves and each other—unfamiliar in the evidence offered, strategies deployed, and conclusions drawn.

I place the "rise" of the novel, for example, in the supposedly lyrical period of Romanticism; what rose, however, was not just the number of individual novels, but novelism as well. By *novelism* I mean the habitual subordination of writing to the novel which made writing, by the end of a century initially obsessed with its dangers, comfortable—as in the flow from work to play we feel today as we reach for the bedside paperback and from the strange to the familiar as we include novels in multicultural syllabi. Comfort, though, has a price, and I conclude by locating the cost in what I call *The Great Forgetting*—a term for the various ways in which the disciplinary narrowing of Literature was also an act of gendering, largely leaving out writing by women.

Conceptual Goals

In turning to population and labor statistics in the last chapter and in coordinating figures for periodical fiction and for the novel in Chapter 7, I have an experimental purpose in mind—a purpose overlaying the local arguments: to help to reconceive literary study by mixing different kinds of data into it. I am not, of course, claiming to be the first literary scholar to work with numbers; in fact, my point is not only that *more* work should be done, but that we need to make effective use of what has *already* been done. Quantitative inquiry has been treated habitually as an admirable but isolated and minor part of the overall enterprise of literary study, its findings of telling importance only to others working the same vein.

That isolation will continue until the discipline starts to reconsider what Steven Johnson calls its "burden of proof" (50). The result need not—should not—be a wholesale conversion to "scientific" standards, but rather a recognition that different kinds of questions may require different kinds of proof: from, let us say, a numerical total, confirming the novel's rise, to a feeling, informing an aesthetic judgment. Johnson observes, for example, that literary critics with historical interests, who seek to understand change by zooming out from individual texts to a more inclusive system, would be in particular need of a solid understanding of the constituent parts of that larger whole. *Solid* and its sister terms such as *rigorous* and *hard* are, of course, matters of disciplinary and interdisciplinary agreement—of a shared sense of what the words mean and where and when data of that kind are desirable. By trying out different kinds from different disciplines—the numbers already mentioned, historical chronologies of education and copyright, sociological descriptions of the professions, communication theory—I seek not to impose or even propose a new consensus for literary studies, but to highlight the need for one.

To say *new* is not to suggest that there has been a prior period of calm consensus—Graff and others have detailed the frequently loud disagreements—but to indicate that the common ground that hosted those debates is itself shifting, thanks to the current historicizing of Literature. Since the specific strategy of this study is to move it into the history of writing, my efforts to reconceive Literature's disciplinary burden of proof carry with them two related conceptual goals. First, in weighing what kinds of material we should bring to bear upon arguments regarding writing, we need to engage the materiality of writing itself. By arguing that writing was a new technology in eighteenth-century Britain, I am asserting a historically specific capacity to make something. "Means of communication," in Raymond Williams's words, "are not only forms, but means of production, since communication and its material means are intrinsic to all distinctively human forms of labour and social organization, thus constituting indispensable elements both of the productive forces and of the social relations of production."[54]

The tendency *not* to engage writing as a productive, material practice arose, in fact, from the very set of social relations to which, in the eighteenth century, writing became indispensably related: the reorganization of work into mental versus physical labor. As writing became increasingly implicated, during that century, in (disciplinary) acts of knowing, and those acts were, in turn, valorized under the rubric of mental labor, the work of writing was idealized as a cipherlike medium for the power of mind. Again, this is not a matter of the technology losing its effectivity, but of the effects being naturalized—that is, relocated into the explanatory matrix of individual, human psychology.

This same hierarchical binary of mental over physical was reproduced even within writing itself, splitting it into the creative versus the critical. Reworking that distinction is thus another conceptual goal of this book as well as a link to its predecessor (*Historicity*

37–63). On the macro level of system, the problem, in the words of Peter Hohendahl, is whether "the structural position" of criticism is "opposed to, or within, the totality of literature."[55] Taken to the micro level, the fundamental nature of this problem of position—of whether the critical belongs inside—becomes clear: it challenges the integrity of what we conventionally think of as individual texts and distinct genres.

In what ways, for example, are the "lines" of verse which we call "Tintern Abbey" separable from the critical features with which they were initially mixed, including not only the Advertisement, Preface, Appendix, and Notes, but also the collective structure that mixed them with other lines according to a principle of mixed forms (lyric/ballad)? And cannot the eighteenth-century novel, written to amend the romance and read to recuperate the real, be profitably reconceived as itself a critical form? Certainly the amending and recuperating were not just performed by the part we partition off as "creative": the "story." To recover more fully what was done and how, might not a more inclusive rubric, such as *novelism*—embracing the full range of strategic features with which the story mixed, from prefaces and narrative frames to advertisements and reviews—be more useful? One might even argue that, as writing about writing produced more writing during the eighteenth century, all writing became—at that time and in that self-reflexive sense—critical. For us to cordon off certain features as inherently "critical" rather than "creative"—and thus, in Romantic terms, separate and inferior—may be to miss the historical point: what we take now to be secondary may have functioned, back then, as a primary condition and product of the act of writing itself, as long as that act was still experienced as new.

Specifying *where* as well as *when* is crucial to reconceiving how that writing worked. My initial decision to focus on Britain turned on two issues: a need to assert limits that would make the project feasible and the hope that such a focused study would effectively complement such geographically ambitious efforts linking writing and nation as Henri-Jean Martin's *The History and Power of Writing* and Benedict Anderson's *Imagined Communities*. I come away still admiring the power of such comparativism, but with a new respect for difference[56]—both as to how writing worked, genre by genre, in different nations, and as to the workings, nation by nation, of nationalism. Not only was the course of nationalism in Britain, as I mentioned earlier, peculiar to a newly united kingdom, but the nationalist workings of a genre such as the novel were also uniquely shaped—in Britain—by that genre's particular relationship to another genre, the periodical.

Gender has been the other surprising form of difference. The surprise was not that it played a central role in the changes in knowledge and labor I describe, but how swiftly and systematically gender differentiation was deployed—from the exclusion of women from the disciplinary adventures of the Royal Society[57] to the formation of protoprofessional groups that effectively screened women from occupations that had previously been open to them. Familiarity with the results today—how disciplinarity currently "fragments" the study of gender "so that," in the words of Ellen Messer-Davidow, "we locate it everywhere and, as it seems, significantly nowhere"[58]—hardly lessens the jolt of seeing earlier forms of fragmentation and dislocation at work. To gauge the extent to which that work was the work of writing, I have, in this book, situated gender both everywhere—it is engaged in every chapter—*and* somewhere—it is the main topic of the concluding section.

Literature emerges in that section as something made—to use the word I introduced earlier—*safe,* raising important political questions as to what and who were saved and why. As I frame this history, however, the safety of Literature is not only a matter of what is in it—Literature was and is, of course, a major and compelling carrier of political *content*—but of how the technology that does the carrying works and is understood to work.[59] Literature, this book argues, is, in important ways, a historically specific reply to a question about writing: How safe is the technology? As the fate of Harry Kaufman demonstrates graphically, that question presses upon the present with an urgency that recalls the past.

I DISCIPLINARITY

THE POLITICAL ECONOMY
OF KNOWLEDGE

1 Writing Havoc

> Fire in each Eye, and papers in each hand,
> They rave, recite, and madden round the land.
>
> —"An Epistle from Mr. Pope to Dr. Arbuthnot," 1735

> We Poets in our youth begin in gladness;
> But thereof come in the end despondency and madness.
>
> —W. Wordsworth, "Resolution and Independence," 1807

Writing and Madness

These poems appear to tell similar tales of writers threatened by madness, but my argument here, and throughout this book, is that the seventy years between them saw a dramatic shift in what threatened writers and why. To gauge the change, let us start with something the poems share: leeches—in vertebrate and invertebrate form. In the earlier poem, the Leech-gatherer is the speaker, and the leeches—although not labeled with that specific word—are human. Pope depicts himself as the unwilling target of aspiring hordes of writers who hope they can ride his fame to market: "All fly to *Twit'nam*, and in humble strain / Apply to me, to keep them mad or vain" (21–22). In the later version, however, the gatherer is an "old Man" who invites the leeches onto his body so that—after they apply themselves—he can carry them to market. Leech gathering, from being a "maddening" activity in Pope's poem, becomes, by the end of Wordsworth's, a double cure: it brings to physicians the means to bleed their patients while offering the Poet a thought to which he can cling—"'I'll think of the Leech-gatherer on the lonely moor!'" (140)—and thus soothe his "madness." The stickiness that threatens to derange Pope becomes a saving stick-to-it-iveness (old Man to task *and* poet to old Man) in Wordsworth.

Leeches are not, of course, either the threatening or redemptive agents, but they do provide a clue as to what has changed. The word *leech* itself did shift in meaning between the two poems; the variation that Pope's description of human behavior seems to anticipate—"one who 'sticks to' another for the purpose of getting gain out of him"—is cited by the *Oxford English Dictionary* as first appearing in 1784 in Cowper's *Task*.[1] As that negative definition gained currency, the word's positive associations with "healing" began to fade, particularly its use as a synonym for "physician." Although leeching remained an important medical practice during the nineteenth century,[2] it faced increasing competition from other practices as medicine assumed its modern, professional form.[3] With growing prestige and fees, those physicians still labeled *leeches* earned the title less for their use of the worm than for the size of their bills.

Wordsworth, then, had all of these meanings at hand—*leeches* as "worms," as "physicians," and as "human parasites"—but he explicitly uses just the first, and what we learn about the worms comes only in glimpses and in fragments of conversation. In the stanzas initially describing the old Man, we do discover how to gather leeches—"he the pond / Stirred with his staff, and fixedly did look / Upon the muddy water"—but the description of that primitive technology points to a technology of another kind: "which he conned / As if he had been reading in a book" (78–81). This strange occupation is thus made familiar by a simile comparing the moving staff and fixed gaze to the work of writing and reading.

The strange old Man—initially made even more strange by comparisons with "a huge stone" and "a sea beast" (57–63)—is also made familiar, but not simply as another human being. The speaker's persistent inattention to their conversation—the details of the old Man's life were "Scarce heard" (198)—ensures that we must come to know him in other terms. "What is it," asks Steven Knapp, that "paces continually, laborious and opaque, across the field of the poet's and the reader's consciousness?" What is it that "repeatedly makes a pause and then the same discourse renews?" What is it that in its "persistence" is so indifferent "to any particular thematic content?" It is not an old man or what he said, Knapp argues, but the form in which both are written:

> the condensed Spenserian stanza (measured, antique, opaque, elusive) whose persistent and finally pointless repetition constitutes this very poem. The Leech-gatherer is nothing other than a materialized deposit, a kind of personified sediment or precipitate, of the stanzas that serve as the deliberately awkward and alien medium of the speaker's meditation.[4]

Just as the act of gathering leeches is written up and made familiar as a kind of "reading," so the gatherer can be read as a form of writing. We are left, concludes Knapp, with the "peculiar sense that one is encountering a familiar character who is at the same time no more than a cipher for the very medium that makes him seem familiar" (120). As with the persistent push on Twit'nam's door by the literary types Pope's poem helped to make familiar, the "medium" that motivates all—"If Foes, they write, if Friends, they read me dead" (32)—is the message.

In other words, what haunts both of these poems is the technology they share: a combination of practices used in different ways at different times. *Writing*—as I've emphasized, my shorthand for the entire configuration of writing, print, and silent reading—is not only something people do, more or less often and more or less well; by calling it a *technology* I am acknowledging it as something other, something to which people must adapt, something that can, in a sense, be done to them. In fact, the difference between that sense of otherness and the assumption that writing is a difficult but simply natural human behavior points to what changed so significantly between "Arbuthnot" and "Resolution."

Writing is a force that invades and pervades Pope's poem. Despite the opening repetition—"Shut, shut the door" (1)—it enters everyone's life. In the way it seems to spread, and in its effects, writing is represented as a kind of contagion—"What *Drop* or *Nostrum* can this Plague remove?" (29)—making Arbuthnot the ideal recipient of what Pope termed his "Bill of Complaint." As a writer as well as a doctor—he was a member of the Scriblerus Club and a playwright—Arbuthnot could have read the complaining knowledgeably for both its literary and medical grievances and for how they inform each other. Pope presents "this long Disease, my Life" (132) as—from birth to death—something so thoroughly made by writing that he cannot quite make out the difference: "was I born for nothing but to write?" (272). Being read and written to death is offered as a fitting end—in a poem that ends with the fitting ends of Pope's father, mother, and friend—for a child who "lisp'd in Numbers" (128).

Those numbers, Pope writes, "came." The child is certainly precocious, but also, just as certainly, not in control. Whereas Wordsworth's youthful poets are by their "own spirits . . . deified" (47), Pope's does not make his fate but must learn to handle it. He uses the epistle to describe what he has learned, for that genre, from Horace and the New Testament to Dryden and Young, had functioned as an important didactic form for dispensing judgments and advice. Here, Pope uses its potential for intimacy and immediacy—in being addressed to a friend on a particular occasion—to infuse the force of personal, confessional experience into an informal "how-to" guide to the technology of writing: "what sin to me unknown / Dipt me in Ink, my Parents', or my own?" (125–26). The answer is neither, for writing, in this poem, is like original sin: a given. Choice is only at the level of coping. In a fallen world, a world already filling up with writing, one must try to master what one cannot avoid.

The "Clerk" who "pens a Stanza when he should *engross*" (18), for example, has no choice but to write—as with more and more of his contemporaries, it is part of his job ("engrossing" as transcribing documents in a large, clear hand)—however, in writing poetry, he has chosen the wrong kind. This multiplicity of kinds of writing is matched by a multiplicity of venues for it, so that the "Stranger" who hawks his "Packet" to the "Stage" can, if rejected, turn to booksellers like Lintot to "print it." Every choice, in turn, enhances writing's power by extending it to others: the Clerk's turn to verse "cross[es]" his "Father's soul," and the Stranger needs Pope to influence Lintot's publication decision. Writing's web of "Int'rest" appears to reach everywhere in "Arbuthnot," and even when the connecting strand appears spurious—"Poor *Cornus* sees his frantic Wife elope, / And curses Wit, and Poetry, and *Pope*" (25–26)—the belief in writing's penetrating power augments that power: it leads, that is, to more writing, including the lines just quoted.

This kind of proliferation—in which the interrelated practices of writing, reading, and print feed each other—points to the irony of Pope's position. The saner his efforts to master writing, to control it by controlling himself—

> If want provok'd, or madness made them print,
> I wag'd no war with *Bedlam* or the *Mint*.
> Did some more sober Critic come abroad?
> If wrong, I smil'd; if right, I kiss'd the rod. (155–58)

—the more out of control his life becomes, as his very success attracts the maddened leeches to his door. The resulting "bill of complaint," of course, only furthers the proliferation of writing which he is complaining about, by adding to it the new and recirculated materials—at least two passages had already been published earlier (*Pope* xxiii–xxiv)—which make up the "Epistle." Writing is not only represented in that poem as a relentlessly productive technology; it also works that way. More writing also makes for more—often unintended—effects, ranging from the obvious embarrassments of Pope's incompetent "fool[s]"—"One dedicates in high heroic prose, / And ridicules beyond a hundred foes" (109–10)—to his own "dire dilemma" (31) in which writing at its most competent invites the maddening onrush of friends and foes.

That crowd embodied for Pope the threat posed by writing's heightened productivity. Not only was more written, but improved circulation raised the efficiency of print as a one-to-many means of communication. Pope's complaint against the "many" he helped to produce, however, did not assume our modern shape of the nameless masses versus the valorized individual. In fact, "Arbuthnot," like *The Dunciad*, is a difficult and strange read today precisely because so many are named. Startled from the exclamatory start of the poem, Pope names names on the fly not only because doing so functions within satire as an effective targeting strategy, but also because of how he makes sense of this new multiplicity. For us, the crowd is a mystery we need to explain by naming *it* rather than those who make it up.[5] For Pope, the active agent was writing itself; the crowd was thus a disturbing, but not mysterious effect—one that invited target practice. Learning the names and tracking the allusions cannot quite quell for us the dizziness induced by so much specificity nor the desire for what we are used to: the comforting counterpoint of a strong, subjective center.

That is precisely, of course, what Wordsworth gives us. The problem is no longer writing producing too many writers, but the individual writer failing to produce more writing. This turnabout is naturalized in a very literal way: the poem puts us deeply *into* "nature," both temporally—the first line recounts the weather that has already past—and spatially—the "Traveller . . . upon the moor" leaves behind "all the ways of men" (15, 21). "Far from the world," and thus safe from the human leeches of Pope's crowd, Wordsworth's poet worries only that the distance will produce a debilitating "solitude" rather than a healthy "independence" (33–35). Avoiding that distress is the responsibility of the individual who must learn to take "heed" of himself (42); unless paired with "resolution"—as in the title—"independence" gives way to "madness."

Between Pope and Wordsworth, then, concern has shifted, as I suggested earlier, from the potentially disruptive power of the technology of writing to the possibly disrupted personalities of people who wrote. In generic terms, an epistolary user's guide to a technology gives way to carefully "measured" (95) tale telling intended to heal the individual. As Knapp's analysis linking the Leech-gatherer to the poem's distinctive stanza makes clear, that tale is told through the form as well as the content. Seen as a "condensed Spenserian" (nine lines down to seven), this stanza—in echoing the past and yet persisting into the poem's present—conveys a continuity capable of countering the discontinuity (gladness into madness) threatening the speaker.

Both in the number of lines and in the rhyme scheme (*abab bcc*), Wordsworth's formal experiment bears an even closer resemblance to a still older model: Chaucer's Troilus stanza. "Resolution and Independence" does, in fact, echo that tragedy's threatening shifts of fortune and concern with how to communicate.[6] Since Chaucer's formula was renamed *rhyme royal* after being used by James I of Scotland, Wordsworth's variation may also carry a play upon the contrast between the Leech-gatherer's lowly state and his

> Choice word and measured phrase, above the reach
> Of ordinary men; a stately speech;
> Such as Grave Livers do in Scotland use. (95–97)

Most importantly, however, by extending the seventh and final line into an alexandrine—an innovation he employed elsewhere[7]— Wordsworth turned the stanza from its straightforward narrative functions to the grander task of monumental inscription. The result conveys healing continuity not only by repetitive tale telling but by pronouncing conspicuously—by underlining problems and cures rhythmically with extended last lines:

> But thereof come in the end despondency and madness. (49)

> I'll think of the Leech-gatherer on the lonely moor! (140)

The first of these pronouncements sets up a now standard tale of individual development in which the self that must grow faces a self-induced ("by our own spirits") crisis. The second turns the solution into a mental issue of what the "I" "think[s]." One could say, in the language of 1960s "Consciousness" criticism of the Romantics, that whatever bothered Pope and those at his door was "internalized" as a matter of mind.[8] As I have pointed out elsewhere, however, criticizing Romanticism in its own psychological terms only reifies what it purports to explain.[9] What is needed are alternative grounds for the explanation of change—grounds that I have sought to stake out here by identifying Pope's problem as the proliferation of writing.

Wordsworth's efforts then materialize *in* a history of writing; there, they can be seen as pointing to and participating in the specific changes in working and knowing which accompanied, and finally domesticated, that proliferation. In terms of content, the turn to *mind* cast writing as mental labor and valorized that labor as inherently useful (see Chapter 5). In regard to form, remeasur-

ing stanzas to fit conclusive pronouncements into sustained narrative proved conducive to professionalization—a process that re-
vamped how specific occupations pronounced knowledge. Who
says it? How? To whom? And to what ends? The particular pronouncements I have quoted above speak directly to those issues:
by casting shifts in fortune—"gladness" to "madness"—as problems in human development rather than as arbitrary or as divine,
Wordsworth helped to authorize a tale that was not only about
work but did work: it helped to secure for a new range of professions an ongoing supply of clients. In that tale, development is
idealized so that it can *always* be pathologically interrupted. Those
interruptions, after all, are opportunities for professional intervention and surveillance—the ongoing pronouncing of disciplinary cures.[10]

I say *disciplinary* because the final pronouncement of "Resolution and Independence" turns upon two central meanings of that
term. The speaker hopes to take heed of himself—to control his
own behavior—by thinking of the Leech-gatherer as a model of
self-discipline. But of what will he be thinking? In what way is that
"mind" "firm?" Its firmness consists throughout the poem in being
able to stick to what he does and knows. Following the logic of disciplinarity I proposed in the Argument, it is the very narrowness of
that knowledge, and the Leech-gatherer's ability and willingness
to persist in it, which makes him so formidably deep. In fact, given
how he is presented in the poem, one could say simply that it
makes him: initially presented as less than human—a (mindless?)
"sea beast"—he comes to be identified in memory as the embodiment of his specialty: the (firm-minded) Leech-gatherer.

The speaker pays little attention to that specialized knowledge
because he embodies expertise of a different kind. His world features a basic division between "We Poets" and "others" (48, 40).
Work informs personal identity to such an extent—an issue I address further in Chapter 4—that this tale of individual development becomes a lesson in disciplinary concentration and professional survival.[11] Failure to work well can jeopardize an identity
grounded in that work, making the threat of madness—understood as a loss of identity—*real* in a new, historically specific way.

As the disciplines and their associated professions assumed their modern form, tightening work's grip on personal identity, madness materialized in occupational units: from mad writers to mad scientists to mad doctors to mad hatters.[12]

Writing, as the technology whose proliferation helped to elicit disciplinary and professional control, figured in all of these behaviors. But those who turned to it for a living were cast as particularly vulnerable—especially since that option was not even available in Britain until the eighteenth century—putting the newly forming category of Literature into a special relationship with madness. "Resolution and Independence" widens its scope in the Chatterton stanza to warn against that danger, offering a portrayal of a tragically loony late eighteenth century that persists into present-day literary histories. In doing so, what appears initially to be a tale of individual redemption opens up into a prototype—aesthetic issues aside—of one of the twentieth-century's best-selling genres: the professionals' *how-to-succeed* book.

Although we are accustomed to thinking of Romantic writing as more personal and private than the work that preceded it, Pope's poem not only features more individual names and details than Wordsworth's, but it also, in the final lines, collapses social distinctions—"Kings shall know less joy than I" (405)—into the leveling intimacies of family, friendship, and death. Far from defining a professional identity, disciplinary expertise easily switches hands: in the end, Pope becomes Arbuthnot's doctor. Pope himself cannot be cured, for his problem is with writing and not the writer. The threat of madness, made immediate by the knocking at the door, can only be left unanswered. Paradoxically, not answering would have been an effective answer *if* it had meant not writing back—a response to writing's proliferation that death, the "Epistle's" end, would have made final.

Wordsworth did claim to find an answer to the apparently less immediate ("there may come another day," 34) threat of professional *in*firmity which he faced. His solution, however, exacerbated Pope's problem. "Internalization," as an event in the history of writing, made mind matter in very specific and quantifiable ways: more discipline and greater professionalism increased the flow of writing, naturalized the increase as a matter of doing one's job, and even turned death itself toward newly productive ends. Under the rubric of developing a "firm mind," Wordsworth transformed not only Chatterton's suicide into more writing, but his own demise as well: the deliberately posthumous publication of the story of that "mind"—what became known as *The Prelude*—contributed significantly to writing's ongoing proliferation in both kind and quantity.

Pens and Periods

Starting with this comparison of canonical texts by canonical writers highlights some of the ways a history of writing can depart from traditional histories of literature. The two poems provide a chronological framework for focusing on the chapter's central issue: writing's capacity to wreak what Hume called "havoc" on itself and its users. Two crucial markers in Britain's relationship to writing have been identified: its proliferation as a technology, depicted by Pope as a threat, and its subordination, in Wordsworth, to disciplinary and professional ends. The productivity of writing led, it appears, to the formation of newly proper subjects—both bodies of knowledge and individuals that embody them.

Before pursuing that connection in this chapter and the next, however, we need now to acknowledge an important limitation in the initial evidence: both canonical poets addressed so far were, not surprisingly, male. And, as Alan Bewell points out, "Resolution and Independence," in particular, "presents a starker, more patriarchal conception of poetic origins, and a more general effacement of the female imagination, as Wordsworth rewrites the supernatural origins of poetry in more masculine terms, as madness within himself and the Leech-gatherer."[13] In order not to replicate that effacement here, we need to turn back briefly to the issue of proliferation with the gender of the writer—and the issue of gender in the writing— in mind.

When that proliferation initially accelerated in Britain at the turn into the eighteenth century, it shocked everyone who participated in it. Dryden, for example, began the Preface to *Fables Ancient and Modern* (1700) by casting his experience of writing in tales of an overpowering excess: "'Tis with a poet, as with a man who designs to build, and is very exact, as he supposes, in casting up the cost beforehand: but, generally speaking, he is mistaken in his account, and reckons short of the expense he first intended. He alters his mind as the work proceeds, and will have this or that convenience more . . . I have built a house, where I intended but a lodge" (*Dryden* 740). The struggle with such excessiveness is then cast in epic terms—"I ought in reason to have stopp'd," writes Dryden of his prolific translating, "but the Speeches of *Ajax* and *Ulysses* lying next in my way, I could not balk 'em." Whether argued in architectural images or heroic ones, the point remains the same: writing, to use the verb Dryden settled upon, "swell[s]."

In the hands of Dryden's contemporary, Sarah Egerton, that swelling arose as the problem of the "Enlargement" required by her "Subject." Her Preface to "The Female Advocate" (1686) domesticates the proliferation of writing in a pregnant image of how "Books come abroad in the world" despite authorial efforts to "hinder the Publication." Her only option, given this reproductive imperative, is to try "to put a Period to the intended Length of the insuing Lines, lest censuring Criticks should measure my Tongue by my Pen, and condemn me for a Talkative." This feminine foreshortening of masculine length, however, is but a strategy to ensure that writing will proliferate even further: if the "small Venture . . . passes the merciless Ocean of Criticks" there can be another "adventure the next time."[14]

More writing required more reading, and thus the anonymous author of *Constantia* (1751) prefaced that novel with a strategy for making "the majority of mankind" esteem reading as "a thing necessary." The prescription was, of course, more writing—this time of a critical kind—for every book must be presented as doing more than just "kill[ing] time." "A certain standard" must be written up—and the author proceeds to do so—"for books of amusement as well as for books *of every other kind*" (emphasis mine).[15] So frequently was this interplay of writing and reading played out in the late eighteenth century,[16] that E. S. Dallas was only repeating a commonplace early in the next century when he observed: "it is an age of books and papers—of much reading and writing. The chief movement of the age rattles upon a causeway paved with reading-desks and writing-desks."[17]

Whether working as a he, a she, or in anonymity, those who trafficked in writing during the long eighteenth century spared no metaphors—from houses to boats to roads—in conveying how and how much it proliferated. Gender did not absolutely determine the mode of participation, but certain strategic patterns do appear. Among the most prominent and persistent was the use by women of variations on Egerton's "period" tactic: adjusting to the obstacles they faced as women by acquiescing to limits in ways that made those limits occasions, sooner or later, for more writing. Egerton's period not only increased the likelihood of picking up the pen again, but it also served as an immediate subject to write about.

Examples from two women writers, one at each end of the eighteenth century, illustrate both the ongoing pressure to "put a Period" and the often heavily ironic results. Both Anne Finch's Preface to the folio volume in manuscript of her poems (about 1702) and "A Tour to the Glaciers of Savoy," anonymously published under the name of Eliza (1796), feature women facing landscapes that invite description. Finch mixes forms to convey her mixed response:

> Like mighty Denhams, then, methinks my hand,
> Might bid the Landskip, in strong numbers stand,
> Fix all itts charms, with a Poetick skill,
> And raise itts Fame, above his Cooper's hill.

> This I confesse, is whatt in itts self itt deserves, but the unhappy difference is, that he by being a real Poet, cou'd make that place (as he sais) a Parnassus to him; whilst I, that behold a real Parnassus here, in that lovely Hill, which in this Park bears that name, find in my self, so little of the Poet, that I am still restrain'd from attempting a description of itt in verse.[18]

Putting a period to one kind of writing, verse, enables another kind. The prose confession—faced by a "real" Parnassus, she does not feel like a "real" poet—is gendered not only by the contrast to a male writer, Denham, but by the context: an extended discussion of Finch's fear of being mocked as a "Versifying Maid of Honor" and the resulting struggle to "keep within the limmitts I had pre-scrib'd myself."

Almost a century later, Eliza updated the scene and the poetic skill needed to describe it but plotted a strikingly similar confession. Whereas the neoclassical hill required Denham's "strong numbers"—a reference to his reputed mastery of the rhythms of the closed couplet[19]—the "romantic" vale of Chamouny calls for "fire":

> For though many a vale we had passed,
>   And o'er mountains, whose heads were gigantic,
> Yet this vale of all vales, at the last,
>   Was beyond every thing most romantic.
>
> I wished for a genius of fire,
>   I wished for a thousand of quills,
> Of paper far more than a quire,
>   To sketch out each beauty it fills.
>
> For though I no genius was born,
>   From such wishes I am not exempt;
> Your pen would the subject adorn:
>   You might soar,—but I must not attempt.[20]

The concluding diction here precisely echoes Finch, who describes herself as restrained from "attempting," and, although the context is more verse rather than a switch to prose, it too highlights gender as the issue: not only is the "soar[ing]" "you" a male poet, but in the very next stanza, as the task switches from poetic description to the physical ascent of the glaciers, Eliza emphasizes the need to lay aside "female fears."

Once again, the basic irony of the self-imposed "period" is the resulting output: the period itself becomes a topic to write about, and, as with Finch, another kind of writing is authorized. Without a romantic fire to tend, Eliza can transform what she calls an "epistle" into an extended comic ballad. The billowing "ocean of ice," for example, elicits the following unheated lines:

> If to wonder it makes you look old
> Such wonder of wonders are in it,
> Muse but how those billows are rolled,
> You'd be ninety years old in a minute.

By the conclusion, the most effective fire is clearly the most mundane:

> Then in our hot beds we reclined,
> Each served with a basin of whey;
> Yet withal, 'twas a wonder to find,
> We had none of us colds the next day.

The point here is not whether these lines are more or less appealing than fiery ones, or whether women could or did write lines of another kind, but that these pieces represent an important pattern of proliferation—a gendered pattern demonstrably common to women writers but certainly not restricted to them (or them to it): proliferation through limitation. That is not to say, of course, that the pressure to "put periods" did not in many cases severely restrict productivity, but to acknowledge that limits did work in surprising ways. We are, that is, more used to what may appear to be the opposite and more logical relation: productivity and free choice—in this case, the freedom to write what you want. Coleridge, for example, did not hesitate to stoke the romantic fires in his poem on the vale of Chamouny written a few years later (1802); in fact, he felt so free to "attempt" the vale that he did so without ever having seen it.

Such freedom actually follows Finch's formula, the "real" poet, again a male, can still "make" a "real" Parnassus without even beholding one. Like Finch, Coleridge negotiates this issue by supplementing his verse with prose. However, he does so not to confess to his lack of firsthand experience or any other limitation; rather, at the end of a prefatory note full of names and details that raise the stakes, he seems to challenge the audience to detect his caper:

> Who *would* be, who *could* be an Atheist in this valley of wonders? If
> any of the readers of the *Morning Post* have visited this vale in their
> journeys among the Alps, I am confident that they will not find the

sentiments and feelings expressed, or attempted to be expressed, in the following poem, extravagant.

Here is where the ironies of gendered proliferation proliferate.[21] De Quincey, taking up this challenge in 1834, accused Coleridge of "unacknowledged obligation" to a German poetess.[22] This prime example of high romantic writing—precisely the kind that Eliza, as a woman,[23] would not even attempt—may well have been a rewriting of writing by a woman.

Where do these episodes leave women writers? They suggest that the workings of gender in the proliferation of writing were all the more powerful because they were *not* fixed, either by intention or by biology—a fact that does not deny but can help to explain the particular trouble they generated for women. The last tale demonstrates both the capacity of women to produce in the face of limitations and the power of those limitations. One woman cannot write what she wants, another loses credit for what she did write, and, in our traditional literary histories, the lone male gets almost all of the attention—not only for his writing, but also for, as Wordsworth might have put it, his infirm mind.[24]

A history of writing—by not veering into the individual psyche, psychologizing and essentializing on the way—can redistribute that attention. What we can attend to are behaviors *in* writing and how they function in writing's different kinds. I want now to pursue, from poetry into philosophical prose, the various ways in which writing proliferated through the articulation of limits. Those exertions of control for the sake of growth, I will argue, helped to effect the large-scale behavior we call disciplinarity: the dividing up of knowledge into proper subjects. I will begin with that branch of philosophy which concerned itself explicitly with the regulation of growth: political economy. Its fate, during the period covered by this book, was to grow so successfully that it, in a sense, disciplined itself, fragmenting in the mid nineteenth century into the modern subjects of political science and economics. I will begin at that moment and work back, turning first to a passage that turns strangely upon the absence of women.

Productivity and Proper Subjects

"Philosophy and the study of the actual world," wrote Marx and Engels, "have the same relation to one another as onanism and sexual love."[25] The masturbators, of course, were the Young Hegelians—those who appear elsewhere in *The German Ideology* (1846) as "bleating" "sheep" (thus raising a less lonely but still unflattering sexual scenario). Having replaced "wrong ideas" with more *idealizing*, they have missed the materialist point. "The products of their brains," as Marx and Engels put the problem the Hegelians perpetuated, "have got out of their hands." To suggest that they had something else in hand is to invoke the now standard developmental narrative in which masturbation is a mark of adolescent male immaturity. The *Young* Hegelians will be left "'behind' and below" by those who progressively engage the actual world.

By casting that engagement as "sexual love," Marx and Engels tried to underline the progressive element in practical terms: sexual love is better because it can *produce* something. The proper kind of study, in other words, would not feature barren bursts of interpretation but encounters *with* the real world which can bear the fruit of change. This criterion of productivity—specifically, the capacity to produce progress—was Marx and Engels' means of articulating what I am calling the work of writing. Their efforts to redirect philosophy can be seen not only as testimony to their particular revolutionary fervor, but also as evidence of their participation in this ongoing debate about that technology's productive powers. Even as they mounted a critique of capitalism, their argument about what kind of writing mounts best furthered the phenomenon central to it—what Henry Abelove calls the "privileging of production."[26] In fact, by applying so forcefully the criterion of productivity to the differentiation of kinds at the tail end of the long eighteenth century, Marx and Engels confirm, in Abelove's words, that period's "dramatic rise in virtually *all* indices of production."

The *historical* force of their simile—"Philosophy and the study of the actual world have the same relation to one another as onanism and sexual love"—only becomes clear when we take into account the one particular index central to Abelove's now infamous article, "Some Speculations on the History of Sexual Intercourse during the Long Eighteenth Century in England." Citing recent demographic studies linking the population boom in eighteenth-century England to a rise in fertility, and that rise to more and earlier marriages as well as more illegitimate children and prenuptial pregnancies, Abelove draws the astonishingly simple conclusion that there must have been "a remarkable increase in the *incidence* of cross-sex genital intercourse" during the latter part of the century—"the particular kind of sexual expression which we moderns often name tendentiously 'sexual intercourse,'" he asserts, "became importantly more popular" (126–27).[27]

What Marx and Engels offer up, then, as a natural preference—productive sexual love over onanism—turns out to be in England a statistical and thus historical phenomenon with very specific and material political dimensions—some of which, in regard to women, I pursue in detail in Chapter 9. Correlating the popularity of "the sexual act which uniquely makes for reproduction" with the general privileging of production, Abelove can speculate that "behaviors, customs, usages which are judged to be nonproductive"—whether they be "plebian conception[s] of time," such as rest on "St. Monday," or "nonreproductive sexual behaviors"—all came "under extraordinary negative pressure" as their productive counterparts became "discursively and phenomenologically central in ways" they "had never been before" (128–29). The result was a sweeping reorganization and reconstruction of the human according to the criterion of productivity, including—and, in many ways, transpiring through—the increasingly important behavior of writing.

A key discursive location for the working out of that criterion was in eighteenth-century philosophical narratives, specifically the articulation within moral philosophy of the branch we call political economy. From its start in the late seventeenth century, political economy took shape explicitly as an effort not only to discuss productivity but *to be productive*; in the words of David McNally I cited earlier, it "represented an attempt to theorize the inner dynamics of these changes [toward capitalism] *in order to shape and direct them*" (1; emphasis mine). Two major changes invited such activity. "Political economy came into being," Engels declares in the opening sentence of his "Critique," "as a natural result of the expansion of trade."[28] This is still the most often cited change, for the expansion was significant: "between the early part of the seventeenth and the middle of the eighteenth century alone," according to Eugene Rotwein, "England's foreign trade had increased roughly seven-fold."[29] The less frequently cited, but still crucial, change had to do with the land. "Between 1690 and 1750," McNally points out, "there was a major shift of property away from the peasantry and lesser gentry and towards the large landowners" (10).

To shape and direct these two changes—concentrated land ownership and increased trade—the narratives of political economy conformed to Bacon's model of experiment—a methodology "in which," as McNally puts it, "knowledge of nature would be acquired by acting upon it," for "it is by acting on nature (through 'works') that," Bacon advised, "we acquire genuine knowledge of things" (37). The method alternated empirical practice, proceeding from sense experience, with the formulation of general propositions, advanced by abstract reasoning regarding quantity and number. The practitioners of social Baconianism became very active by the end of the seventeenth century, and their Experimental Philosophy Club often met at the lodgings of the writer whom Marx and others cite as the first political economist, William Petty.

As one of the largest landowners in Ireland, Petty, like his fellow experimental philosophers, believed, as McNally points out, "that reform of husbandry was the key to reform of the commonwealth. In particular, they saw agricultural improvement as the primary solution to the problem of poverty and unemployment" (McNally 40). Experimental reform thus produced writings that were configured to effect change by embracing the details of empirical practice—physically measuring different types of land— along with the formulation of theoretical propositions—abstractly determining "'the naturall and intrinsick'" (McNally 49) value of that land. These early versions of political economy could thus facilitate the ongoing redistribution of the land into fewer hands as it sought, explicitly, to relieve the social problems that arose, in part, from that very redistribution.

The increase in trade was also engaged experimentally, but with a crucial twist to the alternation of the empirical fact and the abstract generalization: the latter was used to recast the former. Under mercantilism, as Engels scathingly put it,

> People still lived in the naive belief that gold and silver were wealth, and therefore considered nothing more urgent than the prohibition everywhere of the export of the "precious" metals. The nations faced each other like misers, each clasping to himself with both arms his precious money-bag, eyeing his neighbours with envy and distrust. . . . The art of the economists, therefore, consisted in ensuring that at the end of each year exports should show a favourable balance over imports; and for the sake of this ridiculous illusion thousands of men have been slaughtered! (Marx and Engels III.418–19)

The experimental work of political economy was thus to convince people that the actual metals they held, sensually and empirically, in their laps, were not actually equal to their, or the nation's, wealth. Since political economy posited that wealth abstractly as a self-regulating totality generated by the circulation of capital, it needed to invoke another data set if it was to help discursively to shape the fate of trade.

Social Baconianism—with its imperative that, in the words of Edwin Greenlaw, "everything that relates to the state of learning . . . should be treated *historically*"[30]—once again supplied a narrative strategy: the experimental data would come from the past. History, that is, in the form of developmental narratives—natural histories—became, by the middle of the eighteenth century, a central feature of the experimental philosophy we know as political economy. Hume, for example, as Rotwein points out, used a "historical framework" to argue against the "'narrow and malignant opinion'" that "all trading nations are rivals and cannot flourish except at one another's expense" (lxxiv). This empirical argument for "free" trade can be made *historically* because, in Hume's own words,

history is not only a valuable part of knowledge, but opens the door
to many other parts, and affords materials to most of the other sciences. And indeed, if we consider the shortness of human life, and
our limited knowledge, even of what passes in our own time, we
must be sensible that we should be for ever children in understanding, were it not for this invention, which extends our experience
to all past ages, and to the most distant nations; making them contribute as much to our improvement in wisdom, as if they had
actually lain under our observation.[31]

History, according to this argument, extends our empirical reach
by bringing more experience into view. Since data of that kind
were precisely what political economy needed to conduct its "experiments" concerning human behavior, the solution was to mix
the two.

History also mixed productively with natural philosophy, as
the recent work of Charles Bazerman on Priestley and electricity
has shown. "Through a comprehensive view of the [earlier] literature" in his 1767 book *The History and Present State of Electricity*,
Priestley establishes, concludes Bazerman, "the corpus of communal experience and organizes it around problems and principles
that define an evolving state of knowledge and research agenda. A
list of generalizations emerging from that communal history provides a common knowledge base for continuing work."[32] In this
experimental history of earlier experiments, in other words, the
recounting of the progress of knowledge productively enables further progress. What Priestley's systematic historicizing of experience, discovery, and theory configured, observes Bazerman, was
a "discourse directed at an inward-facing community concerned
with shared research problems . . . a prototype discipline" (38).

The direction in which the community faced is the crucial point
here; the *inward* turn was a form of limitation. It set a boundary
that delimited subject matter and audience. But those controlling
exclusions were made for the sake of growth—the eliciting from
that audience of more writing on that subject. Priestley's mixing of
natural philosophy and history, in other words, was yet another
example of proliferation through limitation. In being subject spe-

cific, however, it points to the role of such mixed forms in the advent of modern disciplinarity: they produce not only more writing and more knowledge but also more kinds of knowledge. That differentiation of knowledge, I am suggesting, was the *product* of Baconian efforts to conform writing *to* the criterion of productivity.

The paradox this entailed for British philosophical writing was particularly evident in practitioners such as Hume, whose extensive philosophical branching—into political economy, for example—so clearly contravenes our own disciplinary standards. That branching was enabled by the experimental procedures we have already discussed—empirical observation of experience extended through history, alternating with general propositions. The developmental narratives of progress and refinement they constructed from that extensive database authorized what McNally calls "all-embracing theories of social life" (158) within which inquiries that we now find diverse could be conducted. This kind of productive writing thus provided the unity underlying that diversity *even* as it accelerated diversity into difference. In the short term came the extraordinary outpouring of knowledge we associate with the Scottish Enlightenment; in the slightly longer term came the separation of knowledges that characterize modernity.

The narrative structure of Hume's *Enquiry Concerning Human Understanding* (1748) exemplifies this transformation. The object of enquiry may initially appear to be singular—human understanding—and the database simply "cautious observations" of our experience of it, but as that database is extended *historically* the "it" becomes, increasingly, earlier kinds of writing *about* it. Thus, each of the twelve sections of the *Enquiry* proceeds according to one of two alternatives established in the opening parts: either an assessment of the progress of kinds, as in Section I on "the different species of philosophy," or, a priori assertions of common human experience, as in Section II, which "Every one will readily allow."[33] The first alternative proceeds through various classifications, from interrelations among philosophy, geometry, algebra, arithmetic, and theology to a comparison of the moral versus the mathematical (25, 40, 60). The second alternative accumulates

what is "evident" about "principle[s] of connexion" and "probability" in all of our "mind[s]" (23, 56).

The conclusion Hume draws from that latter accumulation of
evidence is, of course, skepticism. But that is not the *end* of *An
Enquiry Concerning Human Understanding;* it is the *means* to its
end, for the function of skepticism is to establish, in Hume's own
words, "narrow limitation[s]" (163) for our enquiries. The literal
end of human understanding—by that I mean both the final words
of this particular treatise *and* the conception that Hume helped to
make real for us—is disciplinarity: the concluding paragraphs provide a catalogue of kinds of knowledge which *insists* upon difference. In fact, so strongly is difference emphasized that the very last
image is of a systematic ravaging of the stacks of knowledge:
"When we run over libraries, persuaded of these principles," asks
Hume, "what havoc must we make?" (165).

That havoc is now our institutions. After Hume, what we understand about human understanding is, again in his words, its
"proper subjects" (163). These are not the Section I "different
species of philosophy"—the *of* indicating the older organization of
knowledge, in which every kind was a branch connected *to* philosophy; difference became an insistent principle of reorganization
only when mixed with the historical empiricism of Section II,
where Hume's observations of common human experience suggested that the "natural powers of the human mind" are best suited
to limited enquiries.

The *Enquiry* enacts that tale not only as content and as mixed
form, but in its publication history as well. It began as the *Treatise
of Human Nature* (1739–40) including branches into such matters
as our "ideas of space and time." Those were cut when Hume recast
it, dividing "human nature" into separate enquiries into "understanding: (1748), "morals" (1751), "passions" (1757), and "religion"
(1755). He arranged for their publication together posthumously as
Essays and Treatises on Several Subjects (1777). Whether his assessment of the lack of success of the original *Treatise*—"going to the
press too early" and "negligences" in the "expression" of a "juve-
nile work" (vi, viii, 2)—was accurate is open to debate.[34] What the

record of revision clearly does tell us, however, is that his writing proliferated and became successful as, in the latter half of the eighteenth century, his philosophy found its proper subjects.

Disciplinarity and the Middle Class

Since that time, if one wants to produce institutional havoc by challenging what is proper—propriety *and* property—then, like Marx and Engels, one must struggle with the force of disciplinary difference. Under the criterion of productivity, writings such as *The German Ideology* and *The Poverty of Philosophy* were thus understood by their authors to be necessary revolutionary activity. Disciplinary change became a prerequisite for larger-scale institutional and social change.

Both kinds of change, as Hume's cry of havoc makes clear, entail violence; the body of knowledge, like the body politic, was to be sliced up in new ways. Hume's writing contributed to both operations. Although his difficulties with "real" connections and cause-and-effect certainly lend themselves to Marxist charges of philosophical onanism, his ventures into political economy helped to forge a powerful analytic tool. In a letter to Turgot in 1766, Hume provided one of the first uses of *class* in its modern sense. The word had previously referred primarily to lectures "restrained to a certain company of Scholars"; in those instances when it did point to divisions among people, the referent was the hierarchical ordering of Roman citizens.[35]

Two of the initial uses of class as a socioeconomic *and* political division in modern society occurred in Hume's letter and in a treatise by Jonas Hanway—a man who wrote about the "dissoluteness" of the "lower class" but whose more striking contribution to the history of class was decidedly middle, as he was the first person to carry and to use an umbrella on the streets of London (Calvert 14–15). Hume's written reference was *to* that middle—in fact, it helped to constitute that middle as a distinct socioeconomic entity by naming it as an object of taxation: "besides merchants," wrote Hume,

> I comprehend in this Class all Shop-Keepers and Master-Tradesmen of every Species. Now it is very just, that these shoud pay for the Support of the Community, which can only be where Taxes are lay'd on Consumptions. There seems to me no Pretence for saying that this order of Men are necessitated to throw their Taxes on the Proprietors of Land, since their Profits and Income can surely bear Retrenchment. (Rotwein 209)

Classification into classes, then, followed a criterion of productivity—taxation became the disciplinary index of one's level of production—and that is precisely what happened to the body of knowledge. Hume, as we have seen, wrought havoc by insisting skeptically on narrowness and limitation—not as caps to, but as the enabling conditions of, productivity: disciplines made narrow could become deep and thus serve to induce *and* control the proliferation of writing and knowledge. Cast in that form, these newly differentiated kinds of knowledge, as with social classes, could then be made subject to arguments about their relative productive value: the distinction of kind between a dominant philosophy and its subordinate branches collapsed and was replaced with a new hierarchy of degrees—degrees of productivity. *The German Ideology*, in identifying a social class with a discipline (the bourgeoisie and philosophy) for the purpose of making such an argument (both are, insist Marx and Engels, relatively unproductive), thus exemplifies the consequences of Humean havoc.

By "commit[ting] to the flames" all volumes that do not concern either "quantity or number," on the one hand, or experiential reasoning on human "existence," on the other (165), Hume also helped to institute our now familiar distinction between the sciences and the humanities. Marx and Engels, of course, aligned their work with the sciences—scientificity signaling productivity. That left the humanities within the category of the nonproductive, a category that, as Abelove puts it, came "under extraordinary negative pressure." The result for sexual behaviors of that type was not, he points out, that they disappeared but that they were "relegated and largely confined to the position of the preliminary": they became "foreplay"—a tellingly accurate rendering of how society and even many humanists have tended to see the humanities. They can be exciting and, sometimes, even worthwhile, but, finally, they are only a warm and fuzzy prelude to the real thing: science's productive engagement with the actual world.

At the end of the twentieth century, we are again at a conjuncture of debates over middle-class taxation and disciplinary change—with *retrenchment*, socioeconomic and academic, a key word in both arenas. Disciplinary stability is threatened from without—tax cuts mean budget cuts in education—and from within, by the intellectual efforts to reclassify nicknamed theory. We are now faced, that is, with the prospect of significant change in the political economy of knowledge, perhaps on a scale comparable to Hume's moment of havoc.

Posed in the universities by administrators looking for savings, our current choice appears to be a matter of preserving the most proper of proper subjects: something, we are told, may have to go—be it classics, sociology, or mechanical engineering—so that something else does not. Comparing Humean havoc with our own, however, suggests a choice of another kind, for what took shape in the eighteenth and early nineteenth centuries in Britain was "proper subjects" as a way to produce, circulate, and consume knowledge. My argument in these opening chapters is that those were behaviors that allowed Britain to come to terms with the newly proliferating technology of writing in ways that formed the modern disciplines. It is not surprising, then, that today's havoc is occurring at another moment of technological change.

Given the onanism argument, the irony of this historical connection between disciplinarity and productivity has been the apparent absence of women from its formation and operations. The next chapter begins by addressing the first issue, for my focus in this one on a kind of writing historically dominated by males—the various versions of political economy—has only laid the groundwork for describing the advent of disciplinary behavior. I turn next to other kinds, from different branches of philosophical prose to verse to letters to fiction to a variety of critical forms, in which the proliferation of writing by women can help us to continue the tale.

2   Engendering Disciplinarity

§☞ "Alas, poor Plato! All thy glory's past:
   What, in a female hand arrived at last!"
   "Sure," adds another, "'tis for something worse;
   This itch of reading's sent her as a curse."
   "No, no," cries good Sir John, "but 'tis as bad,
   For if she's not already crazed, I'm sure she will be mad."
   —Elizabeth Thomas, "An Ode," 1722

§☞ The Mahometans, indeed, enslave their Women, but then they
teach them to believe their inferiority will extend to Eternity; but our
Case is even worse than this, for while we live in a free Country, and are
assured from our excellent Christian Principles that we are capable of
those refined Pleasures which last to Immortality, our Minds, our better
Parts, are wholly left uncultivated, and, like a rich Soil neglected, bring
forth nothing but noxious Weeds. —Eliza Haywood, from *The Female
Spectator*, 1744–45

As writing proliferated during the eighteenth and early nineteenth
centuries in Britain, so did the strains of madness associated with
it. To those we identified in the last chapter as troubling Pope and
Wordsworth, add the clearly gendered one articulated above by
a male character in Elizabeth Thomas's ode. For Thomas, of course,
the "real" (line 78) madness was clearly male, for she saw the problem as not being with women, books, or the act of reading, but
with threatened British men. Unlike their French counterparts,

Thomas claimed, those men, feared "learned ladies" (73), an opinion also held by Eliza Haywood. Both women deplored the contrast between that behavior and the ideal of British "liberty" (86), attributing it, in Thomas's case, to "avaricious soul[s]" and "greedy eyes" (80–81) and, in Haywood's, to jealousy: "they would be apt to think . . . the Admiration we profest for Learning, was only a Veil to cover our Admiration of the Person who possessed it."[1]

In all of these scenarios and in others like them, writing held a special place in Britain as a technology of what Thomas called "war" (76): a tool capable of altering the behavior of those who used it. Depending on the point of view, men otherwise dedicated to freedom became maliciously oppressive, or virtuous and sensible women became lustfully crazed. Thomas and Haywood and, as we shall see, many other writers both before and after them, envisioned peace in the metaphor that concludes the second epigraph above: the "cultivation" of women's minds through education. The first part of this chapter uses this discourse on female education to link gender to the controlling behaviors of disciplinarity. It then examines how notions of cultivation were, in the writing of Burke and others, "sublimed" by the early nineteenth century into the modern concept of *culture*—an arena where, in the late twentieth century, particularly in the "free" West, issues of gender and disciplinarity are erupting into a new set of wars.

Education and the Engendering of Discipline

By *engender* I mean that the division of knowledge in the eighteenth century was informed by divisions of gender. Modern disciplinarity, that is, was not first constituted and then later altered by gender difference; rather, that system has functioned from its inception to articulate and enact those differences. Because gender was such a popular topic in the eighteenth century, influence of some sort was highly likely, but I have in mind a more direct and pervasive discursive connection. On the one hand, writings by both women and men on their hierarchical interrelations turned relentlessly on the topic of education—whether seen as the key to equality or as the means of ensuring proper conduct. On the other hand, one of the ironies of writing the history of disciplinarity is that, as Keith Hoskin has observed, its "genesis is to be found in [what is still today] the apparently marginal and illegitimate field [of] education." Focusing on the specific ways in which that field was formalized and institutionalized in such eighteenth-century phenomena as the *seminar* and the *laboratory,* Hoskin details education's central role in reconfiguring knowledge.[2]

Gender and discipline thus meet discursively in the eighteenth century in education. That last *in* is misleading, however, because it suggests that education was the more established and substantial location in which the others could converge. On the contrary, not only was there no national system of education in England, but, as Nicholas Hans has observed,

> the existing Grammar Schools and the two Universities were entirely inadequate to the country's need of educated men. [They] were monopolised by the Church of England and in fact became the nurseries of the Anglican clergy. . . . The leading men in the sciences, in philosophy, in social-economic studies, were seldom connected with the Universities and often did not possess English degrees.[3]

The alternatives for men were the Dissenting Academies, universities outside of England, and private vocational initiatives, whereas women were solely "limited to private boarding-schools and home education" (194). Given these problems of access, curriculum, and institutional purpose, education, during much of the eighteenth century, did not function as the same kind of enterprise which we assume it to be today—as a locus, that is, for systematic schooling and knowledge production. Appeals by women to "education" as an equalizer, then, were in large part idealizations—but idealizations that functioned constitutively, bringing about improvement in the supposed means of improvement. Although this was certainly not the only factor, education could be said to assume its modern form only when women came to desire it.

Disciplinarity, I am suggesting, was shaped in part by the articulation of that desire. Features from the discourse on gender difference, through repeated turns to education, helped to reconfigure the organization of knowledge. A key feature linking disciplinarity to education, for example, is development: the seminars and exams cited by Hoskin reshape knowledge into that which can be learned systematically, and thus reproduced precisely, over time. Disciplines, in other words, as opposed to other forms of knowledge, must be mastered through a developmental sequence in which a narrowing—and thus more easily monitored—range of inquiry is supposed to ensure a greater depth of understanding.

Unless we take this developmental logic of "narrow but deep" to be a truth discovered in the eighteenth century, we need to look for the discursive locations in which it first began to make sense—although the initial sense that it made may have been quite different from what it eventually came to mean. In Mary Astell's *A Serious Proposal to the Ladies* (1694), for example, features that point toward the later valorization of developmental depth were specifically articulated as a solution to the plight of women. Her initial distinction between "souls" and "bodies" appeared both earlier and contemporaneously, of course, in male philosophical discourse, but its particular function in this proposal was to posit an alternative for women to the desire "to attract the eyes of men." Spatially, avoiding the gaze from "without" entails, for Astell, a turn *"within."* Temporally, countering the "little time" she says that a woman remains physically attractive to a man occasions an emphasis on intellectual "improvement."[4]

Together, these rhetorical moves configure a female subject defined by the capacity for "improvement within." Astell labels that process "education" and enlivens it with the same organic metaphor we already noted in Haywood's *Female Spectator*—one that remained, through Wollstonecraft a century later, a staple of writing about gender: "The soil is rich and would if well cultivated produce a noble harvest" (6). Astell's plan for how to cultivate well exemplifies the constitutive power of this idealizing of education. She proposes

> a Religious Retirement, and such as shall have a double aspect,
> being not only a Retreat from the World for those who desire that

advantage, but likewise, an Institution and previous discipline, to
fit us to do the greatest good in it. (14)

In its "double aspect"—that is, not only being a permanent
retreat for some, but also a place to prepare others for the world—
this plan prescribes the modern transformation of education.
By positing "an Institution and previous discipline," it uncannily
points to the conditions for the shift to systematic schooling and
knowledge production: first, the need for more extensive institutionalization, and second, the casting of discipline as developmentally preparatory to action in the world.

Linked to monastic discipline—what Astell calls "the service of
GOD"—this disciplinary knowledge continued to take "*necessary*
and *perfective* truths" (18) as its goal. The gendered function of that
will to truth, however, was what she termed "improvement of . . .
minds." Although this desire to improve is now a given to us, for
Astell, it—and the education she proposed to achieve it—was specifically formulated as an alternative to the desire of and for men.
The entire proposal is thus informed by what she posits as her
gender's need to establish proper boundaries. For example, the assertion that improving minds require a "blissful recess" from the
"world" may strike us an "ivory tower" argument, but, for Astell,
it meant a necessary escape from the "eyes of men." She invites
"ladies" into the confines of the school, so that they "shall suffer no
other confinement" (14–5). Transcending the limits of gender, in
other words, paradoxically required new forms of delimitation.

The type of delimiting which takes up much of the *Proposal*
is the confinement of knowledge into disciplines. Two kinds of
boundary making are at work here. First is a principle of selectiv-
ity, for if women are to unmask "the deceitful flatteries of those
who, under pretense of loving and admiring you, really served
their *own* base ends," then they need to distinguish "real wisdom"
from "froth" and "idle tales" (15). Because women *need* to know
what's "real," their most practical option is, in regard to knowledge, to value the narrow over the wide: "Nor need she trouble
herself in turning over a great number of books, but take care to
understand and digest a few well chosen and good ones" (18).

Narrowing is accomplished both through this selecting of "good materials" (20) and, in the second form of boundary making, through categorical exclusion. In Part 2 of the *Proposal,* again with the practicality of her plan in mind, Astell maps out a strategy for ensuring that "Good natur'd" men will "not deny us" and that those who are proud, having failed to "entertain the least Suspicion that we shall overtop them," will not consider it necessary. Her tactic is to divide up knowledge with the men, excluding certain kinds of knowledge from her own institution—"We will not vie with them in thumbing over Authors, nor pretend to be walking Libraries"—to ensure access to other kinds: "Knowledge of the Books of GOD, Nature[5] I mean and the Holy Scriptures" (159).

Astell's image is useful in grasping the various ways in which the behaviors that came to constitute disciplinarity were written up and enacted: while Hume, Priestley, and other moral and natural philosophers were inside the "library" wreaking havoc for the sake of controlled productivity through their classificatory arguments, generic mixing, and revisionary activities, Astell and other writers working in the discourses of gender and education were walking outside, carrying away, for their own developmental purposes, certain carefully "chosen" books.

That kind of activity extended at least as far back as Margaret Cavendish, who, a generation earlier, foregrounded differences among subjects but appears to have been uniquely insistent upon—and strangely successful in—participating in them: "the only woman of her time to write extensively on issues of scientific theory," according to the Folger Collective, Cavendish "insisted on attending a special meeting of the all-male Royal Society, which did not elect a woman member until 1945."[6] She saw herself as linked to "the best philosophers, both Moral and Natural, as also the best Divines, Lawyers, Physitians, Poets, Historians, Orators, Mathematicians, [and] Chymists" by what she, anticipating Pope, called her "disease"—the disease of "much writing."[7]

The way her own writing proliferated was indicative of the kinds of differentiation to come. Her venture into the fast-growing new fields of "useful" sciences—*Observations upon Experimental Philosophy* (1666)—received a tailpiece two years later: *The Descrip-*

tion of a New World, called the Blazing-World. Adding "Fancy" to "Philosophy" was, for her, an inward turn occasioned by gender:

> For I am not Covetous, but as Ambitious as ever any of my Sex was, is, or can be; which makes, that though I cannot be Henry the Fifth, or Charles the Second, yet I endeavour to be Margaret the First. And although I have neither power, time nor occasion to Conquer the World as Alexander and Caesar did; yet rather then not to be a Mistress of one, since Fortune and the Fates would give me none, I have made a World of my own.[8]

In our terms today, this would be a disciplinary pairing of opposites: fancy and reason, fiction and nonfiction, art and science, with the first terms Romantically indicative of the creative mind seeking a natural solitude. Here, however, as with Astell and her proposed retreat, the turn inward is cast in social terms as a matter of female survival in a male world of wealth and power.

By the turn into the eighteenth century, Astell was joined by other women writers articulating similar concerns and strategies, who, despite anonymity, delays, and refusals to publish, were apparently aware of each other's efforts. Elizabeth Thomas, as I pointed out in the Argument, wrote a poem praising Astell, and, in the ode cited in this chapter, even echoed her vocabulary. Women, she argued, "must a serious judgement make, / What to elect, and what refuse" (39–40) if "well chosen books" (48) were to aid them in fending off the proliferation of writing and the greed of men.

Mary Lee, Lady Chudleigh, who also wrote a poem to Astell, responded to that author's *Some Reflections on Marriage* (1700) and to a disturbing wedding sermon she heard with "The Ladies Defence" (1701).[9] It, too, emphasized choice—"all such Toys despise; / And only study to be Good, and Wise"—linking the narrowing of subjects to the inward turn: "my Sex" should "Inspect themselves." The result, she wrote, would be the ability to produce "solid Notions." Since the purpose of the poem was to define proper behavior in marriage, she could not have Melissa, the female character, propose retirement as protection from men; instead, Melissa tells men how to be protective:

If we less wise and rational are grown,
'Tis owing to your Management alone.
If like the Ancients you wou'd gen'rous prove,
And in our Education shew your love;
Into our Souls wou'd noble Thoughts instill,
Our Infant-Minds with bright Ideas fill:
Teach us our Time in Learning to employ,
And place in solid Knowledge all our Joy:
Perswade us trifling Authors to refuse,
And when we think, the useful'st Subjects chuse.

"Solid Knowledge," according to this quasi-disciplinary formula, is the product of developmental "growth" through an "Education" that narrows in on the proper "subjects."

We know from letters to Elizabeth Thomas that Lady Chudleigh, unlike Melissa, did not seek better "Management" from men, but preferred an Astell-like retirement, "the great Part of my Time is spent in my closet; there I meet with nothing to disturb me, nothing to render me uneasy; I find my Books and my Thoughts to be the most agreeable Companions."[10] Such variations on Astell's "confinement" for the sake of freedom argument—itself a variation of what I have been calling proliferation through limitation and control for the sake of growth—were a particularly prominent feature of this discourse on gender and education. Astell's contemporary, Anne Finch, for example, ended "The Introduction" (c. 1702) she wrote for her poems with the image of a "contracted wing" among "few friends" in the "dark," and she titled another effort "The Petition for an Absolute Retreat" (1713).

For many women, of course, a retirement linking knowledge and solitude was less an option to be chosen and petitioned for than, in Lady Mary Wortley Montagu's words, a "retreat to which probably their circumstances will oblige them"[11]; it was a primary mode of survival in a world in which the alternative—marriage— was, "a lottery where there is (at the lowest computation) ten thousand blanks to a prize." In a genre whose very form raises issues of ongoing development, an epistle to a woman who is addressed as "Child," Montagu (also an admirer of Astell)[12] wrote: "The use of knowledge in our sex, besides the amusement of solitude, is to moderate the passions and learn to be contented with a small expense, which are the certain effects of a studious life."[13]

By the mid eighteenth century, when Montagu wrote the letter, the very notion of a "studious life," for women and for men, had been altered by the thematizing and enacting of the behaviors I have been discussing. As with Priestley's mixing of history with description and Hume's transformation of an inclusive treatise into multiple enquiries, the work of writing materialized in altered genres. As the Folger Collective observes, the traditional focus in histories of Literature on novels and novel criticism has "obscured the wealth" of women's "attention" to a "wide spectrum of genres" (xiv–xv). That includes such extraordinary attempts at mixing as Jane Barker's effort to mix much of that spectrum into a single work: *A Patchwork Screen for the Ladies* (1723). Her purpose in placing "Pieces of *Romances*, *Poems*, *Love-Letters*, and the like" in one "SCREEN" was to make writing work like "Needle-Work," and thus please "*Ladies*, in this latter age"—an age in which women were so "differently mix'd": "To wit, *Whigs* and *Tories*, *High-Church* and *Low-Church*, *Jacobites* and *Williamites*, and many more Distinctions, which they *divide* and *sub-divide*, 'till at last they make this *Disunion* meet in an harmonious *Tea-Table* Entertainment."[14] This inclusiveness may seem, at first, to be the opposite of the narrowing we have been discussing; however, in Barker's hands, it worked in a pointedly disciplinary manner, the accumulated divisions and subdivisions highlighting division itself as a principle of organization.

Patchwork assumed its far more familiar guise less than a generation later, appearing as the anthology, a genre that collects other genres in order to bind them together. Elizabeth Cooper acknowledged precedents for her work in the various "Lives" of the poets by William Winstanley and others, and we can add that several Renaissance discourses on poetry featured quasi-canonical lists.[15] But the feature of *The Muses Library* (1737) which, as she put it, "has never been aim'd at any where else," is highlighted in the subtitle: *A Series of English Poetry*. Cooper mixed her biographical and critical work on the selected poets with "some of the most beautiful Passages, or entire Poems, I could *chuse*" (emphasis mine). As with a sonnet series, the point of lining up parts was to produce a unified whole: a "*Poetical Chronicle*" of "this Island" grounded in the works themselves.[16]

The patchwork of the anthology remains, of course, the generic bedrock of the discipline of English Literature, but we are only now beginning to recover a sense of how such disciplinary work was engendered.[17] A major part of the problem has been the very narrowing that these texts helped to naturalize; many texts by women, as I discuss in more detail in Chapters 8 and 9, were left out of Literature. The first step of the recovery has thus been putting texts back into circulation. But, unless they are to be ignored again, they then have to be put into our texts—into, for example, a history of Literature or a history of writing. Put back into the former, Cooper's anthology would be examined for content: how closely her series resembles our current disciplinary list. In the latter, list making is itself a behavior in writing to be studied. From that perspective, the serial anthology can be linked generically to other mixed forms—including forms with less obvious connections to disciplinarity, such as Astell's *Proposal* and related texts on gender and education.

With knowledge divided up and narrowed so as to improve a self that turns "within,"[18] those works do appear to anticipate many of the central features (depth, development) of modern disciplinarity. For their authors, I have been emphasizing, those features made sense in regard to gender, as a means of ameliorating the subordination of women. However, this engendering of disciplinarity somehow became, and still largely remains—despite almost two decades of editorial salvage work—all but invisible.

The Subliming of Knowledge

Discourses, of course, do not simply disappear; frequently, they are overwritten by other discourses that contain some of the same features but subordinate them within a new mix. In Edmund Burke's *A Philosophical Enquiry into the Origin of Our Ideas of the Sublime and the Beautiful* (1759), for example, gender and knowledge mix with other concerns in ways that both obscure Astell's logic and accelerate the advent of disciplinarity.[19]

Obscurity itself, of course, is a central feature of the discourse of the sublime—one that it shares with another, closely related, form of writing in the latter half of the eighteenth century: the Gothic. Horace Walpole's *Castle of Otranto*, subtitled *A Gothic Story*, is a fantasy (in one sense) about the passing of architectural styles. The aesthetic violence that does in the castle is triggered by a transformation of the temporal into the spatial. The past in which Manfred usurped the throne returns in the form of a giant sword and helmet that are too big for the present. The pieces of armor and their owner are overwhelming, leaving the walls and the beholders "prostrate"[20] and permanently obscuring Manfred's dynastic hopes. The experience—the rising "up to" ("sub") and through the tops of the doors ("lintels," "limit," "limes")—literally enacts the word that Burke's *Enquiry* helped to popularize as a label for it: *sublime*.[21]

Although that word describes Manfred's experience, readers have experienced those same moments as ridiculous. "We can conceive," wrote Clara Reeve in 1778,

> and allow of, the appearance of a ghost; we can even dispense with
> an enchanted sword and helmet; but then they must keep within
> certain limits of credibility: A sword so large as to require a hundred
> men to lift it, a helmet that by its own weight forces a passage
> through a courtyard into an arched vault big enough for a man to
> go through . . . When your expectation is wound up to the highest
> pitch, these circumstances take it down with a witness, destroy the
> work of imagination, and, instead of attention, excite laughter.[22]

The distinction made here is extraordinary. Enchanted objects, of the proper size, are okay, and even a ghost is permissible. Apparently, it is fine to be slimed but not sublimed. The sublime takes us to the edge—in fact, it is the edge—between the awesome and the awful.

Karen Swann has recently rewritten that edge in political terms as "The Sublime and the Vulgar," arguing that "the sublime is always in danger of succumbing to gross popularity."[23] Because it always grounds itself in a taste held in common even as it celebrates the singularity of individual experience, the discourse of the sublime "laments . . . the ease with which the novel, obscure, and terrifying become contemptibly familiar with daily and vulgar use." The sublime must therefore court "vulgarity while it legislates against it, as part of its defense of the high" (10). Swann, building upon the efforts of Jonathan Arac, Michael Hays, Neil Hertz, and others,[24] uses this paradox to match Allan Bloom to Edmund Burke. The latter's work, she claims, draws together a similar "constellation of concerns — cultural decline, the fate of the Great Books, the tastes of the vulgar—and . . . lays the groundwork for the charged attacks on the public taste that began to emerge in England during the 1790s and that to this day continue to shape the terms of our debates on education and culture" (11).

To center the sublime in this manner, as a link spanning two hundred years, is to make it, and the late eighteenth-century philosophical and fictional obsession with it, less strange. But simply open Burke's *Enquiry* not to the Introduction on Taste but to the analysis of what tastes good at the end of Part IV, and the sense of strangeness rapidly returns:

> If you have tried how smooth globular bodies, as the marbles with which boys amuse themselves, have affected the touch when they are rolled backward and forward and over one another, you will easily conceive how sweetness . . . affects the taste; for a single globe (though somewhat pleasant to the feeling) yet by the regularity of its form, and the somewhat too sudden deviation of its parts from a right line, it is nothing near so pleasant to the touch as several globes, where the hand gently rises to one and falls to another; and this pleasure is greatly increased if the globes are in motion, and sliding over one another; for this soft variety prevents that weariness, which the uniform disposition of the several globes would otherwise produce. (152–53)

My purpose here in distancing us from Burke is not to challenge Swann. Hers are precisely the kinds of compelling connections my argument about disciplinarity must help to explain. Any such explanation, however, must be able to engage discontinuities as well as continuities. *How* does this particular text *from the past* "continue to shape the terms" of *a different* present?

To place Burke's text in the past requires first that we clarify its relationship to the Gothic—not just the Gothic thematically conceived in terms of pain and violence, but the Gothic as a particular kind of writing first produced in the late eighteenth century. For both Walpole and Reeve, the generic enterprise of the Gothic is the mixing of the "ancient romance" with the "modern romance" or "novel." In the former, argues Walpole, "all was imagination and improbability: in the latter, nature is always intended to be, and sometimes has been, copied with success" (7). Reeve accepts this formula in her "helmet" criticism of Walpole, insisting that the Gothic carefully balance "a sufficient degree of the marvellous, to excite the attention" and "enough of the manners of real life to give an air of probability to the work" (136). By establishing man as an object of knowledge and placing that object in a range of probable (how big is the helmet?) circumstances, Gothicism took as its project the mapping out of the kinds and limits of human behavior.

Burke is engaged in a similar act of knowledge production, but his equipment is of different kinds. Rather than the "marvellous" objects of ancient romance, Burke takes up the sublime figures of (ancient) rhetoric; those are mixed with the "real" in the form not of novelistic depictions of manners but of laws of taste accessed through (modern) Newtonian natural philosophy. This combination of rhetoric and natural philosophy within a historical frame was the prescription for what Hume called "a new kind of philosophy"—a kind capable of producing a "science of man."[25] Burke's project is thus precisely titled *A Philosophical Enquiry*.

Identifying the central concern of that project, however, has proven to be a difficult task. Burke's use of the term *origin,* for example, can be misleading because he does not mean a *why* but a *how*. He specifically rejects any attempt to unravel "the great chain of causes" as a foolish encroachment into divine, as opposed to human, knowledge, mocking Newton himself for reckless speculations about the æther (129–30). Like Newton, however, Burke does seek to identify laws—in his case, laws governing the mechanics not of celestial bodies but of human experience. He wants to classify the ways in which the "natural properties of things" affect the body and thus excite the passions. One of the reasons that Burke's—and the eighteenth century's—obsession with the sublime and the beautiful seems to strange to us now is that we have not carefully attended to *what* these mechanics are supposed to explain about the human. It is *not* primarily what we would now call *aesthetics.* Burke himself notes that "it was not my design to enter into the criticism of the sublime and beautiful in any art." He points out, for example, that "poetry as it regards the sublime and beautiful . . . has been often and well handled already"; even the turn to words in Part V is less concerned with rhetorical evaluations of language than with natural reactions to "natural things" (176–77).

What is naturally at stake? If we turn back to Burke's classical predecessors for a clue, we find, first, that much of Longinus's rhetoric of the sublime is taken up with the textual examples Burke eschews. Second, we discover, as John Baillie did in 1747, that "Longinus has entirely passed over the Inquiry of what the Sublime is,"[26] thus ironically, given Burke's emphasis on obscurity, subliming the sublime. When, however, we reach the end of Longinus's tract, a very specific concern does emerge: "what eats up our modern characters," concludes Longinus, "is the indolence in which, with few exceptions, we all now live, never working or undertaking work save for the sake of praise or of pleasure."[27] The problem, in other words, is making men work—for particular reasons in particular ways.

Burke's *Enquiry* takes up where Longinus leaves off. After an Introduction on Taste establishing our "common nature" (11), Part I, Section 1 begins by trying to define the "active principle" (31) we have in common. It is curiosity that is our basic motivator, argues Burke, but for people "advanced in life to any considerable degree" there must be "other causes" that induce the states of "pain and pleasure" which lift us out of the "state of indifference" (32). To dwell in that state is deadly: "Melancholy, dejection, despair, and often self-murder," warns Burke, are the consequences of staying in a "relaxed state of body." The lesson echoes Longinus's polemic: "labour," insists Burke, is "a thing absolutely requisite" (134–35).[28]

An important continuity in the discourse of the sublime and

the beautiful, then, is the emphasis on the necessity of work. The discontinuity in Burke is the focus on differentiating the motives for and kinds of work. The key difference in kind is between physical labor, which "preserve[s] the coarser organs," and labor that exercises "the finer and more delicate organs" by which "the mental powers act." The incredibly elaborate system of the *Enquiry* serves to distinguish "common labour," as a "mode of pain" suitable for the "grosser" parts, from work that is a "mode of terror" appropriate to the "finer" (136). In other words, Burke's quest to map out how humans work leads him to work itself, which he divides up and hierarchizes into what we would now call manual and intellectual labor.

The hierarchization proceeds by first establishing terror as "the ruling principle of the sublime" (58). Because, for Burke, there is "nothing sublime which is not some modification of Power" (64), he concludes that terror is power's "inseparable companion . . . growing along with it as far as we can trace them" (70). Linked on the one hand to power and on the other to intellectual labor, terror becomes the middle term though which Burke's text empowers the work of the mind.

As J. T. Boulton points out, Burke's turn to pain (and its finer forms, such as terror) as the sole source of the sublime "had no precedent."[29] By starting with an absolute distinction between pain and pleasure as "simple ideas, incapable of definition" (32), Burke was able to desynonymize the sublime and place it into a productive opposition to the beautiful.[30] Addison, for example, had opposed the "Great" to the "Beautiful" and had posited circumstances in which they could combine.[31] Burke, however, by keeping them absolutely separate, allows for what Terry Eagleton terms the "double ideological effect" of a "dialectic": the sublime becomes after Burke a "chastening, humiliating power, which decentres the subject into an awesome awareness of its finitude, its own petty position in the universe, just as the experience of beauty shores it up. . . . [W]e must be both cajoled and chastized, made to feel both homeless and at home."[32] For Eagleton, this dual effect is a corrective to the "commonplace of deconstructive thought" which sees "the sublime as a point of fracture and fading, an abyssal undermining of metaphysical certitudes." "While there is much of value and interest in this view," observes Eagleton, "it has served in effect to suppress just those modes in which the sublime also operates as a thoroughly ideological category."

The "abyssal" reading also fails to account for the specificity and historicity of the term *sublime*. It had been in use in English since Chaucer as a verb describing the chemical reaction in which a substance is heated "to convert it into vapour, which is carried off and on cooling is deposited in a solid form."[33] The vaporizing as the fading into the abyss, in other words, is only a step in a transformation into another substance. Thus the act of subliming, and its now more familiar synonym *sublimation,* were understood in the late eighteenth century to be acts of production. More specifically, they were applied frequently outside of chemistry to acts of knowledge production. "The heat of Milton's mind," observed Johnson, "may be said to sublimate his learning."[34] As a term from chemistry applied to other kinds of learning, the act of subliming was often employed to distinguish among those kinds, as in Burke's description, in the French Revolution tract, of an economist "subliming himself into an airy metaphysician."[35]

The preface to the second edition of the *Enquiry*, in fact, ends with the suggestion that the pursuit of the sublime will help to shape the different forms of learning: "we may not only communicate to the taste a sort of philosophical *solidity*, but we may reflect back on the severer sciences some of the graces and elegancies of taste" (6; emphasis mine). Notice that our strong distinction between the humanities and the sciences is at Burke's historical moment a matter only of degrees of severity. That is why he can engage in the apparently multidisciplinary ventures that seem so strange to us now. Within his organization of knowledge, as I argued earlier, such excursions are branches of one central field: philosophy.

Branching, of course, is the architectonic strategy of the *Enquiry*: an initial absolute distinction—"what I dispose under different heads are in reality different things in nature" (5)—is extended into finer and finer distinctions over more and more specific areas of human experience. Because the analytic imperative is the production of Newtonian laws governing each and every area, the philosophical system comes to contain within itself a variety of rule-based fields of knowledge. These include what we know now as psychology ("qualities of the Mind," 110), ophthalmology ("the whole capacity of the eye," 137), sociology ("Society and Solitude," 43), zoology ("the great bag hanging to the bill of a pelican," 105), even the modern variant of anthropology known as body language (in love, "the head reclines something on one side; the eyelids are more closed than usual . . . the mouth is a little opened," 149).

Even as it branches philosophically, I am suggesting, the *Enquiry* participates in the modern reorganization of knowledge into separate and specialized disciplines. The word *sublime* itself, in linking depth (*sub-*) to transcendence, naturalizes the logic of specialization identified earlier: the valuing of knowledge that is narrow but deep. The role of the *Enquiry* in the construction of specialties is why Boulton, in tracing the influence of Burke's text, finds that it has little effect on subsequent philosophical investigations of the sublime but a great deal over other areas.[36]

The one area of particular importance, of course, is the branch to which Burke devotes a whole part: the concluding investigation of "Words." His claim for writing and reading is a large one: words work in a way that can make them more powerful than the "things they represent" (177). This is the claim that underwrites the reorganization of knowledge which I will detail in the next chapter: the displacement from the center of philosophy by literature. Poetry, claimed Wordsworth, by the turn into the nineteenth century, is "the breath and finer spirit of *all* knowledge" (*Prose* I.141; emphasis mine). As we shall see, the other kinds did not branch off from this new center. It became, instead, the specialization they all held in common—the prerequisite that prepared them to use language's power as a tool for deepening disciplinary differences.

With the claim for that power as its concluding argument, the *Enquiry* as a whole relates to us a remarkable story: the celebration of intellectual labor, the specialization of that labor into increasingly distinct and thus potentially deep fields, and the construction and accessing of that distinctive depth through specialized uses of words. This is, in short, a sketch of the transition we have been tracing to modern disciplinarity. Subliming in Burke's text, to put it another way, functions as a proliferation-through-limitation strategy—one that constructs boundary lines between the legitimate fields of a newly forming organization of knowledge—what become disciplines—and the illegitimate unknown. Writing was sublimed into English Literature, for example, by specializing in a few, supposedly highly "imaginative" kinds. The selection was naturalized as simply tasteful and timeless by dismissing the other kinds, such as the Gothic, as, in Wordsworth's word, "sickly" (*Prose* I.129).

Gender is not absent from this story; Burke clearly identifies men with the sublime and women with the beautiful. But set up, like "self" and "society," as just another pairing fitted to his absolute binary, the categories lose the particular explanatory power and political edge they had in Astell. Women are not only placed on the less powerful side of that binary, but their subordination to men is *itself* subordinated to, and naturalized by, the fundamental distinction in the *Enquiry* between human pain and pleasure. Burke's Newtonian laws sublimed the protodisciplinary concerns with cultivation we identified as gendered in Astell—the turn "within," "improvement," delimitation—into manifestations of a universal human nature. The divisions of labor and of knowledge which his discourse on the sublime help articulate can thus appear as naturally inevitable, rather than, in part, the products of the very hierarchy of genders they reproduce.

Culture and Disciplinarity

I turn now to *culture,* not because Burke uses the term, but because he does not. In fact, historically the two terms become almost mutually exclusive; once the discourse of the sublime helped set the boundaries for the new forms of knowledge, culture stepped in as the inclusive rubric for what had been legitimated. If, in other words, you have wondered, as I have, where the sublime went or if you have struggled to recreate the eighteenth-century fascination with it for students left only with its Freudian poor cousin, subli mation, culture is the culprit. It is also a link from the shift to disciplinarity I have been describing to—as *cultural studies*—the most recent locus for disciplinary discontent.

The thrill of interdisciplinarity in the late twentieth century, like that of bungee jumping, has something to do with the feeling of flying free of certain constraints while staying solidly tethered to the platform of one's own discipline. To do cultural studies, however, particularly as it aspires to greater independence, is to start off by first stretching the tether like a slingshot—stretching it in the hope of empowering a scholarly flight that will transcend previous limits. The danger, of course, as in an episode of reverse bungee jumping I actually saw on television, is that the upward flight ends in a collision with the bottom of the platform, a jarring return to the solidity of disciplinarity. In fact, many who have tried to institute cultural studies programs at their universities are probably very familiar with such collisions, the force of which often knocks individuals or the whole group back where they or it came from.

I want to conclude this chapter, like the last one, with a brief turn to this present situation, so that we do not leave engendering behind as a problem in the past. My argument is that what enables interdisciplinary flight and what enforces disciplinary limits is the tether of *culture* itself: the object of knowledge—culture—and the way we know it—disciplinarity—are inextricably linked. Whether cultural studies should be institutionalized as a separate discipline is an interesting question, but the fact that it is inherently disciplinary is of far greater import for the problem of change. Let me put this as bluntly as possible: the crucial issue for cultural studies is culture itself. If cultural studies is to reshape the kinds and organization of knowledge we produce, then it must turn upon its constitutive noun—not in a debate over what *culture* means but in an analysis of how it came to be at the center of debate.

Eighteenth-century scholars are chronologically positioned to contribute substantially to such an analysis, for, as Raymond Williams carefully detailed almost two decades ago, "*Culture* as an independent noun, an abstract process or the product of such a process, is not important before lC18 and is not common before mC19." Quoting from British and German sources, Williams shows that this rise in importance was not unopposed. In the 1780s, for example, Herder "wrote of *Cultur* [*sic*]: 'nothing is more indeterminate than this word, and nothing more deceptive than its application to all nations and periods.'" The applications that particularly concerned him were the natural histories of the mid and late eighteenth century—histories that generically transformed discussions of the processes of cultivation into narratives describing a standard transition from the state of nature to the state of culture. Such narratives both universalized (the same transition happens everywhere) and hierarchized (the transition is an improvement) those states, leaving Herder to bewail to "Men of all the quarters of the globe" that "The very thought of a superior European culture is a blatant insult to the majesty of Nature."[37]

Herder's purpose was not to formulate an alternative to culture—in fact, his complaint only makes sense within a nature/culture binary—but to put it in the plural so that every group could have one. That move, of course, has led us into the currently ironic position of cultural studies—ironic because those who practice it are increasingly dependent—in work that is supposed to accentuate difference in an egalitarian manner—on a concept that remains both universalizing (cultures may be different, but they happen to everyone) and hierarchizing (there are now more of them to judge). Discomfort with this dependence has surfaced in the social sciences, in recent collections such as that of Münch and Smelser, *Theory of Culture*,[38] and, in the humanities, in work such as David Radcliffe's *Forms of Reflection*. If we want to understand difference, Radcliffe argues,

> why pursue concepts of culture that can be applied to all literatures and societies indifferently? This seems to be the impetus behind discussions of method in recent criticism: while cultural practices are thought to vary, all literatures and societies are thought to behave as cultures. [Can we] recogniz[e] structures of difference other than those articulated by and as culture?[39]

His alternative is to "reflect not on culture itself but on the literary procedures that generate the belief in culture, to reflect on them in ways that do not reduce differences to functions or disfunctions [*sic*] within an implicit totality" (201).

How did this particular totality first arise, and why has it remained implicitly desirable? In this case, our present situation can provide us with a clue to the past. Why do so many scholars now pursue cultural studies? Because, whether they see their efforts as enacting the British model of a collaborative, ongoing political project or the more American emphasis on "reading" a wider range of popular objects, they do cultural studies because it somehow seems, compared with the more traditional disciplines, more real, more relevant, more marketable, more useful. There are, of course, immediate reasons for this desire, such as the defunding of the university, but the specific connection of "usefulness" to "culture" has, as well, a very specific history—one that can further clarify the role of culture in the reorganization of knowledge which brought us modern disciplinarity. In that history, the issue of *use* can be seen as a disturbance that helped to render the older organization untenable.

The usual suspects in histories of knowledge focused on the eighteenth century are the *rise of science* and, after Foucault, the advent of the *human sciences,* with objectivity replacing faith and man displacing God. But, as we have seen in regard to gender, these tales can be misleading; in this case, they obscure a realignment crucial to those changes. The most oft-cited originary event in those tales, for example, the founding of the Royal Society, illustrates the problem. The issue we would now engage as objectivity was raised as a matter of authority in the Society's motto, "On the word of no one." But the turn from another's word was not just a juridical move to empower one's own, but a turn from words to action—very particular actions. "The objectives outlined by Robert Hooke," points out Robert Mandrou, "defined a programme focused upon experiments and practical applications." This was not just an emphasis on the practical, however, but an exclusion of that which was not: "First and foremost," Mandrou continues, "it was explicitly stated that the university disciplines subject to discussion and political controversy (metaphysics, divinity, morals), together with the strictly literary ones (grammar, rhetoric, logic) would not enter into the society's work, which should be directed to improving the useful arts, manufacture, machines and inventions."[40]

This was not simply a matter of separating the trivium from the quadrivium, for that organization was structured not according to the principle of usefulness, but, as David Wagner argues, in terms of different kinds of order.[41] Although those kinds were roughly verbal versus numerical, remember that the latter mixed, in Pythagorean terms, music and astronomy with arithmetic and geometry. When the society met, in what they called *commissions,* the most frequented concerned mechanics, whereas the most poorly attended one was on astronomy (Mandrou 269).

This new conception of usefulness—after all, rhetoric had been seen as a most practical and useful art—and the emphasis on it became the initial and crucial realignment that preceded and was indispensable to modern science and professional scientists. As Margaret Jacob argues in a book that—given my present argument—is somewhat ironically titled *The Cultural Meaning of the Scientific Revolution,* our crucial distinction between "pure" and "applied" science "simply did not exist" in the eighteenth century, for science then "was, perhaps above all else, useful science."[42] She details the mixing this imperative authorized of men of action and of the mechanical arts, of academics, self-taught experimentalists, traveling educators, entrepreneurs, and gentlemen. The knowledge they produced was not subsequently adapted for use by the last two groups but was from the start produced to be used by them.

The early history of social scientific knowledge tells the same story. As we saw in Chapter 1, the man whom Marx and others cite as the first political economist, William Petty, founded the Experimental Philosophy Club in order to improve husbandry by measuring the intrinsic value of the land, a most useful task for one of the largest landowners in Ireland. The growing influence of this club and of the Royal Society thus posed a difficult problem for the arts and knowledge outside of their shared agenda: if those activities were not useful, then what were they? The answer the eighteenth century eventually provided was *culture.* By that I mean not that culture was simply the label for everything "useless," but that the classification of culture worked to redistribute use value by functioning in two strangely complementary ways. First, on the basis of its earlier usage as, in Williams's words, "a noun of process," specifically "the tending of natural growth" (87), it played a crucial role in the aforementioned natural histories—narratives in which *everything* a civilization does is understood to contribute to its transition from nature into a product of the process of culture— that is, into the state of *being* a culture. The marking out of this new common ground, not by rejecting the criteria of usefulness but by extending them, is what I understand John Barrell to be describing in his extraordinary analyses of the eighteenth-century poems, such as *The Fleece* and *The Castle of Indolence*, which most explicitly try to map all kinds of "arts" into this newly inclusive domain.[43]

But—and it is in this conjuncture that the conceptual staying power of the term lies—culture simultaneously functions to reorganize internally the very unity that it has helped contrive. In this second meaning, it identifies a subcategory of the activities of a culture which are cultural activities—roughly what we now call the humanities and fine arts—from which a particular kind of use value can be extracted. What I am describing, in other words, is how culture became the discursive infrastructure[44] for disciplinarity—just as cultivation was for the earlier organization of knowledge. It remains so by providing an inclusive frame—culture as the rubric for all that can be legitimately studied—within which specialization— the cultured part of culture—can be naturalized as the means of maximizing the usefulness of the entire disciplinary enterprise.

What that naturalization obscures is the engendering of all of these divisions. Let me be quite precise here. I am not saying that the discourse of culture ignores gender; as with the category I am arguing it replaced—the sublime—culture characteristically invokes gender difference, and those differences are now, of course, a fixture of cultural studies. But what Gothically haunts those efforts—the problems they center and the solutions they propose— are the interrelations I describe in this book. Every time we invoke *culture* we are reinvoking both a continuity with the *sublime*—the naturalizing of difference—and a discontinuity—the hierarchizing through "usefulness" of the sciences and the humanities. The first move mutes Astell's sense of discipline as a means of redressing inequality, and the second, in measuring all knowledge against the "useful" knowledge of "men of action," institutes the very gaze she wished to avoid. The difference that culture continues to naturalize, that is, is modern disciplinary difference.

To retheorize disciplinarity from the perspectives I have offered here—gender, sublimity, culture—is to confront the historicity of that enterprise and thus some possibilities of change. First, although cultural studies is currently an important location for discussing such change, it may be time to cut the tether—the category of culture, that is, has bound us historically to our present form of disciplinarity. If *inter*disciplinary activity is the final goal—activity that leaves the unit of knowledge intact even as it allows multiple units to interact—then the study of culture is a conceptually adequate enterprise. But if dedisciplinarity,[45] moving *from* the disciplines, is a goal, then we need categories that allow for organizational models other than (eighteenth-century) *branching* and (modern) *subliming*.

Second, having seen how Burke's binaristic theorization of the sublime—leading to finer and finer branching—naturalized differentiation into the narrow but deep, we need now to retheorize theory itself. Today, it is still often understood to be productive of only increased specialization: supposedly narrower concerns articulated in more inaccessible language. However, the extension of theory throughout the disciplines has, in fact, functioned to connect previously discrete domains of knowledge, allowing for what sociologists such as Dietrich Rueschemeyer call *dedifferentiation*—in this case, a remapping of the domains of knowledge such that the new "forms of division of labor . . . are not necessarily more specialized."[46]

Third, and this is why I have repeatedly returned this chapter to the issue of engendering, Astell's *Proposal* offers evidence that can help us recoordinate our practice with the recent functions of theory. It sheds historical light on why the present accelerated entry of women into the universities and women's studies into the curriculum necessarily disrupts disciplinarity; it is a matter not only of content but of the earlier role of gender hierarchy in configuring "education." Astell's turn to "an Institution and previous discipline" suggests how these past remappings have been social and contested rather than simply natural. It also points to the problem of intention, in that an effort to address women's inequality participated in the construction of an organization of knowledge which perpetuated it.[47] As Burke's focus on labor makes clear, that construction also entailed, necessarily, a reorganization of work—one that had, as we shall see in the next section, similar consequences for women. First, however, I want to use the concept of culture to ground my arguments about disciplinarity in the specific geographical and institutional contexts of Britain in the eighteenth century.

3 Scottish Philosophy & English Literature

§☛ Here, My Lord, there seems to be occasion for a little philosophy.
—Thomas Blackwell, *An Inquiry into the Life and Writings of Homer*, 1735

§☛ I do not know what you will think best for me afterwards; but the thing I should most dislike, and, I think, least profit by, would be an endeavour to acquire Scotch knowledge in a Scotch town. Political economy may surely be studied in England. As for metaphysics, I cannot even understand the word. —Lord John Russell, future prime minister, to his father, 1809

What Thomas Blackwell wrote bears little relationship to what we would now call philosophical discourse. Having first turned briefly to theology to "assert that Homer's poems are of human composition," he proceeded to write history (of "antiquity"), geography (of "Asia the Less"), climatography (of the "temperate regions"), political science (of the "early times of liberty"), psychology (of "young minds"), sociology (of the "Grecian manners"), anthropology (of people not "yet taught to be ashamed of themselves"), not to mention literary criticism (of a "poet who has wrote well"). Our label for such a proliferation of inquiries in contemporary academic work is *interdisciplinary,* but that word cannot describe Blackwell's situation. There were so many occasions for a little philosophy in eighteenth-century Scotland not because many *different* disciplines met on that common ground, but because what we now assume to be separate fields of knowledge had not yet been fully differentiated.

That differentiation has been, for me, an occasion for more than a little history of writing. The word I have been using so far to describe this form of proliferation is *branching*—a metaphor to suggest how inquiries of various kinds were understood to share an originary philosophical center. Arthur King and John Brownell have referred to this historical configuration as the *hegemony* of philosophy, explaining that, "until the nineteenth century," it "dominated knowledge through four relations: (1) it provided the unity for all knowledge, (2) although clearly under attack by the sixteenth century, it provided knowledge of reality, (3) it posed and answered epistemological questions about knowledge and knowing, and (4) it directed scientific knowledge toward new goals and opened new paths."[1] Blackwell gives us both a sense of the diversity of those paths and, by placing his work in an institutional and national context—he was a professor at Aberdeen University—a way of approaching their differentiation into disciplines.

During the eighteenth century in Britain, Scotland was the Enlightenment home of philosophical inquiry—so much so that those who wished to follow Blackwell's paths routinely followed the path north from England to the universities of Scotland. Lord Russell's letter to his father, quoted above, was in response to the suggestion that he do just that. But by the early nineteenth century the path no longer seemed so inviting. The preeminence of Scotch knowledge was on the wane, not only because of increased competition from educational institutions elsewhere, but because the organization of that knowledge around philosophy was itself in flux. For the young Lord Russell, political economy was available in England *and* available as a subject separate from what used to be its associated branches in philosophy, such as metaphysics, which—certainly to him—did not appear to be so central anymore.

This change in status was startlingly severe. Between Blackwell and Russell, philosophical writing shifted from being extraordinarily popular—"not just respectable," observes John Price, "but fashionable,"[2] to being a specialized discourse displaced from the cultural center as it became geared increasingly to a limited number of experts. As we shall see, this was not a change inflicted from outside that center—the subject center or the geographical center—but induced from within: metaphysics, for example, was a particular target of Hume's empirically oriented havoc. In Hume's own words, a decentered philosophy became—"besides the immediate pleasure"—"nothing but" the methodological corrections of "reflections of common life."[3]

At roughly the same time, Literature was transformed from that which Samuel Johnson defined inclusively as "learning; skill in letters" to a field of knowledge concerned with writing, and writing about, an increasingly refined version of Elizabeth Cooper's "Poetical Chronicle." This specialization, however, was not a decentering, for the extravagant Romantic claims for canonical works of "this island" pushed English Literature toward the special position it has occupied since the mid nineteenth century: "the breath and finer spirit," again, in Wordsworth's words, "of all knowledge."

My topic in this chapter, then, is the disciplinary displacement of Scottish philosophy by English Literature—a reorganization of knowledge which, to anticipate the next chapter, also marked the advent of modern professionalism in Britain. To give the notion of *reorganization* some material weight, I will sketch out a political and then an institutional history, first picking up the path to Scotland by pursuing the discussion of culture begun in the previous chapter. Once north of the border, I will turn to the history of Scottish education to ground the branching model of knowledge in curricular and pedagogical practice. The chapter will conclude with a trip back across the border to Wordsworth and the English Lakes as they were experienced in writing by John Stuart Mill—a move that, in regard to the chapter, will bring us back home to culture by suggesting how, historically, culture was brought home.

National Unity and Cultural Doubling

In Chapter 2 I argued that culture, as a kind of doubling, became the discursive infrastructure for disciplinarity: it provided an inclusive frame—culture as the rubric for all that can be legitimately studied—within which specialization—the cultured part of culture—can be naturalized as the means of maximizing the usefulness of the entire disciplinary enterprise. That valorized part provides the means both of differentiating among cultures and, within a single culture, of hierarchizing its constituencies according to their access to, or identification with, those definitive practices. While this argument does describe how culture works, it does not explain how it first *came* to work that way. What happened—prior to the appearance of the term in its modern guise—which materially cast the problem of group identity and behavior as a matter of the kind of doubling I have just outlined?

Here is where we need to turn to Scotland, for its relationship to the rest of Great Britain—most visibly and violently manifested in Jacobitism—troubled that nation's identity throughout the eighteenth century. All three of the terms I have just put into play—*culture, nationalism,* and *Jacobitism*—remain, in fact, very troublesome today. The issue of the current culture wars arose in the last chapter, particularly in the form of cultural studies as a rallying cry for disciplinary change, displacing and replacing English departments as it reorganizes publishers' lists. Violence of a more explicit kind has been occurring—in Bosnia and elsewhere across the globe—under the rubric of nationalism, provoking a fresh wave of scholarly efforts to theorize and document how that *-ism* works. Its new incarnations in the United Kingdom have spurred—and been spurred by—renewed interest in such topics as Jacobitism, which has become a touchstone in the ongoing debate over the historiography of eighteenth-century Britain—era of bourgeois individualism or *ancien régime?*—a question that goes, in W. A. Speck's words, to "the very heart of English history" and even to the current crisis over the country's connections to the Continent.[4]

Although there is ongoing confusion and disagreement over the meanings and referents of all three of these terms, the mystery surrounding *Jacobitism* is perhaps the most striking and strange. In fact, that strangeness is nowhere more evident than in the debates over nationalism. Turn to Gerald Newman's important 1987 book, *The Rise of English Nationalism*, and you will not even find the word *Jacobite* in the index.[5] Open Linda Colley's prize-winning book *Britons*, published just a few years later on the same topic (1992), and you will find twelve subtopics and two *see also*s. This apparently absolute difference, however, is just the start of the strangeness, for if you follow Colley into her text you will eventually find yourself entering with her into a scholarly twilight zone—visited at one time or another by almost all of the participants in the nationalism debate—where what are supposed to be *explanations* of nationalism begin to seem like *examples* of it. With a British perspective, secure in profits and Protestantism, as the norm, Colley links Scottish Jacobites to reckless violence prior to and during the '45 and to an "aggressive and sometimes unscrupulous" "attitude toward authority" in their "disproportionate contribution" to the Empire after it.[6]

Voices more sympathetic to Scottish Jacobites and Jacobitism in general have, of course, been raised, particularly in recent years; but there, too, a certain strangeness persists. Rather than disappearing into a shadowy past, as in Newman, Jacobitism has been made to cast, in somewhat mysterious fashion, tremendous shadows over the present. Paul Monod hauntingly concludes his book with "King James III . . . smiling at us so benignly. He recognizes us, and seems to suggest that, if his own titles and authority are no more than myths, so too are ours."[7] J. C. D. Clark's contribution to *The Jacobite Challenge* ends no less dramatically with another time-traveling vision—in this instance, "250 years hence"—when historians are asking

> Was a socialist England ever a real possibility after 1918? Most implausibly of all, can it really have been true that significant numbers of intellectuals, including even historians, subscribed to and occasionally acted on an ideology so "nostalgic and anachronistic"? Such incredulous investigators from a future age might find some suggestive analogies in the re-excavation of Jacobitism in the 1980s. (185)

What kind of thing, we might ask, can occasion all of these responses? By comparing Jacobitism with another *-ism,* socialism, and clearly casting both as "ideologies," Clark avoids the conceptual soul searching with which Monod begins his book. Arguing that Jacobitism has been "too vague to grasp, too volatile to define,"

Monod reviews earlier classificatory efforts before floating "culture" as a possibility. Admitting the ambiguities of that term, he recounts briefly structuralist and poststructuralist uses of *culture,* strangely subsuming Foucault's effort to historicize it within a Derridean "identification of culture with language"—an identification that, finally, authorizes Monod's own solution: Jacobitism, he says, is a "political culture" that should be interpreted as a "system of signs" (7–10).

I say he *strangely* subsumes the issue of culture's historicity—of *when* the term *culture* itself took on the heavy burden of meaning it still bears today—because attending to that date would allow for a very different twist on the problem of Jacobitism. To speak of Jacobitism as a "cultural phenomenon"—despite the considerable value of Monod's work—is, I would argue, to not quite grasp the historical point: Jacobitism is the occasion for the advent of the phenomenon of culture itself as a constitutive category of modern knowledge. That is a reason—not the only reason, but an important one—for its current intellectual celebrity—a celebrity contemporaneous with, as I have just pointed out, that of culture. Jacobitism, to put it another way, helped to make possible the very mode of analysis which Monod deploys to explain it.

To construct this argument, I need to address all three terms, for nationalism was the problem for which Jacobitism provided a solution: culture. Establishing the historically and geographically specific nature of that problem is no easy task; Gerald Newman reveals that a computer search in the mid 1980s came up with "only one document in the entire bibliography of nationalism which focuses squarely on the general problem of an English variety" (xviii). He attributes that lack to "a manifestation in the academic world of the fond old idea that God is an Englishman. Other peoples—the French, the Germans, the Mexicans and Irish—have their nationalism, their amusing beliefs, and silly prejudices about themselves," but the English simply *are* themselves (xix).

Newman, Linda Colley, and others have since filled in the blank on the computer screen, and it is tempting now simply to dismiss this attitude as another silly prejudice. But I also think we can take its assertion of difference as a clue to something that may have been different in the workings of English self-identification. Otto Dann's description of nationalism is useful here. We apply "nationalism," he observes, "to any political movement by which a social group, regarding itself as a nation, aims at political sovereignty in its area of settlement and claims political participation and autonomy."[8]

In eighteenth-century Britain, political sovereignty came first; a group did not aim at political sovereignty, but a sovereign state aimed at forming a group. The problem specific to British nationalism was thus how to form a group—how to address disparate elements as a totality. The solution was to insist on what Newman calls the "fond old idea" that it simply was one. What was needed, that is, was a mode of address which assumed that a totality was always already there, waiting to be articulated—whatever we *call* a culture always functions for us *as* a culture.

By attending to Jacobitism we can begin to understand the shape that totality assumed. With its overlapping forms (political, social, religious) of coherence and difference within a United Kingdom, Jacobitism provided the eighteenth century with a paradigmatic experience of the hierarchical doubling that came to be called *culture*. Even in its most basic political meaning—the restoration of the Stuarts—the hierarchizing aims of Jacobitism—legitimate kings over illegitimate ones as in high culture over low—always served totalizing ends—not Scotland splitting off from England but a newly legitimated and thus coherent whole.

A look at how that whole actually was formed in 1707 can make the connection to the formation of culture less schematic and more concrete. The Act of Union was itself a doubling of the kind I am describing; as a solution to the particular problem of British nationalism, group formation, it sought to ensure a whole by, paradoxically, dividing up into parts. Scotland was to become a part of England by not only remaining, but becoming, in very particular ways, a particularly distinct part. The Act differentiated the political and economic ways from the legal, religious, and thus educational ones—those having to do with the passing down, regulation, and valorization of distinctive traits, customs, and beliefs—in other words, that which we would now call *culture*. The Union, I am sug-

gesting, attempted to produce Britain by producing—articulating—that new category.

By *articulate,* I do not mean that this attempt was made solely
in the language of the Act. It transpired materially, with swiftness
and force, through a process of institutionalization which was itself
a doubling. "A central bureaucracy," argues the sociologist Robert
Wuthnow, "was created by adding new layers of officials to traditional institutions."[9] Scotland's institutional workings became a
suturing of the "centralizing and traditional" which authorized, in
Wuthnow's words, a new unifying "network of political patronage" (252–53). That patronage, in turn, financially brought into
play the proliferation of activities we know as the Scottish Enlightenment. The Enlightenment was not just a flowering of Scottish
culture but a flowering of the *category* of culture itself. Those who
participated in it were linked, through the patronage circulating
through Scotland's newly doubled institutional infrastructure, to
the initial doubling of the Act of Union itself. Virtually all of them,
observes Wuthnow, "benefited from official patronage" (258–59)
made possible by the new politico-economic unity. The totalizing
effort to make Britain a nation thus proceeded *through*—not in
spite of—the articulation of cultural difference. The doubling ensured that difference and unity articulated each other. Scottish cultural activity in the eighteenth century thus did not fail, as many
historians and critics have complained, to induce nationalism; the
surprise was what was induced—British nationalism.

That surprise was the same even in regard to Jacobite activity,
where, in Murray Pittock's words, "the politics and the image"
became "utterly sundered" as King George IV donned the tartan.
For Pittock, this was and is a problem in the discipline of history
itself: "the ultimate triumph of incrementality"—Pittock's word
for the Whiggish workings of Hanoverian history—"having been
to display its opponent as the reverse of itself."[10] I am arguing that
culture became the classificatory tool that enabled such workings,
its doublings the very means by which Pittock's sundered reversals—undoublings—could take place.

It became such a tool *at* that time and *in* that place because
eighteenth-century Scotland was an institutional and discursive lo-

cation for what Steve Bruce has called "the hyperbolic treatment of difference." After tracing the changing but consistently extreme depictions of Highlanders before and after the '45, Bruce concludes that "Walter Scott could safely deploy his highland myths of distinctiveness in an unionist cause precisely because such distinctiveness had been largely reduced to unimportant matters of cultural preference."[11] Here, again, within the category of culture, distinctive difference ensures the very unity it would appear to challenge. Culture does this by regulating, in Bruce's terms, "importance"— what I earlier called "use value."

Such value is generated through the acts of doubling I have been describing, and the doubling in Scotland was as pervasive as the differences were hyperbolic. The fate of those who, officially or unofficially, opposed the Union and/or the king who presided over it, was not to escape or undo the doubling of those within the patronage net but necessarily to double in return. As Howard Erskine-Hill has demonstrated, Jacobites often had to resort to a "cryptic code"—already a doubling in that one thing was disguised as another—but even that code was frequently itself doubled for sometimes the "disguises" were not just camouflage but were in themselves "real and telling historical instances."[12]

The multiplications of meaning which this doubling entailed produced the *effect* of depth—a profundity that Erskine-Hill cannily calls a "*literary* idiom." It was literary in the modern sense of culture as the deep truths of a people, with Literature—as I am about to argue—at its center, as the disciplinary embodiment of the deepest. The contributions of Scotland to what became the discipline of Literature in the late eighteenth and early nineteenth centuries were, in fact, characteristically marked by the feature of doubling—sometimes personified in the doubles that haunt the novels of Hogg and Scott and sometimes more problematically enacted as in the doubling of author/translator, present/past in the forgery controversies surrounding Ossian and the ballad revivals.[13]

My point here is that in Literature, as in history, the category of culture and its particular workings have played a crucial role, configuring how and what we know. And if I am right about the temporal and geographical origins of *culture* in Britain, then we need to stay focused on Scotland to understand the accompanying reorganization of knowledge into the modern disciplines. We are in good company, for there has been a recent wave of work across many of those disciplines—including Pittock in Literature, Monod and Clark in history, and Wuthnow in sociology—which attend to Scotland in innovative ways.

In fact, two substantial books that engage Literature's own history have also focused directly on Scotland: Howard Weinbrot's *Britannia's Issue* (1993) and Robert Crawford's *Devolving English Literature* (1992). Weinbrot describes how, from 1660 to 1760, "the native view of Anglo-Saxon heritage polished by expanding Rome is modified to include Scottish Celtic and Hebrew Jewish cultures." Highlighting specific genres and "historical and intellectual contexts," he presents this acceptance of other cultures as a "continuing change" that points to today, when so "much literature in English is of course in African, American, Australian, Canadian, Caribbean, Indian, New Zealand, Pakistani, and other idioms."[14] What England accepted from Scotland, Crawford mischievously argues, was "English Literature" itself—a product, as he sees it, of a Scottish effort, in light of opportunities opened up by the Union, to improve themselves by clearing Scotticisms in favor of an ideal of "English" which was largely of their own construction.[15] For my purposes, what both authors share is the premise that the status of English Literature as a discipline is tied to the status of Scotland in the Union: the reorganizations of knowledge and of nation go hand in hand.

Instituting Knowledge

The history of Scottish education figures in both reorganizations— but so has the telling of it. "Scottish education and literacy," reads the jacket of a 1985 book on their role in Scottish identity, "have achieved a legendary status. A campaign promoted by church and state between 1560 and 1696 is said to have produced the most literate population in the early modern world. This book sets out to test this belief." After efforts to debunk key parts of the legend, including open access and high literacy rates, R. A. Houston clarifies an overriding agenda in the conclusion:

> when we identify differences and similarities it is vital to assess their importance as genuine indicators of divergent social organizations. Yet all this should not prevent us from trying to further the idea of *British* history. Indeed we should not be slow to follow Francis Bacon who nearly four centuries ago expressed the earnest hope that . . . "neither of these [Scotland and England] are to be considered as thinges entier of themselves, but in the proportion they beare to the whole."[16]

Obviously much is at stake here, and, if *Braveheart* running all night in Scottish movie theaters is any indication, those stakes have risen even higher in the decade since Houston's book. Fortunately, my agenda here is not to intervene in a debate that both sides trace back at least four hundred years; rather, I want to cull it for a few events and features that speak to the issues of reorganization.

The fifteenth century saw not only the founding of three Scottish universities—St. Andrews in 1411, Glasgow in 1450, and Aberdeen in 1494—but also the passage in 1496 of an Act that was, as S. Leslie Hunter observed,[17] the first in Europe to attempt to introduce some element of compulsory education. It directed barons and freeholders of substance to place their eldest sons in school until they had "perfite latyne." Although that Act was officially passed but had little effect, sixty-four years later John Knox and his fellow Reformers offered, in their *First Book of Discipline*, a plan for a national system of education which Parliament officially rejected but which continued, as a model, to have considerable effect. This scheme, offered in the aftermath of the destruction of many Church schools during the Reformation, was also compulsory, embracing rich and poor within an institutional sequence of

> elementary schools in country parishes in which the 5–8 year olds would be taught reading and the elements of the Catechism . . . ; grammar schools in towns of "any repute" in which the 8–12 year olds would study Latin grammar; high schools in important towns

in which selected pupils of 12–16 would study Latin, Greek, logic and rhetoric; and universities in which the most able scholars would pursue a 3-year Arts course followed by a 5-year course in medicine, law or divinity. (Hunter 3)

Although the next 150 years did see the appearance of a fairly widespread network of parish schools serving elementary needs, the number and quality of the grammar or burgh schools were decidedly insufficient. As a result, the universities were filled with boys as young as twelve years old, with most being fifteen or sixteen. Those institutions thus felt two kinds of curricular pressure. On the one hand, they had to fulfill the general education requirements of the absent or ineffective secondary schools, offering a basic exposure to Latin, Greek, and the traditional liberal arts. On the other hand, these young students of varying social and economic backgrounds were perceived as being in need of "useful" knowledge and "practical" training, for intellectual activity and civic life were explicitly linked in Scotland; the University of Edinburgh, for example, was founded by the Town Council on the model of Calvin's Academy in Geneva.[18] That modeling did not occur on the university level in England. To the extent that the need for the useful and practical surfaced there, it was institutionally articulated in a different manner. Following Baconian ideas on educational reform, the Puritans founded schools in their homes which were constituted publicly after 1689 as the Dissenting Academies. Although their curriculum at first resembled that of the established universities, during the eighteenth century the academies began to diversify into modern languages, modern history, and scientific subjects.[19]

At the time of the Act of Union (1707), then, the Scottish universities embodied curricular conflicts that in England had already produced alternative institutional forms. The product in Scotland was pedagogical reform. The deployment of teachers had been yet another way in which most of the universities had resembled secondary schools: the regenting system authorized one "master" to prelect a class of students through every subject in the four-year arts curriculum. The first challenge to that procedure was issued in the late 1500s by the educational reformer Andrew "The Blast" Melville. In what Harold Perkin has called "a typically Scottish device for saving money," Melville substituted for the regents "a smaller number of professors responsible for single disciplines."[20] This change was only widely adopted in the eighteenth century, beginning with Edinburgh in 1708, but it spread rapidly, producing subject-specific chairs in a wide range of arts and sciences.[21]

This new feature completed the peculiar mix that was the eighteenth-century Scottish university, an institutional formation differing markedly from that of England, as G. E. Davie and others have argued, and yet also departing from the continental model it more closely resembled.[22] My point in detailing the construction of difference is not to celebrate romantically uniqueness or individuality for its own sake. I seek, instead, an alternative to the mystifying metaphors that appear where discussions of the university intersect with celebrations of the extraordinary output of knowledge we know as Scottish philosophy and the Scottish Enlightenment. In Perkin's incisive analysis, for example, we are told that "the establishment of separate chairs . . . had an *almost magical effect* on the advancement of knowledge" (32; emphasis mine). *Magic* in this case is Perkin's shorthand for a historical relationship between a particular form of power and specific kinds of knowledge. The end of regenting, in other words, institutionally empowered a new regime of knowledge.

To be specific, the universities, historically configured to provide their youthful and socially diverse student body with a general *and* useful course of education, adopted and altered the continental curricular model of a unified diversity. Working with "a sense of the encyclopaediac unity of all disciplines in philosophy," the Scottish critics—most of whom worked within or were associated with universities—represented themselves, in Gerald Chapman's words, "as investigating a 'branch' of what belongs to a much larger, communal investigation of Man in Nature and Society" (267–68). They thus characteristically wrote lectures and books on more than one subject, and, because each subject, as we saw with Blackwell, was an "occasion for a little philosophy," each lecture or book also branched out from an initial philosophical inquiry into a variety of different fields.[23]

To cast this branching as a *communal* investigation was a crucial maneuver in the Scottish enterprise, for it clarifies the ideological functions of unity as common-ness. Philosophical discourse as the common ground of different fields of inquiry authorized as well a social unity of the community as having something in common. "Though a philosopher may live remote from business," wrote Hume in a statement configured by this dual function, "the genius of philosophy, if carefully cultivated by several, must gradually diffuse itself throughout the whole society and bestow a similar correctness on every art and calling."[24] Philosophy was thus distinguished in part by an apparent openness, in terms of both its disciplinary inclusiveness—Johnson defined philosophy as "knowledge natural or moral"—and its social accessibility—"a philosophical book," observed John Price, "was not thought to require any special reading skills" (174).

Philosophy was, however, also the site of very distinct kinds of discursive mixing. As R. S. Crane observed, rhetoric assumed "in its new philosophical form, the role of architectonic art with respect to all the other particular arts which borrowed its devices or assimilated its ends."[25] Its end in becoming philosophical was to demonstrate "connections with the science of human nature." In George Campbell's *The Philosophy of Rhetoric* (1776), the works of the "poet and the orator" could both "furnish" "lights" on that science or, in turn, could be illuminated by it.[26] The point, from our perspective, is that in their mixing they came to valorize each other. The Scottish twist was that the literary works at issue came increasingly from the vernacular; examples from the student's own tongue were seen as being more easily absorbed and thus more practical as well as more useful in later pursuits of life (Palmer 11–12). The valorization of philosophical rhetoric in Scotland thus entailed the naturalizing of modern, as opposed to just ancient, literature as a valid object of knowledge.

For Campbell, the goal of knowing such an object was not "a correct map, but a tolerable sketch of the human mind." However, the degree of correctness, or tolerance level, varied according to the precise nature of the mix. For writers such as Hume, Reid, and Stewart, scientificity was the element increasingly at issue; their goal of the correct mapping of the mind required what Hume called a "new kind of philosophy"—one that must inform, and be informed by, not just rhetoric, but by Newtonian natural philosophy with its methodological turn toward general principles or laws. That turn, supposedly productive of a more rigorous and precise "science of Man," was nevertheless again configured by the Scottish imperatives of common-ness: a central unity of subjects, on the one hand, as in Hume's notion that this science was a "foundation" for a system of more specialized enquiries, and in Reid's contention that Newton's rules of philosophizing were simply "common sense"[27]; and, on the other, communal accessibility, for Hume insisted that philosophic analysis, as Chapman puts it, "be subservient to the 'easy and humane,' that is, the literate, common-sense, social world, and that the easy and humane criticize and feed back into the 'accurate and abstract'" (272).

The conjunction of these forms of unity is dramatically evident in Hume's *Treatise of Human Nature*. Proclaimed in its subtitle is the first form, the unifying maneuver of "introduc[ing] the experimental Method of Reasoning into Moral Subjects." Supposedly discovered in its pages is the second, communality: Hume's Newtonian law of human science—sympathy as a "kind of attraction" (Chapman compares it to gravity; 273)—explains man as an essentially social being.

To compare this regime of knowledge with our own is thus to recognize as most familiar the proliferation of subject-specific kinds—what we would call *specialization*. What is strikingly unfamiliar, as I have been emphasizing by using the branching metaphor, is the centering of philosophy as the occasion for, and means of, producing in those kinds. Its function, however, once we view it as a site of discursive mixing, should not appear strange: it makes specialization make sense—appear desirable—by ideologically resolving its contradictions in the ideal of communality. Increased scientificity, for example, is philosophically represented not as a turn toward the esoteric, but, as I have shown, an affirmation of humane accessibility to the social world. Such representations require, however, particularly as the century nears its end, more and more discursive effort. Witness Hume's struggle to conclude the first section of *An Enquiry Concerning Human Understanding* by at first seeming to acknowledge the difficulties of his new science and then dissolving them:

> What though these reasonings concerning human nature seem abstract, and of difficult comprehension? This affords no presumption of their falsehood. On the contrary, it seems impossible, that what has hitherto escaped so many wise and profound philosophers can be very obvious and easy. . . . But as, after all, the abstractedness of these speculations is no recommendation, but rather a disadvantage to them, and as this difficulty may perhaps be surmounted by care and art, and the avoiding of all unnecessary detail, we have . . . attempted to throw some light upon subjects, from which uncertainty has hitherto deterred the wise, and obscurity the ignorant. Happy, if we can unite the boundaries of the different species of philosophy, by reconciling profound enquiry with clearness, and truth with novelty! (15-16)

If philosophy is no longer the happy center of our profound enquiries today, *our* in-depth specializations, then what, if anything, is? Although there is no single discipline that performs precisely the same functions, there is one that incorporates elements of the Scottish philosophical mix and which, in certain of the same ways as philosophy, claims the center. Three parts of that mix were, we saw: a new psychological emphasis on rhetoric (as mapping the mind in terms of the effects of language); second, a turn toward the vernacular; and third, an emphasis on the general and accessible. What I am suggesting is that writing as the imaginative product of mind ("Literature"), as the best examples of the national language ("English Literature"), as something to be taught, shared, and cherished by that nation (the "discipline of English Literature") appropriated many of the centering functions of Scottish philosophy. "Of all subjects," insisted William McCormick in 1889, "it is the most generally interesting: it touches more nearly than most studies our nature as men and women—our every day life and character."[28]

In his collection of *Three Lectures on English Literature*, McCormick's opening argument on "English Literature and University Education" is followed by an essay on Wordsworth. The connection is a telling one, for the period we call Romantic—as Coleridge's notion of Wordsworth as the first great philosophical poet suggests—saw a switch in subject status: poetry came to embrace philosophy rather than the other way around. The explicit maneuverings, in pieces such as the Preface to *Lyrical Ballads*, transpire on temporarily shared ground:

> The first volume of these poems . . . was published, as an experiment, which, I hoped, might be of some use to ascertain, how far, by fitting to metrical arrangement a selection of the real language of men in a state of vivid sensation, that sort of pleasure and that quantity of pleasure may be imparted, which a poet may rationally endeavour to impart. (*Prose* I.118)

The argument offers a rational appeal to scientificity (the collection is an "experiment") as a gesture toward commonality (how all men are pleased) within a rhetorical situation (which quantifies the effects of real language). The point of Wordsworth's argument, however, is not to confirm philosophy as a common ground but, instead, to valorize literature—a distinctly national literature—as stylistically worthy of being centered as the "finer spirit of all knowledge."

Wordsworth's subjects in the ballads themselves suggest the national turn. As Alan Bewell has claimed in *Wordsworth and the Enlightenment*, Wordsworth's marginal, rustic figures are in fact domesticated versions of "the ethnographic descriptions of other peoples provided by [eighteenth-century] travel narratives (30)." To "bind them to an English place" within ballads, I would add, places this act of domestication within the extraordinary list of late eighteenth-century literary activities that were constitutive of what historian Gerald Newman calls *The Rise of English Nationalism*, including

the chartering of the society of Antiquaries to study *English* history
(1751), Johnson's preparation of a dictionary of the English language
(1755) . . . the preparation of the *Biographica Britannica* (1747–66),
the production of the first edition of the *Encyclopedia Britannica*
(1768–71) . . . [and] the writing for the first time of the histories of
English painting (1762–80), music (1776–89), and poetry (1744–81).
(112)

The slippage here, and still in our current usage, between *English*
and *British* actually confirms my earlier argument about the particular nature of this group formation: whereas the contribution of
Scotland to Britishness was to function as an *other,* England, as the
central and dominant part, often substitutes synecdochically for
the whole.

Recognizing Wordsworth's participation in this construction
of the nation—his later poetry, of course, is explicitly obsessed
with it—can help to clarify the displacement of Scottish philosophy; it is not that Scotland is the foil in this valorization—France
was by far the most important locus of negative comparisons—but
that the turn to nationalism entails the recasting of common-ness.
Rather than ideologically justifying an idealized philosophical
community of educated men, it functions in Wordsworth to construct a purpose for the specific kinds of writing which became Literature. The problem with "the present state of the public taste in
this country," argues the poet, requires a turn to this "literature" as
the only type of "knowledge" which can produce "healthy" community (*Prose* I.120): England *needs* its literature.

The nature of literature was, of course, the other issue. Hume's
description of his own "passion for literature" and "love of literary
fame" confirms John Price's observation regarding the eighteenth-
century "inseparability of literature and philosophy" (175) as classificatory terms. The former's specialization into highly imaginative
kinds was thus another major part of Wordsworth's Romantic enterprise. He dismissed philosophy as an ineffective kind of writing,
one that cannot produce "health" because, in Bewell's words, being
"void of images [it] cannot act upon habitual feelings" (11). Poetry,
however, not only provides images but also enlivens them with

meter. It is more innately valuable than prose because it connects the reader directly with human life. For Wordsworth, Literature is a matter of what he calls "style," and his style, as defined in the Preface to *Lyrical Ballads*, is to keep the "reader in the company of flesh and blood" (I.130).

Connecting with the reader was not a goal foreign to Scottish philosophical writing. As a practice configured around communality, it had been the locus of stylistic efforts to engage a growing reading public through then innovative gestures of sympathetic identification. In Hume's philosophical history, for example, the historian and the reader are manipulated into bearing, in Louis Kampf's words, "the burden of making the proper connections" between the past and present.[29] Literature, however, appropriated those efforts as an end—what we think great writing really does— rather than as a means of communicating other content. Literary activity, in other words, was institutionalized as the profession of Literature by taking as its *job* the stylistic engagement of the reader. When that task was specialized as the disciplinary property of the creative writers, critics, and professors who practice English, the other kinds of knowledge became specialties.

As such, they constituted their authority by abjuring the use of style as a strategy for appealing to a larger community, deploying it instead as a tool for deepening the sense of disciplinary difference. This new organization of knowledge as specialties, in other words, was enabled and rationalized by the centering of English Literature as a field whose specialization is what we are supposed to have in common. By providing both useful knowledge (the skills of literacy necessary to learning an expert language) *and* the self- and class-authorizing ideology of the aesthetic (the taste by which one knows great authors and thus one's own greatness) Literature altered the interplay between knowledge and power. The result was the modern professionalized state with Englishness (as the nation) and Literature (as a shared body of work) providing common ground. The change, let me emphasize, was not just in *what* was common, but in how common-ness figured in the production of knowledge. Unlike Scottish philosophy, English Literature has not been an "occasion" for *branching* into other related kinds, but a *prerequisite* for entering autonomous professional fields.

Making Culture

"Men are men before they are lawyers" proclaimed John Stuart Mill in an 1867 inaugural address at a Scottish university,[30] compressing the tale of specialization into its essential stages. It is important to be precise here: men cannot become lawyers until they are *first* made into men. One must specialize *from* a prior state of fullness. Mill, as we know from the *Autobiography*, understood himself to have been broadened by a literary experience: he required a heavy dose of Wordsworth prior to attaining professional success. "Work without hope," in Mill's own words borrowed from Coleridge, was transformed into work with "joy."[31] I end this chapter with the narrative of that transformation, but rather than casting it in psychological terms as a personal escape from depression, I offer it as testimony to the newly central role of a national Literature in an age of culture: it inscribes that discipline as a specialized prerequisite for the intellectual work of the modern professional, including, as in this case, the professional philosopher.

The problem troubling both self and world in Mill was progress—not (and this is the crucial twist to the whole scenario) the failure to improve but the consequences of doing so: "if the reformers of society and government could succeed in their objects . . . the pleasures of life, being no longer kept up by struggle and privation, would cease to be pleasures" (1072). Mill must make progress—professional success and the social improvements it occasions for the nation—make sense by linking it to pleasure: developmental change, to use Wordsworth's words, can be experienced as "gratulant" when "rightly understood" (XIII.389).[32] Literature's job as a discipline was to produce the right kind of understanding. It helped, that is, to construct and naturalize new relationships between knowledge and power, underwriting the intellectual labor of what Mill called "the most confirmed habit of analysis" with a guarantee of joy—joy that "had no connection with struggle or imperfection, but would be made richer by every improvement in the physical or social condition of mankind" (1073).

I emphasize that this was Literature's job *as a discipline* to clarify how the work was performed. The reorganization of knowledge which I have been describing occasioned a shift in the relationship between *doctrine* and *discipline* which turned upon the concept of property. Etymologically, *doctrine,* which the *Oxford English Dictionary* refers to as "the property of the doctor, or teacher" had been "more concerned with abstract theory, and 'discipline' with practice or exercise." But with the advent of specialization, as subject areas became rule-based fields of knowledge mastered through vocationally plotted educational schemes, the discipline itself became the doctrine—the property owned by the specialist. To *have* a profession, at the historical moment that the qualification was no longer being a gentleman but having a skill, meant that what one possessed was the right to exercise certain modes of knowledge production.

Mill, then, was not cured by Wordsworthian doctrine; he learned to discipline himself by producing knowledge within a particular discipline—literary knowledge. There are no quotations from the poet in the paragraphs describing Mill's recovery; they detail, instead, the intellectual work by which the poet was found and valued. First, the competition is winnowed away, Byron being cited and then rejected. Then Mill makes intra-Wordsworthian discriminations, turning from *The Excursion* and "beautiful pictures of natural scenery" as he tries to focus only on "the precise thing" of value. By assigning value, Mill himself *makes* what he says he discovered through Wordsworth: neither beauty nor—remember the historical sequence I described in Chapter 2—sublimity, but "culture." What is *in* Wordsworth, therefore, is not really the point; since culture doubles as both the inclusive frame for all that we do together as a nation and as the exclusive frame for what pleases us most, this ability to make culture provides the guarantee Mill requires—the ongoing presence of pleasure in all other forms of making. Mill, like Lord Russell before him, did not need to cross the border to do philosophy.

II PROFESSIONALISM
THE POETICS OF LABOR

4 The Georgic at Work

§ Poets, painters, and musicians;
  Lawyers, doctors, politicians:
  Pamphlets, newspapers, and odes,
  Seeking fame by different roads.
    —Mary Robinson, "January, 1795"

§ A Lawyer art thou?—draw not nigh!
  Go, carry to some other place
  The hardness of thy coward eye,
  The falsehood of thy sallow face.
    —William Wordsworth, "A Poet's Epitaph," 1799

Mary Robinson, who had considerable firsthand experience with
the law thanks to a bankrupt husband and a treacherous royal lover
(the young George IV),[1] shared William Wordsworth's opinion of
lawyers: "Oh, keep the shrewd knave and his quibbles from me,"
she wrote in 1797.[2] Her purpose in "January, 1795," however, was
less to condemn the lawyers and other professionals occupying
the first couplet above than to explain how they worked. Each
type seeks fame through different forms of writing. The stanza as a
whole, that is, maps professional success by linking behaviors to
genres. In a sense, that is my purpose throughout this section on
professionalism. I start this chapter with a text by a newly occupied
professional—an author able to write for a living—and try to name
the genre; then I focus on a genre—*georgic*—and try to identify the

professional behaviors it authorizes. A turn to the lyric in Chapter 5 allows me to identify the forceful role of gender in this redistribution of tasks.

Matching professions to genres is not only a practical concern of those on the road to fame; it is also, for those who study professions, a tactic that acknowledges the particular nature of their subject. The sociologist Eliot Freidson, for example, argues that any attempt to theorize the professions must recognize

> that there is no single, truly explanatory trait or characteristic—including such a recent candidate as "power"—that can join together all occupations called professions beyond the actual fact of coming to be called professions. Thus profession is treated as an empirical entity about which there is little ground for generalising as an homogeneous class or a logically exclusive conceptual category. The task for a theory of professions is to document the untidiness and inconsistency of the empirical phenomenon and to explain its character in those countries where it exists.[3]

In denying that there is an essence to the category of profession, Freidson turns the grouping of occupations within that category into a historical process. In the phrase that Ralph Cohen uses to theorize literary genres, *profession* becomes an "open category"[4]; like *lyric* or *novel*, it needs to be studied not as determinate but as necessarily changing over time and place—its particular mix of "traits" at any one moment and location dependent on its interrelations with competing and connected categories.

By bringing the large-scale categories of writing and knowledge to bear upon work, I am making the following historically specific argument. The proliferation of writing, during the eighteenth and early nineteenth centuries in Britain, not only helped to occasion through limitation the re-forming of knowledge into disciplines—including Literature as the disciplinary home of writing itself—it also altered work, enabling and valorizing newly specialized forms of intellectual labor. The alterations followed the fate of writing I outlined in Chapter 1: Pope experienced the work that writing enabled as an uncontrollable surge of activity; Wordsworth valorized that activity as a means of controlling his mind. To be a professional—remember what Wordsworth calls the Leech-gatherer—is to become what you do.

The results are not always pretty, as with the cowardly and sallow-faced lawyer in the stanza quoted above. Add in Robinson's disgust, and it is quite clear that *professional* was and is an ambiguous term—something one may want *and* dread to be. That is the paradox of attacking a whole range of professions in a poem entitled "A Poet's Epitaph": to do so is not to reject *profession* as a category but to reinforce it through claims of hierarchical superiority. To be a Poet is to be a member of the *best* profession.

Today, however, even the very category of professionalism has become increasingly problematic, something both threatened and threatening. The threat it faces is most dramatically evident in the scenario that sociologists call *proletarianization*.[5] Figures from 1985—almost a decade before Bill Clinton declared a health care crisis—show that almost half (47 percent) of the physicians under thirty-six years old were already no longer independent practitioners but employees of the large companies constituting the new health care market; that figure compares with less than 20 percent for those over age fifty-five.[6] Independence among either age group, however, has only invited proletarianization in another form, as evidenced in Michigan where physicians carrying picket signs rallied in the streets of the state capital to protest rising insurance costs. The double bind is obvious: every such effort to preserve their independent financial status as professionals erodes both their public image and self-image as autonomous professionals.[7]

Despite their difficulties, the doctors will probably not get much sympathy from professionals facing even more immediate and drastic threats: professors in the humanities, for example, confronting decades of job lists only a few millimeters thick. Neither will they draw much sympathy from a public that understands professionalization not as concept under siege, but as a force that has gone too far. Just consider how many images we have for professional excess: yuppies who are too ambitious, specialists who are too narrow minded, experts who are too elitist, theorists who are too esoteric. We yearn instead for what professionalism has supposedly disguised: an individual whose deep human feelings have somehow survived the chill. "The problem," as one literary professional has recently put it, "is that you can't talk about your private life in the course of doing your professional work."[8]

Suggesting an essential opposition between professionalism and the subject of private life, however, misses a major historical point: for the past two centuries professionals have talked about little else. Their apparent detachment from their own private lives while working on others' has been but a blind to the productive power of such talk: far from preceding and being increasingly suffocated by professionalism, private life was and is a product of the same discourse. Without individual privacy of body, soul, and property, professionals would have nothing in which to intrude. Their power, as Robert Dingwall has observed, lies in the license

> to carry out some of the most dangerous tasks of our society—to intervene in our bodies, to intercede for our prospects of future salvation, to regulate the conflict of rights and obligations between social interests. Yet in order to do this, [professionals] must acquire guilty knowledge—the priest is an expert on sin, the doctor on disease, the lawyer on crime—and the ability to look at these matters in comparative and, hence, relative terms. This is the mystery of the professions.[9]

As we saw in Chapter 1, Romantic writing such as Wordsworth's deepened that mystery by producing the deep, developmental self. Such development, I argued, is always idealized so that it can *always* be pathologically interrupted. Those interruptions are the opportunities for professional intervention and surveillance; the authority to convert knowledge of the deep self into prescriptive expertise is what makes professional behavior a central form of modern power.

So central is that power to our society that the exercise of it is a staple of our popular culture. In an episode from the 1980s television show *Miami Vice,* for example, Sonny Crockett is shot, and as he lays near death his professional friends from the force have flashbacks focusing on their personal debts to him. The scenario repeated again and again involves the first time each of them blew away a suspect. Sonny rids all of them of their debilitating remorse with the line he himself learned from his lieutenant: "It's your job, man." Two hundred years ago, a job was "petty, piddling work," or a "low, mean, lucrative, busy affair,"[10] and it certainly did not make absolute sense of personal identity, morality, or fate. For that to happen, the concept of work had to be rewritten from that which a true gentleman does not have to do, to the primary activity informing adult identity; the tales that tell of it and the features associated with it were altered to produce a myth of vocation.[11] This was not just a work ethic, for it made work more than necessary: it made work desirable—and necessary for personal happiness.

Crockett's formulation—you are, finally, your work—is Wordsworth's. Some members of the lower social ranks, of course, had been identified with their work as millers or smiths, but this kind of link between the first-person pronoun and an occupation was different: in many cases, it came to function as a claim to social mobility and privileged status. The exercise of such privilege—rationalized now by knowledge rather than blood—entailed a recodification of human behaviors. As one of the traditional "gentle" professions, for example, medicine had not needed an additional or special code of ethics, since gentlemen already had the obligation to behave like gentlemen. Thus, through the eighteenth century, Hippocrates was attended to not for his oath but for his techniques of passive observation and humoral pathology.[12]

Works such as Thomas Percival's *Medical Ethics* (1803) helped to empower modern professionalism by the particular way they first rewrote gentlemanly commitments into occupational codes. "Perhaps the most striking feature of Percival's book," observes Ivan Waddington,

> is that, whilst relatively little space is given to a consideration of ethical problems in doctor-patient relationships, a great deal of space is devoted to establishing a set of rules for regulating relationships between practitioners. Moreover, the advice which Percival gives to practitioners in this context is much more concrete and more detailed. (156–57)

Doctors professionalized themselves, in other words, by learning how to relate to each other as professionals, writing up and thus regulating the appropriate behaviors.

Professionalization has become an increasingly popular subject in English, sociology, and other disciplines, but the history of the *constituting* of professional behavior has remained obscure. Attention has been paid, on the one hand, to the mid and late nineteenth-century statistical "rise" in the number of professionals, while, on the other hand, writers such as Geoffrey Holmes have focused on the early eighteenth-century "development" of the professions.[13] The figures recorded by the census do, at first glance, seem to leave the late eighteenth and early nineteenth centuries out of the picture: at the end of the first three decades of the nineteenth century, for example, only four hundred respondents classified themselves as professional authors whereas more than thirteen thousand did so by the century's close.[14] This numerical difference could be read as a confirmation of the conventional period difference—a few enthusiastic Romantic amateurs versus the many sober Victorian professionals—but doing so does not explain the change.[15] How did an England in which Samuel Johnson defined *profession* as, simply, "known employment,"[16] become an England that less than a century later made professional employment into a *written* object of professional knowledge—recording, classifying, and reclassifying, from the census of 1841 onward, the occupation of every individual in the nation?

The answer was, in part, writing. The word *profession-al,* for example, as an adjective describing a kind of behavior, had to enter the language. It made its first appearances in Britain at the end of the eighteenth and beginning of the nineteenth centuries, a moment that was also marked lexically by the debut of terms of difference such as *amateur.* What we think of as Victorian professionalism, in other words, had to be written up, word by word, before it became "real" and widespread. For most of the eighteenth century, professional behavior had been idealized as the behavior of gentlemen, for only gentlemen were supposed to have the status to enter the professions[17]; this new vocabulary, however, was part of a new way of writing about work—of mixing genres in ways that rearranged the relationships among—and the functions of—character, identity, status, work, money, education, property, and propriety.

Name that Genre

As an example of such mixing, I want to turn to a text that was so thoroughly worked and reworked by its author that it continues to provide work for many other authors even today. Wordsworth's decision to publish *The Prelude* after he perished seems particularly strange to us today—an era in which the absolute imperative of print is spelled out even in the titles of our software programs— *PUBLISH IT!* Literary scholars have followed that punctuation zealously, compensating for Wordsworth's delay by publishing every version of *The Prelude* they can identify: two-part, thirteen-book, fourteen-book, etc. I want to take a step back from this editorial abandon to ask: what are we publishing? To answer that question we need to ask, first, what were *The Prelude*s to Wordsworth? Did they function for him in a way that made nonpublication make sense? These questions place us at the intersection of worker and work, where, in the case of writing, we need to consider issues of authorship and ownership.

Wordsworth's birth happens to correspond almost exactly with the event commonly cited as the birth of modern copyright: the 1774 decision by the House of Lords in the case of *Donaldson v. Becket*. The date requires an asterisk, however, since that decision did not detail a concept or mechanism of copyright, but it allowed for the enforcement of the statute that did. The Statute of Anne had been enacted in 1709 but circumvented in practice and in lawsuits for sixty-five years. That span, like most spans in our histories of the eighteenth century, has most frequently been written up as a *rise*—this time, not of the novel or the middle class but of the Author. Certainly the century that ended with the "creative geniuses" of Romanticism did see the consolidation of the Author function. However, to view the changes in copyright solely in terms of that consolidation is to risk misconstruing the actors and actions of the copyright story thereby turning its climax into paradox: the *Donaldson v. Becket* decision that supposedly topped off the rise of the author actually denied the author's claim to a perpetual common-law copyright in favor of the limited fourteen-year terms of the 1709 statute. "That statute," as Lyman Ray Patterson has observed, "was not intended primarily to benefit authors. It was a trade-regulation statute enacted to bring order to the chaos created in the book trade by the final lapse in 1694 of its predecessor, the Licensing Act of 1662, and to prevent a continuation of the booksellers' monopoly."[18]

The 1662 Act had sustained that monopoly through the granting of perpetual copyrights to anyone who registered a work with the Stationers' Company; the only other form of copyright was the limited-term protection offered by printing patents granted for certain classes of works, such as those on law. The legislative activity that culminated in the Statute of Anne was thus initiated primarily by the stationers themselves in attempts to perpetuate the perpetual copyright after the 1662 Act had expired.

Parliament did respond by legislating copyright, but not of the duration desired by the petitioners: previous copyrights were set to expire after twenty-one years, whereas new ones were limited to fourteen, with an additional term of the same length granted to authors still alive after the initial term. This extension was the highlight of the statute for authors, for its truly "radical change," in Patterson's words, "was not that it gave authors the right to acquire a copyright . . . but that it gave that right to all persons" (145). The legislative object, in other words, was not authors with rights but booksellers with a monopoly.

That monopoly required perpetual copyright not only to ensure ongoing profits from selling older, popular works; as perpetual property, the copyrights themselves could be treated as stocks sold at auctions.[19] Expiration dates would obviously negate their investment value. The booksellers thus reacted to the 1709 limits by ignoring them in practice and seeking in the courts a new conceptual basis for perpetuity. Whereas they had earlier used censorship laws as the stalking horse—their ongoing monopoly would help protect the kingdom against seditious works—the new strategy was to insist upon the common-law right of authors in having a natural right of property in their works. So weak was the position of authors in relationship to the monopoly in the eighteenth century that, from the booksellers' point of view, a perpetual copyright for authors was a copyright in perpetuity for them.

Authors, that is, were a means to a specific economic end for the monopolists — a weapon wielded by the booksellers which their opponents managed to turn against them. An apparent victory for the sellers in the case of *Millar v. Taylor* (1769), in which the author's common-law right was upheld, was precisely the opportunity that the Lords needed to end the monopoly in two strokes. The questions posed to the twelve common-law judges who advised the House on *Donaldson v. Becket* were structured such that the booksellers could be taken on their own legal ground. In the judges' advice and in the debate that followed, the author's right was affirmed, thereby bringing the monopoly within legal range, but so was the notion that the right was "taken away by the Statute of Anne."[20]

This was a crucial moment in the advent of the modern system of letters we call Literature,[21] but not primarily because the Author had risen. The redistribution of property involved more than the authorial. As Trevor Ross has so shrewdly noted, the canon of English Literature, which had been designed rhetorically "in accordance with the immediate needs of speakers and 'makers' [poets]," became, after *Donaldson v. Becket*,

> valued as public domain: as one contemporary account put it, "the Works of *Shakespeare*, of *Addison, Pope, Swift, Gay,* and many other excellent Authors . . . are, by this Reversal [of *Millar v. Taylor*] declared to be the Property of any Person." Never before in English history had it been possible to think that the canon might belong to the people, to readers. From that moment, the canon became a set of commodities to be consumed; it became literature rather than poetry.[22]

This new world of literary commodities certainly opened up, in the long term, extraordinary financial and artistic possibilities for authors, but, in their being pawns in the struggle over monopoly, they had paid a price. "Henceforth," as Hugh Amory has observed, "an English author's 'natural' right to his work was . . . perpetual and unlimited only so long as he never published it."[23]

We are back, of course, to Wordsworth's strange decision. I am not suggesting, with this sketch of copyright, that he withheld *The Prelude* to perpetuate his natural right to that work, but rather that both the decision and the right need to be considered within a more comprehensive set of socioeconomic and literary concerns. What the writer gained as Author was not just the opportunity to earn money from selling individual works. The demise of one type of monopoly in the making of the Author had engendered monopolistic possibilities of another kind—expert control, for example, over the commodification process itself—which also seemed worthy of protection in perpetuity. If we begin to think about the form such protection might take, the strangeness of Wordsworth's decision may begin to lessen. Does not every academic have a piece of writing he or she never publishes, at times allows to circulate, and always revises? At its most effective, it attempts to expand autobiography to epic dimensions by recounting supposedly heroic acts.

The Prelude is, quite simply, the most extraordinary résumé in English literary history. Wordsworth referred to it as a "review" of what "had qualified him for such employment," the "such" referring to the writing of a long poem (*The Recluse*) which he considered "the task of my life."[24] Its primary function was to present an individual's training and qualifications for performing his life's work: it "conducts the history" of the candidate "to the point when he was emboldened to hope that his faculties were sufficiently matured for entering upon the arduous labour which he had proposed to himself."[25] This vita-like detailing of personal identity turns maturation into a preoccupation with occupation: in this case, how to become, behave like, and perform as a professional poet. Such status is described in a now familiar sequence in which personal background (the influence of Nature), formal education (Cambridge and books), and significant life experiences (the French Revolution) all contribute to a concluding epiphany of *professional* purpose: "what we have loved, / Others will love, and we will teach them how."

The Prelude concludes professionally in the sense isolated by the sociologist Magali Larson: modern professionals, she observes, "constitute *and control* a market for their expertise."[26] What they own is the right to define and exercise their expertise. Their specialization-in-depth *is* the property that once earned must be preserved beyond any statutory limits. This is the principle that is surfacing so frequently today in divorce proceedings; property settlements now increasingly turn upon assessing the value of the professional status—the right to labor, the productive capacity— achieved by one or both partners during the marriage.

Literary professionals certainly have their share of divorces, but we rarely read about the value of their specialized labor in today's gossip columns. Nor does it figure prominently in scholarly efforts by Larson and others to detail the advent of modern professionalism; they focus instead on medical doctors, lawyers, and accountants. I would maintain, however, that literary activity, including the production of literary knowledge, was crucial to that advent. Rather than focusing on that activity as something that was passively professionalized, we need, as I suggested earlier, to recognize that professionalization itself has a history, and central to its tale is the very labor—the production, circulation, and valorization of writing—which became Literature's area of expertise.

If *The Prelude*'s concluding emphasis on "what we love" and on the "joy" it brings seems too fuzzy and sentimental a frame for such expertise, we need only take a quick chronological detour to gauge how powerful an ideological prescription it turned out to be. A century after the first versions of *The Prelude*, on July 1, 1901, a group of workers met in Paris to organize a new union: the Confederation of Intellectual Workers. And how was this class of labor defined? "The intellectual worker," wrote William McDonald in his 1923 description of the movement, "works primarily from love of the task, from subtle but conscious joy in performance or achievement."[27]

This is not simply a matter, as I shall emphasize in the next chapter, of whistling while you work, for what is at stake are the hierarchical differences between kinds of work and the criteria for who gets to do them. Both work and desire had to be rewritten before they could so naturally come together. The developing *I* of the résumé came to define itself in terms of its happiness at work as certain kinds of work were valorized as worth doing for the sheer joy of doing them. The ideological circle was completed, of course, by the fact that the privilege and high pay attending that valorization actually made the job all the more lovable.

When we reclassify *love* with *work* in *The Prelude* (1850), the organization of the longer versions of the poem begins to make a new kind of sense. Previous critics have puzzled over both the turn in Book VIII[28] to a "Retrospect" Wordsworth called "Love of Nature Leading to Love of Mankind" and the concluding emphasis in Book XIV on "intellectual love." Without calling into question the psychological, philosophical, and religious speculations of those critics,[29] we can, when we see *The Prelude* as résumé, recognize how it helps to naturalize the division of labor into physical and mental by claiming, for the poet's work of writing, the higher (and thus deeper) motivation of love instead of money. The raw material of that work—and the new object of knowledge of all of the then innovative disciplines of the human sciences—is, of course, what Wordsworth in Book VIII is "naturally led to": "Man."

The entire résumé privileges "intellectual love" as a kind of "work" productive of a "joy" that "complete[s] the man" (1805, XIII.185–202). *The Prelude*'s tale of masculine completion—love of nature, love of man, love of work—is the gendered counterpart of the marriage plots of nineteenth-century romances and domestic novels. In both cases what is at stake are the socioeconomic order and one's place in it. Love, in the masculine version, is not just what works—it *is* work. The spatialization—falling in love—functions in both to idealize the completion of self as a parental- and class-transcendent act of knowledge production: in the feminine, a disciplined knowledge of self through the other and, in the masculine, a knowledge of a discipline through the self. An intellectual worker "falls" in love by "deeply" specializing in a particular kind of work.

As love thus became a key element in the new catalogue of professional behaviors, the possibilities of selfhood were configured along a professional/amateur axis. The drawing of that axis was crucial to resolving the negative ambiguities attached to the professions in the eighteenth century. As the province of second sons, the status of the professions had been tainted by an unseemly need for income. Once the motivation became love, however, money became a permissible consequence of work—work that was now linked, as we have seen, not to unfortunate circumstances but to happiness. Thus as home and work became separate, gender-encoded realms at the end of the eighteenth century, love assumed a strategic role in both: "falling in love" eclipsed parental blood-lines as the mythical key to both domestic bliss, with one's true love, and, as we have seen, to worldly success, doing the work one loves.

That fall, however, is anything but a free fall; rules were imposed, for example, by the introduction of *amateur* into English. The amateur, of course, is one who loves but, in regard to the professional norm, either too idealistically ("understanding, and loving or practicing . . . without any regard to pecuniary advantage" read one definition in 1803) or too enthusiastically (Edmund Burke warned in 1797 of "the greatest amateurs . . . of revolutions").[30] Propagating the norm became the imperative of education, which institutionalized into the various disciplines "what" was loved and "how" it was to be taught. The discipline of literature, as a means of *optimizing* production in this new system of knowledge, can be related generically and historically to the branch of philosophy devoted, under the old system, to optimizing capitalism: political economy. In fact, keeping in mind R. S. Crane's definition of *taste* as "the capacity to receive pleasure from aesthetic objects,"[31] literary knowledge as it appears in Mill and in Wordsworth ("What we have loved, / Others *will* love") is a political economy of taste. It attempts to encourage and rationalize social progress by measuring the *value* of things.

The comparison with political economy is valuable because it helps us to isolate the dual nature of literary study since the late eighteenth century. Like political economy in the work of David Ricardo, on the one hand, and Adam Smith, on the other, Literature is concerned with both "regulating [the] distribution"[32] and maximizing the growth of that value. These are not just different emphases in Literature but coordinated functions. The study of Literature was institutionalized, as Ian Michael's recent survey of textbooks and curriculum has detailed, by combining what had been rhetorical instruction in the skills of literacy with the construction and appreciation of newly defined chronologies of "great" works. The first regulates standards of literacy in order to distribute its skills hierarchically, whereas the second, as we just saw in Mill, employs canon making to naturalize growth—the Wordsworthian desire for "something evermore about to be."

These functions correspond to the two conceptual categories that sociologists use to identify modern professionalism: *technicality*, which "refers to the extent to which a systematic body of knowledge is utilized in the justification of competence or expertise," and *indetermination*, which points to "the bases of [an occupation's] mystique . . . the elements of its ideology [as they] underpin its monopolistic position and successful resistance to external authority."[33] Literature, in its dual nature, maintains what sociologists term the professional *ratio* between the two by insisting heavily upon the mystification of taste that is the canon (indetermination), while also deploying a systematic body of knowledge governing literacy (technicality).

That ratio is what professors of Literature have *possessed* since *The Prelude*, a text that is both a "masterpiece" of indetermination—something that is so much "something evermore about to be" that, during Wordsworth's lifetime, as well as now, through our incessant editorial efforts, it never at any point just *is*—and, as a résumé, a document of technicality detailing the training necessary to master a required body of knowledge. To see *The Prelude* now as both, and thus as an embodiment of professional behavior, is to begin to recognize the place of Literature *in* the history of professionalization and *as* the centered prerequisite.

The concept of technicality returns us to the issue of delayed publication, for it points toward the professional need for rewriting and expansion: as Wordsworth systematizes into knowledge what he has come to love, additive revision becomes the "natural" form of writing. It is now a given for us that the knowledge that constitutes a profession is always in flux and is always growing—one's professional education should never come to an end. This systematic open-endedness also functions as a strategy of indeter-

mination, mystifying the profession to enhance its value. Wordsworth's most stunning mystification, of course, was the refusal to
publish *The Prelude* during his lifetime, an act that embedded his
life and his oeuvre within an inclusive tale of professionalization as
an ongoing struggle for self-improvement.

The other parts of that oeuvre tell other parts of that same tale,
so that, as William Galperin has pointed out,[34] Victorians familiar
with *The Excursion* were neither startled nor overly impressed with
The Prelude when it did appear. The former, after all, concludes like
the latter with a grandiose plea for education—in this case, a national education system that would supply everyone with the "intellectual implements and tools" required for the work of civilization: "The discipline of slavery is unknown / Among us,—hence
the more do we require / The discipline of virtue." Such disciplinary turns in Wordsworth's writing, early and late, and their
connections to professionalization have, however, since Matthew
Arnold, been obscured by the supposedly aesthetic need to filter
the "philosophy" out of the "poetry." But the ubiquity of that need
even to the present time is not testimony to Arnold's "critical" sway
over Wordsworth's "creativity"; it attests instead to the power of
the discourse of the professional, which Wordsworth helped to
generate, to configure our understanding of our relationship to
Romanticism along lines of difference which Arnold found natural
and which we are only beginning to historicize.

Instead of attending to the supposedly inferior didacticism of
The Excursion, we have attended to *The Prelude*, and not *The Prelude* as a text that generically configures professional behavior but
The Prelude as a strictly literary story of imagination, creativity, and
love of nature. My point in trying to shift our attention is that we
need not just admit the discourse of the professional into our literary histories of the past two hundred years but that we recognize
that the history we have held is its product—*and* that such a history naturalizes itself as fact by obscuring the origins of its own
production. The professions, observes Dietrich Rueschemeyer, "inform the dominant understandings" we have of them and the conditions and consequences of their behaviors (138).

M. H. Abrams, for example, gives us a grip on *The Prelude* by isolating within it the "typical Romantic design" of the "spiral journey back home."[35] The problem lies in how that typicality is cast; classified within a range of different philosophies (e.g., "neoplatonism," "post-Kantian"), the spiral argument[36] gives *The Prelude* a grip on us, causing us, like Abrams, to lose sight of it as a work about the problem of work. To keep that social function in view, we need to recognize that the motif works[37] by spatializing value (of the individual) as depth (of imaginative self-knowledge). But *depth* itself— of feeling, character, and meaning valorized in poems such as *The Prelude*, novels, and criticism—has, as I have been arguing, prescribed modern professionalism: as the metaphor of specialization (knowledge that is narrow but deep), depth has made common sense out of the very pattern of division of labor which rationalizes our professionalized society. The specific kind of professional labor which Michel Foucault has called *commentary*[38] is thus an intellectual reenactment of *The Prelude*'s spiraling journey: the critical circling around a "primary" text in which we return to it to say it again, but never in a fully repetitive nor fully adequate way.

Georgic Heroes

Although Wordsworth correctly understood this spiraling, self-descriptive conduct to be at that time "a thing unprecedented in Literary history" (*Letters* 586–87), we are now so used to poets talking about themselves at great length that I want to denaturalize that expressiveness by showing it to be something *made* out of far less familiar parts. The most unfamiliar part to modern audiences is, not surprisingly, the georgic-descriptive. I say "not surprisingly" because that is the element of the poem which has to do with the value of work, precisely the aspect of *The Prelude* which our generally Romantic readings usually ignore. We are far more familiar, for example, with its lyric elements, such as the first-person pronouns and the numerous apostrophes, which confirm the standard emphases on the creative spontaneity of the poet's personal voice.

The English georgic has its origins in the middle element of the three-fold Virgilian oeuvre which the Middle Ages developed into the *rota Vergilii* or wheel of Virgil. Pastoral, georgic, and epic served as the basis for a scheme that divided not only poetry, but life, society, and human personality into three interrelated parts. They are written, according to Anthony Low,

> in three styles: low, middle, and high. They correspond to three social ranks or occupations: shepherd, farmer, and soldier. They may take place in three locales: pasture, field, and castle; and they may be symbolized by three kinds of tree: the beech, the fruit-tree, and the laurel . . . above all, the three kinds of poetry correspond to three basic human activities, into which almost everything we do in life may be divided: pastoral celebrates play and leisure, georgic celebrates work, and epic celebrates fighting.[39]

The basic form of work which Virgil celebrates in the *Georgics* is husbandry, but he explicitly connects agricultural labor to all other forms of work so that the major emphasis is on the value of working hard. Because it opposes action to the ease of the pastoral, and construction to the destruction of the epic, it is understood to be the proper mode for nation building and the affirmation of personal and civic virtue.

Among English poets, however, its propriety has varied considerably depending on how the connection with laboring on the land was interpreted. When the emphasis was on the base nature of that laboring, as during the Tudor and Stuart reigns, it was displaced by an idealized pastoral.[40] Beginning with Milton's emphasis on the patriotic labor of rebuilding England—Low notes that Royalist poets would have considered Milton's phrase "noble task" oxymoronic—the georgic grew in importance, assuming a place "under the overarching epic framework of *Paradise Lost*" (310) with its broad movement from Edenic pastoral to redemptive work-in-the-world. Spurred by Dryden's translation in 1697, the georgic rose even further in the eighteenth century as a didactically descriptive form interrelating art, work, and politics, the detailing of rural life, and the promotion of the landowners' virtues.[41]

The Georgics was a compelling model for articulating those interrelations not only because it thematized *work,* but also because eighteenth-century writers identified, as the particular strength of

that genre, the capacity to naturalize what it articulated. Its growing importance for them as a descriptive form lay in the way that it
transformed the procedure of description itself. "This kind," wrote
Addison, in an anonymous essay prefixed to John Dryden's 1697
translation of *The Georgics*, "raises in our minds a pleasing variety
of scenes and landskips whilst it teaches us, and makes the dryest of
its precepts *look like* a description" (emphasis mine).[42] For the next
one hundred years literary activity was empowered by this georgic-
descriptive ability to make rules appear to be simply an account of
what's out there. The pedagogical twist for those writers was that
didactic assertions became "pleasing" facts; our historical perspective can now clarify the social and political turn: the world of work
"out there" was both rationalized and *constructed* in these very acts
of description.

Writing in the form of the georgic thus proved to be a crucial
tool in the making of modern professionalism. It was the means by
which the work of writing itself came to be seen as a potentially
heroic activity, its practitioners possessed with considerable redemptive power.[43] Dryden, for example, wrote texts—and has
since been written up as a text—that clarify this peculiar interaction
of the heroic and the professional. We have, quite simply, construed the extraordinary circumstances surrounding his translation
of *The Georgics* in an extraordinarily revealing way. The undertaking that set the generic stage for the problematizing of work in the
oft-repeated georgic-descriptive performances of the eighteenth
century was itself occasioned by a problem at work: Dryden, at the
age of fifty-eight, lost his job. With the accession of William and
Mary, Dryden's Catholicism meant the end of his £300 per year
stipend as Poet Laureate. He returned for a time to his earlier occupation as playwright, but by 1692 he had found new work that
worked for him in a new way. Translation published by subscription proved to be a lucrative combination. Dryden's Virgil was
only the fourth publication of this type in Britain, netting its author, for less than four years of work, almost £1500.[44]

The transitional position of this mode of production between
patronage and the marketplace has, of course, received literary historical and critical comment—although Pope's *Iliad* is the more

oft-cited example. But for our purposes what is striking in the tales told about this last phase of Dryden's life, this period of occupational change, is typified by the "Biographical Sketch" heading the Cambridge Dryden:

> had the poet died just before the Revolution, his name would survive as that of the greatest writer of the Restoration period, but his personality would not seem in the least remarkable. Twelve years of toil remained to him, years hampered by old age, by poverty, and by illness. By his performance during this period Dryden showed himself still the undisputed prince of English letters; his character, meanwhile, acquired an elevation in which it had hitherto been lacking, and commands our respect and admiration. (lvii)

In narratives such as this one, the poet who, as Robert Folkenflik points out, helped to change our notions of heroism by shifting from spokesman for the crown to a celebrator of poets, playwrights, painters, and composers,[45] himself becomes heroic. As a princely character whose "triumph was a triumph of character," Dryden appears as his own most important work of art, for his written "works cannot stand to us for all that the living man meant to his own generation."[46] The fifth edition of the *Norton Anthology* even stamps the man it calls "the *commanding* literary figure" of his time with the word that became so central to Romantic and Modern descriptions of artistic heroism: "Though his enemies accused him of opportunism, he proved his *sincerity*" (emphasis mine).[47]

It is no accident that the vocabulary and logic ("Dryden rose to his greatest in failure") of the artist as hero have spread so densely over this generative moment of the georgic-descriptive. The subordination of the work of art, understood as both the labor and the products of that labor, to the individual "life" naturalizes the shift toward professionalization as the realization of human potential—a process of character building. This naturalization does not, let me emphasize, do violence to Dryden's text; my historical point is that its centering of the georgic-descriptive helped both to prescribe changes in the nature of work and to establish, through what Addison saw as the descriptive power of that genre, the terms by which those changes would appear natural.

Thus the dedication of *The Georgics* to an aging Earl of Chesterfield sets up the poem's "facts" about rural occupations as commentary upon the problem posed by a long life: how to produce a "green old age." The answer—the ongoing work of cultivation—is most forcefully articulated in the description that begins Book Two: "Much labor," writes Dryden, "is requir'd in trees" (line 85). This labor is not required for survival; the "vigor of the native earth" (line 69) is sufficient for maintaining life. It is, rather, a matter of greening, of making productive. In learning to labor, man becomes the final object of that labor, and only then, like the immediate object, the tree, does his life bear fruit.

As this georgic conjunction of life, labor, and productivity was described and redescribed during the eighteenth century, the very concept of work itself was rewritten to produce the myth of vocation we discussed earlier: the *I* defining itself in terms of its work. However, since the kinds of *I*s and the kinds of *work* mutually delimited each other, the georgic-descriptive had yet another function to serve: it set the terms for the eighteenth-century debate over the division of labor—a debate that became the discursive arena from which our modern notions of heroic activity and professional competence emerged.

The peculiarities of Dryden's translation help to clarify those terms. His diction and heroic couplets reshape Virgil's arguments into a specific and consistent binary opposition between the "salvage" and the "artful." The trees, for example,

. . . receiving graffs of other kind,
Or thence transplanted, change their salvage mind,
Their wildness lose, and quitting nature's part,
Obey the rules and discipline of art. (lines 71–74)

The opposition of nature to art may not at first glance appear to be an innovative feature; the seventeenth-century debate between the two is most familiar to us, of course, in the exchange between Perdita and Polixenes in *The Winter's Tale*. However, when that feature is extracted from romance and mixed with the georgic both that form and the feature are transformed. The debate is no longer an occasion for identification and transcendence—"so over that art /

Which you say adds to Nature," argues Polixenes, "is an art / That
Nature makes" (IV.iv.90–92)—but rather an occasion for encompassing both Nature and Art within "real"-world distinctions regarding behavior and productivity. Repeated use of the word
"salvage," for example, allows Dryden to describe the reality of Nature—etymologically evoked as *silva*, the forest—in naturally normative, and negative, terms: "wild," "uncivilized," "low," and worse.
Thus, only twelve lines after the reference I cited above to "salvage
mind," grapes that are "turpis" to Virgil (deformed, foul, nasty)
become, in Dryden's version, "salvage grapes" (line 84). Good taste
becomes, georgically, a matter of the right type of work. The grapes
require the farmer's cultivation of the vine. The aging Chesterfield
preserves his own flavor by cultivating himself; the work of what
Dryden, in the Dedication, calls "knowledge" gives a "seasoning
to retirement, and make[s] us taste the blessing."[48]

With nature as savage, the arts—whether the arts of the vine-
yard or the arts of knowledge—became, as Dryden put it, "discipline[s]." In thus describing the work of art in terms of a necessary
disciplinarity, the georgic pointed both to the importance of that
work—such discipline is necessary—and to the problem posed by
its variety—there are many different disciplines. Combined with
other forms, the georgic was used throughout the eighteenth century to engage the latter problem. Thomson, for example, mixing
romance with the georgic instead of displacing it, built *The Castle
of Indolence* using features we have already seen in Dryden. The
father of the "Knight of Arts and Industry" who rescues Britain
from the spell of the Wizard Indolence is a "Knight of old" named
Selvaggio, the Italian for *salvage*. The industrious son is born of the
"Dame *Poverty*" after a coital event that Thomson depicts in appropriately mechanical terms: "Her he compress'd, and fill'd Her with
a lusty Boy" (II.54).[49]

The boy himself turns out to be filled with discipline, and thus
disciplines; he excels "In every Science, and in every Art" (II.74),
evincing, as John Barrell has argued, the gentlemanly "ideal of a
patriotic statesman, who . . . reanimate[s] the public and private
virtues of society"[50] by disinterestedly embodying its diversity—its
variety of fruitful work. Barrell focuses insightfully on the politics

of the poem, arguing that the point of the idealization is to show that such variety is "still capable of being understood as a unity, and of being understood by men who thereby justify the privileges and the authority they claim as members of the ruling class" (50). I would add, however, that in this georgic romance, a form precisely suited to the portrayal of heroic work, the gentleman is not the only hero whose privileges and authority are at stake. The issue of the artist as hero is raised within the poem and by the poem. The character who speaks out against the Wizard in the first canto and helps the Knight do battle in the second is a dwarfish bard modeled on Pope. His heroic action is to represent to others their own enthrallment which, of course, is also Thomson's *job* in writing the poem. I emphasize *job* to clarify the politics of this heroism: to celebrate it is to empower a historically particular kind of work and the hierarchical distinctions it authorizes.

Professional Power

The moment of the artist as hero, in other words, was the historical moment of profession*al* behavior in Britain. That behavior was no longer simply the behavior of gentleman—and not only because the professions were being opened to other ranks; more importantly, it changed because the task at hand, in an increasingly complex culture, was no longer to embody, like the gentleman/Knight, but to *represent*: to write up new kinds of knowledge by writing them down. Gentlemanly disinterestedness was supplanted as a rationale for power by claims of professional competence—command over a field of knowledge.

Prose georgics, such as Adam Smith's *The Wealth of Nations*, functioned as command strategies for mapping the fields, assigning values, and making new precepts "look like" description. The most famous description, of "the important business of making a pin" being "divided into about eighteen distinct operations," asserted the most obvious precept: "The division of labour . . . occasions, in every art, a proportionable increase of the productive powers of labour."[51] But the act of description itself pointed to another kind of division: between those who simply performed the operations and those privileged few who could "examine"[52] them, and thus, like Smith, represent them and turn them into objects of knowledge. Although Smith, writing up the moment of transition between gentleman and professional, presented the *few* as those "who, being attached to no particular occupation themselves," had the "leisure" for such privilege, the privilege itself became an identifying feature of another group: those who did have occupations, but of a specific kind. Modern professionals, as we saw earlier, have a mandate to define their own work, setting "the very terms of thinking about problems which fall in their domain."

In the domain of art, writers such as Sir Joshua Reynolds reformulated the divisions Smith had encoded into his prescription for a wealthy *nation*. Addressed to an Academy that—by excluding engravers from its membership—institutionalized the hierarchical specialization of the arts,[53] Reynolds's discourse mixed georgic and pastoral into a natural history that articulated and justified the prerogatives of intellectual labor: "whilst the shepherds were attending their flocks, their masters made the first astronomical observations; so musick is said to have had its origin from a man at leisure listening to the strokes of a hammer." Reynolds's argument transforms that leisure into a superior kind of work, for such activity provides the most important "advantages to society" through the "gradual exaltation of human nature."[54]

Thus exalted, the professional work of knowing—whether about the stars or about the arts—became, during the eighteenth century, the newly heroic work. Foucault's formulation of the fate of the epic at that time points to the same tale: "the artist was able to emerge from the age-old anonymity of epic singers only by usurping the power and meaning of the same epic values. The heroic dimension passed from the hero to the one whose task it had been to represent him at a time when Western culture itself became a world of representations."[55]

Let me rephrase that for a British context and a history of writing: "culture" did not become a "world of representations"; Britain's world of representations—made so by the proliferation of writing—produced the category of culture, and, within that category, artists carry the power that had previously belonged to their heroes. Writing's world of representations is thus the world of professional power, and the power of that particular representation has been to turn our knowledge-making capacities upon the writer as individual heroic author. Our subject became, by the end of the eighteenth century, the Subject; the work that century georgically initiated became the full-time lyrical work of the period we call Romanticism: the construction and naturalization of the artistic hero's interior depths.[56]

This transformation proceeded even when the descriptions were of occupational inadequacy, as in the efforts of such mid and late eighteenth-century writers as Collins and Goldsmith.[57] Since the heroism lies in behaving professionally—and thus taking the job personally and seriously—the bewailing of an inability to match the achievements of one's predecessors still functioned to present the writers' efforts as heroic, or—even more familiarly now—as antiheroic. The latter alternative, in fact, serves the production of psychological knowledge particularly well, as we find ourselves "finding" in these authors and texts—as Wordsworth did in Chatterton—deep inadequacies and meaningful madness.

By tracing the georgic into *The Prelude*, we can see how the healthy version was constructed. The fate of that genre in Romanticism has, until recently,[58] been largely ignored in favor of analyses focusing on the pastoral,[59] describing the Romantics' love of nature, and the lyric, celebrating the poet's expressiveness. But the georgic does not disappear at the end of the eighteenth century; it enters into new combinations with other forms with some surprising results. Most immediately important for our purposes is the mix of the lyric with the georgic: the "I," in other words, that works—that identifies itself in terms of its developing capacity to work. This combination informs the entire *Prelude*:

> When, as becomes a man who would prepare
> For such an arduous work, I through myself
> Make rigorous inquisition, the report
> Is often cheering. (I.146–49)[60]

To detail personal identity in this manner turns, as we have seen, maturation into a preoccupation with occupation. The nature of that occupation, however, remains at issue. It may be arduous, but certainly not in the way that Virgilian husbandry is arduous: Wordsworth returns to the land, but not to till it.[61] His text, then, is innovative both in linking the development of the *I* to work *and* in the way it redefines that *I* by redefining and valorizing a particular kind of work. The latter task required yet another manipulation of literary kind, this one set up by the Miltonic echo that opens *The Prelude*. At the end of *Paradise Lost*, Adam and Eve leave their home, walking from Paradise "hand in hand with wandering steps and slow" to meet their georgic fate of work in "the world [that] was all before them" (XII.646–49). The situation and the language are mimicked as *The Prelude* begins, with the poet faced by a world that appears new but is actually the home from which he has strayed. Is he returning to the ease of a pastoral Eden or getting down to work?

His description of himself in prefatory prose as "a Poet living in retirement" (*Prose* III.5) begs the question by playing upon an ambiguity: one can retire to an occupation or retire from it. In the initial verse paragraph the emphasis does seem to fall on the pastoral, Milton's image of human activity—"wandering steps"— echoed here in the natural image of a "wandering cloud" (I.17). A few lines later, however, the pastoral and the georgic appear together as the poet thanks the breeze without and the "correspondent breeze" within for "breaking up a long-continued frost" and bringing "with them vernal promises, the hope / Of active days urged on by flying hours,— / Days of sweet leisure, taxed with patient thought" (I.40–43).

When Milton juxtaposed the pastoral and the georgic he did it to show, as Anthony Low has put it, "delight in leisure because he has worked for it, because he is content to seek it not as a permanent state but as a well-earned respite from labor" (314).[62] In Wordsworth, however, the rationale is not so clear cut:

> It was a splendid evening, and my soul
> Once more made trial of her strength, nor lacked
> Æolian visitations; but the harp
> Was soon defrauded, and the banded host

Of harmony dispersed in straggling sounds,
And lastly utter silence! "Be it so;
Why think of any thing but present good?"
So, like a home-bound labourer I pursued
My way beneath the mellowing sun. (I.94–102)

Set within the pastoral, this reference to work is capped by an image of a "home-bound labourer" who should, in the Miltonic formula, be getting a well-earned respite. But the justification for imaging this poet as a labourer is unclear, for he has produced nothing, and the extent of his effort does not appear to be at issue.

Pastoral is also a given, and not a separate reward, when the prospect of "humbler industry" is raised again in the next verse paragraph. The failure to produce is not just accepted here—"Be it so"—but explicitly naturalized:

The Poet, gentle creature as he is,
Hath, like the Lover, his unruly times;
His fits when he is neither sick nor well,
Though no distress be near him but his own
Unmanageable thoughts: his mind, best pleased
While she as duteous as the mother dove
Sits brooding, lives not always to that end,
But like the innocent bird, hath goadings on
That drive her as in trouble through the groves;
With me is now such passion, to be blamed
No otherwise than as it lasts too long. (I.135–45)

When, two hundred lines later, it does appear to have gone on too long, making the poet feel "Like a false steward who hath much received / And renders nothing back" (I.268–69), he defends himself by beginning the review of his life—his résumé—with the same question about the years of professional preparation which has since been asked in moments of self-doubt by graduate students struggling with their dissertations, lawyers befuddled by the bar exam, and doctors exhausted by their internships: "Was it for this?" (I.269).

The ensuing tale of "I a Poet" which erases that doubt continues to mix, not juxtapose, the pastoral and georgic, for it is that mixture that prescribes two of the most important characteristics of the professional ideal. First, it presents professional work as desirable work—an Edenic georgic. Since the pastoral is not offered as a separate source of happiness, the georgic activity with which it is intertwined is taken to be a means to that end. Second, the mixture naturalizes what many sociologists consider to be the distinguishing characteristic of modern professionalism: the claim to autonomy. When the domain of work is assumed to be a personal Eden, the professional assumes ethical sway over his or her own actions: the Wordsworthian phrase "Be it so" signals the self-authorizing power of professionalism. Understood generically, in other words, Wordsworth's retirement can be seen as not just the peculiar act of a poet but also a representative moment of professional privilege.

My argument about the work of writing becoming both heroic *and* professional is not, therefore, that the texts I have cited present writers as professionals and professionals as heroes, for we do not hold the latter view. My point is that the deep aura of heroism obscures the middle term; we see these intellectual laborers sentimentally and psychologically as individual heroes and anti-heroes and *not* politically as professionals wielding a central form of modern power: professional status. To look to the eighteenth and early nineteenth centuries for the georgic evidence of how the artist was cast as hero is to uncover one of the primary ways that the professions configure what we know of them and of the effects of their behaviors. We can then begin to see how specific genres of writing helped to empower professionalism, both by generating the discourse of professional behavior, and, by rewriting the discourse of the hero, turning our professional attention from it. My purpose in the next chapter can perhaps best be described as an attempt to recover some of what we missed.

5   The Lyricization of Labor

§☞ And if the rustics grew refined,
Who would the humble duties mind?
They might, from scribbling odes and letters,
Proceed to dictate to their betters.
— Jane West, "To the Hon. Mrs. C[ockayn]e," 1791

§☞ They advanced at first with much Insolence, avowing their intention of cutting to pieces the Machinery introduced in the woollen manufacture; which they suppose, if generally adopted, will lessen the demand
for manual labour. The women became clamorous. The men were open
to conviction and after some Expostulation were induced to desist from
their purpose and return peaceably home. — A Somerset magistrate
describing "the Depredations of a lawless Banditi of colliers and their
wives," 1790

Given the purchase of writing on professionalization—its increased
use both in particular occupations and in representing the value of
those occupations to society—the possibility that odes might upset
the division of labor did not seem so remote at the turn into the
nineteenth century. As with other kinds of work, the act of writing
was subject to conflicts over who could and should use the technology, in what ways, and with what consequences. Writing was
also instrumental, however, in spurring conflicts over those other
kinds. By focusing on the genre that embraces odes (the lyric) and
on the issue of gender (whether it belonged in women's hands),

this chapter addresses both the specific instance of writing and its effect on the overall reconfiguration of work. Like the colliers' wives, who "had lost their work to spinning engines," women poets faced a changing workplace—changes that also affected men but not in the same ways. What left women "clamorous" made men "open to conviction." To make historical sense of these changes in conditions and behaviors, I turn to genre as a system for identifying shifts in poetic patterns, asking whether those shifts were also enacted on a larger scale in other kinds of work.

The Lyric in History

On the great roller coaster of traditional literary histories every genre has its ups and downs. But for the genre that is supposed to supply our literary highs—the lyric, writes Daniel Albright, is "a lifting at right angles from the usual axis"[1]—rising and falling seem a particularly appropriate fate. Thus, in reading a typical history of the lyric, such as Felix Schelling's 1913 effort (reprinted in 1967), we should be able to sit back and enjoy the ride from the "Lyrical Decline" of Chapter V to the "Romantic Revival" of Chapter VI.[2] After all, it is a literary historical commonplace that the turn into the nineteenth century saw the writing of more, and better, lyrics. Schelling's description of the bottoming-out, however, is now, at the turn into the twenty-first century, inadvertently arresting.

After quickly passing by Blake, as "quite impervious to contamination by actualities and facts," Chatterton, as the "marvellous boy," and Burns, as educated at the "tail of a plough," Schelling then accelerates through Joanna Baillie, Lady Nairne, Hannah More, Mrs. Mary Robinson, and Anna Barbauld before coasting nonchalantly into a moment of extraordinary clarity: "it might almost be said that the lyric by 1795 had fallen into the hands of women and children, ploughmen and mad folk. But the day was at hand, and the lyric was shortly *to come to its own*" (148; emphasis mine). Gravity and momentum do not fully explain this trajectory; instead of simply falling into any set of "hands," the lyric comes into its own by coming *to its own*—that is, the proper hands come to own it. Those into which it almost fell are, in this normative narrative, just that: "fallen." Falling and rising, in other words, cease to be simply natural and solely amusing when we begin to specify what and who are down and up.

Property changes hands here, and, if we look closely at the parties involved we begin to see how this exchange was effected. In the hands of the new owners—Schelling initially names Coleridge and Wordsworth, Landor and Lamb—the lyric enclosed *as subjects* the females and lesser males who had "almost" possessed it. Those who had represented became representations. "Women and children, ploughmen and mad folk" were shuffled and dealt out lyrically in now familiar combinations: the mad mothers, idiot boys, ancient mariners, and poor shepherds of *Lyrical Ballads* as well as Landor's maid who "cannot mind" her wheel and Lamb's "childhood" ending "in a day of horrors." This was obviously more than a "rise"; it was as if the lyric turned and bit—actually swallowed— the hands that had fed it.

The metaphor of consuming is important here, not because I am describing some ahistorical instinct of lyric in particular or literature in general; rather I want to connect this event *historically* to yet another act of consumption. In a manner I shall detail later, the category of lyric came, during the eighteenth century, to comprehend other forms of writing, encircling them from within as their essence. "Of all kinds," wrote Joseph Trapp in 1711, the lyric is "the most poetical."[3] By 1797 Mrs. Barbauld identified it as "pure Poetry,"[4] even as poetry, within an aesthetics of imagination, expressiveness, and intensity, assumed a central role in constituting the new category of Literature. As we have seen, only by the end of the century did *literature* begin to refer solely to special kinds of deeply imaginative writing: poetry of the lyrical kind being, of course, the deepest.

Specialization is thus the link between the lyric, as the most special kind of poetry, and what we now know as Literature—the grouping into a specialty of special kinds. For John Stuart Mill, "Lyric poetry . . . is . . . more eminently and peculiarly poetry than any other; it is the poetry most natural to a really poetic temperament, and least capable of being successfully imitated by one not so endowed by nature."[5] The semicolon divides the definition in two. The first part affirms the special literary status of lyric, whereas the second extends the logic of specialization to the writer. With that move, we are right back on Schelling's roller coaster. When the lyric is defined in terms of who is "natura[lly]" "endowed," then its history becomes a matter of *coming to* those who are.

The lyric, I am suggesting, came to its own *as* it came to inform the new body of knowledge called Literature. Being in the proper hands, as I argue in detail in the final two chapters, was thus a condition of the formation of Literature. How extraordinary a condition that was, particularly in regard to gender, is only now beginning to come clear. The archival and editorial work of Ferguson, Lonsdale, Rogers and McCarthy, Spender and Todd,[6] and others demonstrates that the number, productivity, and popularity of women writers were strikingly high at the very moment at which they were excluded, as not well endowed, from the ranks of Literature.

My purpose in historicizing the lyric, then, is to link changes in the division of labor—toward a specialized professionalism that altered the occupational fates of women and men—to the changes we have traced in the organization of knowledge—toward a disciplinarity that fostered narrow but deep subjects such as Literature. Since these divisions are neither inevitable nor permanent but historical, they need to be understood in relationship to each other. Here is where the lyric—figuring both in the knowledge we call Literature and in the ordering of work by which it, in Schelling's words, came to its own—exercised a crucial historical role.

Unfortunately, of all the categories and concepts I have put into play so far, work on that genre has remained most persistently outside of history. In fact, compared with the strong current of sociopolitical analysis of the novel, running from Watt through Armstrong, Bender, and McKeon,[7] the relative paucity of similar treatments of the genre so central to our conceptions of Literature is astonishing. That is not to say, of course, that the lyric has not been the subject of a great deal of very productive literary criticism, but that much of what has been done has been criticism of other than social and historical priorities.

When the English Institute held sessions on the lyric twenty-five years ago, New Criticism—linked symbiotically to the lyric through the ideal of organic unity—was giving way to what appeared to be new theoretical maneuvers. The 1970 Institute volume ends with Paul de Man's "Lyric and Modernity," a title that appears to invite historical concerns. But, in a characteristic turn I have detailed elsewhere,[8] de Man absolves his argument of the need for chronological, and even national, specificity in order to ask a question that could "be asked of any literature at any time."[9] In the intervening decades, his concern with "the ambivalence of a language that is representational and nonrepresentational at the same time" (175) and an interest in what Patricia Parker calls "the invasion of voice by inscription or writing"[10] have informed many of the recent approaches to the lyric. But, as Jonathan Arac observed in the Afterword of Parker and Hošek's 1985 collection, *Lyric Poetry*, many of these ventures "do not so much surpass New Criticism as renovate it through revision: less 'Beyond the New Criticism' than a 'New New Criticism'" (346).

The difficulty of innovation is apparent in Annabel Patterson's compelling contribution to that volume. She begins by raising a generic issue:

> "Lyric" remains a name for an ill-assorted collection of short(er) poems; but the genre continues to be defined normatively, in ways that exclude dozens of poems that their authors once thought of as lyric. The reason for this is clear. The modernist view of lyric as an intense, imaginative form of self-expression [is] a belief derived from Romanticism. . . . The newer criticisms—structuralist, deconstructive, Marxist—have, it seems to me, done little to resolve this modernist impasse. (151)

Patterson's essay does offer a resolution, but not of this problem in genre criticism; instead, Gramsci's *Prison Notebooks* is invoked "as a theoretical model for a new *societal criticism*" (161–62; emphasis mine), a move that cannily resolves contradictions regarding her chosen author, Ben Jonson, but does not address the generic issue of what the lyric, in her word, "name[s]."

The difficulty in addressing that issue is not with Romanticism per se, but with the assumption that a genre can be defined according to a particular feature or set of features. Patterson is concerned with "exclu[sion]"—that no single trait marks an entire class of texts over time. But, even if we could find a universal mark, using it to identify a genre would, as Ralph Cohen argues, "presuppose that the trait has the same function for each of the member texts."[11]

Thus, to historicize the lyric we must turn once again from essentialistic definitions to the concept of mixing. In the next section I will ask: what does the lyric mix with? The answer allows me to posit the lyric as something very different from what appears in our literary histories. From the eighteenth through the early nineteenth centuries, it was what I shall call a disciplinary venture: a kind of writing which functioned experimentally to organize itself and other kinds into rule-based narratives of "deep" knowledge. Lyricization, in this sense, calls our attention to the reorganization of knowledge which first valorized such narratives as Literature and political economy—a reorganization that helped to determine the once contested, but now clichéd, forms of modern labor with which I conclude: "Bring home the bacon"—from by-employments to occupation; "Whistle while you work"—from combinations to trade unions; and "Look Ma, no hands!"—the advent of mental labor.

Critical Mixtures

I can best dramatize what is at stake in my retheorizing of the lyric by pointing to one of the humorous consequences of the roller coaster history of the lyric. If the lyric rose at the end of the eighteenth century, and if it is defined, essentialistically, as the form of private emotion, then the history that results is that strange but powerful developmental scenario in which, after decades of dry reason, late eighteenth-century Englishmen finally got in touch with their feelings. This notion has been countered either by rethinking the lyric or by rethinking feeling. A straightforward version of the former was offered in 1924 by Eric Partridge, whose book *Eighteenth Century English Romantic Poetry* simply identified a group of pre-1798 poems as early Romantic lyrics.[12] A more sophisticated version appeared in 1989 in a book subtitled *The Char-*

acter of Augustan Lyricism. "When we speak," writes Richard Fein-gold, "of the decline of lyric expression in Augustan art, we are missing its presence in works whose shape, though not nominally lyrical, is yet ultimately adequate to the impress of . . . personal pressures" (93).

The other corrective, one in which I have participated (*Historicity* 11–12), is to place the *personal* under the rubric of *subjectivity* and then show how that—the subject—is historically constructed. Despite the dispute over the date of construction—was it in Shakespeare's sonnets[13] or *The Prelude?*—this maneuver still seems to me to be basically sound. However, even with its emphasis on historical difference, what it and the other correctives leave unchallenged is the identification of the lyric with personal, subjective feeling. I do not question the fact that this has been a feature associated with the lyric, but—I will go out on a limb here—in the eighteenth and early nineteenth centuries, it simply was not the point. To assume that these writers were only finding their personal voice in the lyric or spontaneously expressing themselves in lyrical form is to erase a layer of representation which was crucial to the use of the lyric at that time. The very act of writing in that form represented one's participation in a larger discursive project—Wordsworth's "experiment"—in which lyrics effectively functioned as data in hypothetical narratives of knowledge linking past to present.

To highlight this function is not to deny that the lyric also had, or came to have, what we now understand to be expressive and aesthetic functions; it is, rather, to denaturalize them by insisting upon their historical relationship to this other kind of lyrical work. The overall disciplinary project to which the lyric contributed involved a wide range of endeavors—in different forms—which were brought to fruition within a relatively short period of time. They included, as we saw in Gerald Newman's list in Chapter 3, the chartering of learned societies, the opening of museums, the preparation of encyclopedias and dictionaries, the writing of national histories of the various arts, and the publication of purportedly historical collections such as Percy's *Reliques* (1765).

The importance of the idea of the lyric to the narratives that were specifically literary, as well as to the overall master narrative of human development from nature to civilization, is readily apparent in the *Reliques*. The songs, ballads, and other forms of what was called the lesser lyrics were assembled as part of a very specific argument: "The first attempts at composition among all barbarous nations are ever found to be poetry and song. The praises of their gods, and the achievements of their heroes, are usually changed at their festival meetings. These are the first rudiments of history."[14] This is the logic that helped to insert a mediating layer of representation into the eighteenth-century revival and use of the lyric. That form was understood both to have been the actual form of history in the ancient past and, more importantly, to be, in the present, data for the construction of new histories—ones in which the linking of that past to the present would demonstrate what Percy called "the increase of knowledge" (340).

The imperative behind this construction project was Baconian in the sense we saw in Chapter 1: it was to be historical in order to provide empirical data for experiments. By thus "acting on nature (through 'works')," to quote David McNally on social Baconianism again, "we acquire genuine knowledge of things."[15] The lyric was thus employed experimentally both in terms of the work of recovering past works—the actual finding of "reliques" as well as the occasional falsification of data we know as literary forgery—and in terms of the making of new ones.

What suited the lyric to the experimental purposes of knowledge production—of producing a new kind of knowledge linking pasts and presents, whether of society or of individuals—was not only its musical status as, supposedly, the *originary* form of history, but also, to return to the theoretical question I posed earlier, its relationship to other kinds of writing. Because we connect the lyric so directly to the creative, its interrelations with what we take to be the opposite, the critical, have been overlooked or seen—except for what the criticism might explicitly argue—as irrelevant to the problem of identifying the lyric as a genre. But, from very early on, the English lyric has mixed with the critical, both in terms of poems being juxtaposed with critical writing and in terms of the incorporation within those poems of critical features.

In studying collections of lyrics from the mid and late sixteenth century, for example, G. K. Hunter observed that "the poems themselves are . . . continually hedged about with explanations designed to infringe their independent status." The poet, he notes, "cocoons them in literary criticism."[16] In addition to such cocooning, certain lyric forms, such as the ode, develop traditions of what Stuart Curran calls "self-reflexiveness"—odes about odes— in which the form itself became the forum for critical judgments and comparisons.[17] The linking of shorter lyric forms into longer combinations, such as sonnet sequences, also provided the formal opportunity for self-critical maneuvers, executed within each lyric part or through the cocooning devices of dedications, prefaces, titles, and notes.

I am not pointing to this interrelation of the lyric and the critical as a defining feature of the former. As with any other such mix, it may be more or less present, or absent, at any particular historical moment; even when present, its functions may shift from one appearance to the next. It has, of course, long been apparent to literary historians of the mid and late eighteenth century that the period saw, with Johnson, Grub Street, and the reviews, a "rise" of criticism, and, with the reappearance of ballads, songs, elegies, and sonnets, a "revival" of the lyric; but this conjuncture, I would argue, was not just a matter of more criticism *about* more lyric poems. The conjuncture itself *was* a lyric feature; at this historical moment, the already existing interrelation became more frequent as it assumed a new function. The self-critical turns it enabled conformed productively to the need within the Baconian experimental method[18] to alternate (think of the repetition of the chorus in ballads, the strophic sequences of the ode, the apostrophic turns of sonnets) between episodes of empirical practice (its lining up of finely detailed images) *and* the formulation of general propositions (its epodic marshaling of those details into large-scale claims about temporality and humanity). The very abruptness of these alternations between the empirical and the general left an aftereffect: what is usually experienced as the lyric's supposedly defining trait of personal intensity.

Working within the now established discipline of Literature and thus having invested our own sense of expertise in the emotive, expressive, imaginative aesthetic of the lyric, we have tried to write off this interrelation as something extraneous—a distraction or blemish either to be apologized for or explained away. Thus we have ignored, dismissed, or, at best, offered qualified praise for Augustan lyrics borne down by too much "reason" and the absence of "deep" emotion; and we have even more uniformly fallen—and still do fall—for Matthew Arnold's Great Decade view of Wordsworth, in which any trace of the poet's critical "philosophy" is editorially excised.

I am not asking for a reversal of aesthetic judgments but for a historicizing of them—an effort that recognizes both that all genres are mixed and that identifying the mixtures is crucial to our ability to understand how they were produced and what kind of work they performed. Quick glances at Norman Maclean's sweeping survey of eighteenth-century theories of the lyric,[19] as well as— more recently—Lonsdale's additions to the Oxford anthology, confirm:

1. that more lyrics were written during the eighteenth century than we tend to assume;
2. that they not only embodied critical features but were thoroughly mixed with critical theories of the specific kinds being produced, particularly the ode and later the song and ballad; and
3. that the increasing production of all lyric forms toward the end of the century—the "rise" of the lyric—represents not a new level of emotional health in Britain but the capacity of the lyric—as a mixed genre—to be used as an experimental form.

The other eighteenth-century form with features that proved particularly amenable to the experimental construction of narratives of deep knowledge was the form innovated upon by Bacon: essays and extended essay sequences, such as chapters of what we call a *book*. Like the lyric, the essay had historically provided both internal formal opportunities to alternate empirical practice and general propositions, as well as precedents for external mixing and embeddedness. In fact, scholars such as Clifford Geertz and Ralph Cohen have already laid some of the theoretical groundwork for understanding the essay itself as a lyric form.[20] Here I want only to indicate that the experimental functioning of the lyric and the essay helped to occasion related forms of differentiation: the division of writing into the literary versus the nonliterary; and the accompanying division we have been tracing of eighteenth-century moral philosophy into, on the one hand, the cultural domain of the arts—including the deep narratives of aesthetics and English—and, on the other, the social scientific deep narratives first generated within political economy.

The scholarly efforts of Howard Caygill and John Guillory as well as David McNally and Stephen Copley[21] have recovered traces of common origins: political economy's reliance upon theories of language and conceptions of "beauty" and the transmutation within aesthetics of taste into value. This evidence highlights the conceptual importance of a history of organizations of knowledge: what we may see now as simply similarities between separate economic and literary realms—similarities based only on analogy or on shared imagery and themes—may, under an earlier organization, have been mutually constitutive features. With that possibility in mind—as well as the interrelatedness of divisions of knowledge and divisions of labor—I want now to consider the relationship between the forms of modern work I cited earlier and the forms of knowing which emerged from lyric experimentalism.

Rewriting Work

Recent critiques of the very idea of an Industrial Revolution should make us very wary of employing that narrative to help us understand changes in work during the late eighteenth and early nineteenth centuries. John Foster, for example, contains the figural momentum of *revolution* by discussing what it "did *not* bring about": it did not introduce "essential capitalist institutions" because, by that time, "they were already" in place; it did not bring about mass mechanization, for "the *bulk* of industrial technology would remain primitive—scarcely mechanized at all—for a long time to come"; and it did not suddenly industrialize the work force, for "the proportion of industrial occupations . . . only rose from a minimum of perhaps 30 percent in 1780 to around 40 percent in 1820."[22]

"To say anything more positive," he concludes, "means going back to theory": in this case, the starting up of the "boom-slump cycle" of industrial capitalism. "While economic fluctuations were, of course, nothing new," argues Foster,

> they had previously been largely the result of harvest failure and war. The new form of crisis was very different. It marked the arrival of the *industrial* stage of capitalist development, one demanding an increasing body of fixed investment which would only be sustained by the fundamentally contradictory private profit incentive. As in any system where goods are produced for profit (and so exchange at labour value), the ultimate, collective result of any burst of cost-cutting investment could only be to lower prices (and profits). And from the mid-1780s this is the pattern one begins to find in England—bursts of investment followed by falling prices and suspended investment: 1785, 1788, 1793, 1797, 1800. (19)

The change that clearly deserves the name of *revolution* was this cycle. The first set of them resulted, ironically, from the economic area that had not been fully revolutionized: the "incomplete mechanization of the cotton industry." That situation brought "direct competition with the more cheaply fed workers of the continent" who were edging "England out of continental and later even some colonial markets for woven cloth." For more than two decades, until "the mechanization of weaving finally got under way in the 1820s," the "biggest section of the industry's labour force was exposed to an incessant downward pressure on its real wages" (21).

It was this kind of pressure which was central to the reorganization of work during those decades, and not the imperative of efficiency proclaimed by Adam Smith in linking "the division of labour" to the "productive powers of labour." As Stephen Marglin points out, "the social function of hierarchical work organization is not technical efficiency, but accumulation."[23] For the workforce to be hierarchized, and thus capable of being quickly resized in response to the cycles, lines had to be drawn through it, and those turned out to be what we now know as the constitutive boundaries of modern professionalism: age, skill, character, and gender.

- Age: the chronological narratives of qualification for specific kinds of work were rewritten from apprenticeship to professional education;
- Skill: levels of skilled craftsmanship gave way to a new hierarchy fixed by a dominant division between physical and mental labor;
- Character: within all skill levels, workers held their place according to the degree of *self*-discipline—Andrew Ure's *Philosophy of Manufactures*, the 1835 advice to every owner "to organize his moral machinery on equally sound principles with his mechanical,"[24] meant that owners and professionals as well as manual laborers had to organize themselves;
- Gender: the division of labor according to gender was rewritten in terms of all three of the previous boundaries—in fact, in the largest sense, primogeniture as a system of excluding women from property can be seen to have been replaced, with the rise of bourgeois forms of accumulation, with these restrictions on the new kind of property—the possession of professional skills (the status of any occupation as a profession has been shown by sociologists to be indexed inversely to the number of women who perform it).

These divisions should sound familiar, for, slightly reordered—gender and age, skill and character—they are the fallen hands in Schelling's history of the lyric: "women and children, ploughmen and mad folk." And, just as those who came to own the lyric thrust those hands *into* representation, so the white males who hold the professions do so by "taking care" of those same groups.

The rewriting of apprenticeship took place within the context of what I earlier called "Bringing home the bacon"—the shift from by-employments to occupation. This change in forms of compensation has often been construed in terms of the Industrial Revolution inaugurating wage labor. But research has confirmed that such labor was very common even centuries earlier: "by the year 1314," concludes R. A. L. Smith, "the economy of the Kentish estates of

Christ Church rested almost entirely upon a money-rent and wage-labour basis."[25] What changed was who did how much and in what combinations. "Regular, full-time employment at a single job," observes R. E. Pahl, "was exceptional in the eighteenth century."[26] In fact, he observes, "the notion that there should be, in general, one waged worker or 'breadwinner' in a household who, typically, should be male is, in historical terms, a very odd idea" (41). The previous norm involved each adult working more than one job—by-employments—and more than one adult contributing to what Pahl calls the "household work strategy" (20).

Jobs, in other words, became an occupation in the sense that a single job occupied all of an individual's work time. The cycles of employment and unemployment required the worker to be individualized in this manner so that he would work full-time during the boom and be immediately available after the bust. Apprenticeship became crucial to this issue of availability when, in the late eighteenth century, it began to represent entirely different functions for the workers and the owners. The former, viewing it as the traditional means to restrict access to their trades and therefore maintain the value of their kind of work, petitioned Parliament to enforce in all trades—including those that had been exempted—the provisions of the 1563 Act regarding apprentices known as 5 Elizabeth. For the owners, however, apprenticeship had come to offer a very different kind of advantage. They capitalized on abuses in the ratio of apprentices to masters in order to garner the largest number of workers at the lowest possible wage: according to an 1804 petition from calico printers seeking to end this practice, one factory had fifty-five to sixty apprentices to just two fully paid workmen.[27]

As an institution whose functions had become so radically destabilized that it could simultaneously serve absolutely conflicting interests, apprenticeship could not be preserved. The committee reporting to Commons on the petition acknowledged the abuses but saw no middle ground: "either all restrictions ought to be abolished, and the masters and journeymen left to settle matters between themselves, or an additional restriction ought to be introduced to counteract the evils obviously resulting from the restrictions which already exist."[28] Only one option, however, was really a possibility, since the committee prefaced this finding by initially declaring the general principle that "they are not friendly to the idea of imposing any restrictions upon trade." The petitions, in other words, were doomed to produce the opposite result from what was intended. It took another decade, but despite more than 300,000 signatures on petitions submitted in 1813–14 urging a return to the old form embodied in 5 Elizabeth, that Act, as the only legal basis for apprenticeship, was neither enforced nor extended but repealed—leaving neither master nor apprentice with a claim to expert wages for jobs that no longer required months, let alone the traditional seven years, of training. To assume that the institution simply disappeared, however, is to miss the historical point.

To find it—to make sense of what happened—we need to turn to contemporaneous ways of making sense. As a central technology then, and as a primary source of evidence now, we habitually turn to writing, but not to writing classified in what appear now to be nonrelated categories: in regard to "economics," categories such as the "literary," particularly in its more personal and expressive forms. But to see the lyric as a mixture participating, in the specific ways I have outlined above, in the *making* of those categories is to raise its evidentiary value. In the case of apprenticeship, for example, we can turn to Wordsworth's experimental maneuvers in *Lyrical Ballads*, specifically the characteristic way that distinctions of kind are displaced by distinctions of degree.

Just as the poet's act of lyricization was supposed to collapse the traditional distance between poet and man, poetry and prose[29] (thus altering who was qualified to perform particular kinds of work), so, in other forms of labor, the established gap between master-worker and apprentice-laborer was closed. But, in both cases, the closure functioned to open a new hierarchy of degree: poets more "sensitive" than men, poetry more "pleasurable" than prose, and certain kinds of work and workers raised professionally by degree—with the late eighteenth-century advent of written examinations, literally by degree—over less sensitive and pleasurable forms of work. Apprenticeship as one kind of developmental nar-

rative which linked father to child within a occupational category—
calico printer to calico printer—was reconstituted within a newly
professionalized system of expertise. The result was a new kind of
developmental narrative, one that was lyricized—that is, the relationship between past and present was experimentally recast to correspond with new divisions of knowledge. Now the child was supposed to improve upon his father's lot through an ongoing process
of education in which periods of accumulating details lead to—
alternate with—new levels of propositional authority: a movement
upward in gradations—actually, graduations—which can occupy
an entire lifetime.

This improvement by degree is, of course, "something evermore about to be," its formal equivalent in poetry being the em-
bedding of elegiac features into the conclusions of pastoral medi-
tations. Canonically, that is the moment in "Tintern Abbey" when
the speaker imagines his own death so as to subject his sister to
Nature's relentless pedagogy; to catch more fully the gendered
irony of this move, however, one should turn to a poem such as
"On my own little Daughter, Four Years Old" published anonymously by "a lady" in the same year.[30] There, the pair also communicate through reflections in the other's eye, but the remembering here is sad, for they have been abandoned by the father. The
daughter tries to reassure the mother that she will not do the same,
that she is "here," and it is at that moment that the mother elegia-
cally places herself somewhere else, imagining her own death and
transferring pedagogical responsibility to a male on whom she
hopes one *can* rely:

> Oh heavenly Father, guard my infant child;
> . . . and teach her all she ought to hope or fear.

At these lyricized intersections of death and teaching, parental
aspirations take on a peculiarly modern form: a better education
for the kids—one that will ensure their ongoing development.

I want to reemphasize here that I am not presenting a simple
cause-and-effect scenario: my point is not that this lady, Wordsworth, or any other poet, wrote lyrics that produced these changes
in the forms of labor. Rather, my argument is that the work of writ-

ing, and how writing worked, changed in the same kinds of ways in which other kinds of work changed. The connections, although not unilaterally causal in either direction, were, nevertheless, historically specific and thus able to function in some mutually constitutive ways: with the population and publication booms of the last two decades of the eighteenth century (see Chapter 6), writing itself became work for more and more people, and more and more kinds of work directly involved—or were in more ways affected by—writing. The turn I have just described, from by-employments and apprenticeship to occupation and an ongoing developmental education—moves that made more people write more—exemplified this mutual proliferation.

The lyric, with its formal capacity for self-critical turns, became—in the late eighteenth and early nineteenth centuries—an important location for both adding expressively to that proliferation *and* for trying out ways to contain it, even as it was itself contained within the professional and disciplinary boundaries so memorably articulated in Schelling's narrative. Without claiming causation, we can find in the lyric—and in its fate (i.e., in whose hands it ended up)—ways to make sense of contemporaneous regroupings of knowledge and labor. The developmental turns of the lyric, for example, require a characteristic—self-discipline—which we can also locate canonically within Wordsworth's lyric maneuverings: the various strategies by which the lyricized ballads force the reader to assume responsibility for the work of making the poem. The gap between the poem's detailing of what has passed and the ability to know what it means in the present is filled by an *I* that can, in Wordsworth's word, "think." That is not only the overt message of "Simon Lee"—"It is no tale; but should you think, / Perhaps a tale you'll make it" (79–80)—but also, as I have shown elsewhere, the central feature of Wordsworth's definition of the "lyrical" in the 1815 Preface: since poems "cannot read themselves," then the reader, in the absence of the actual lyrical instrument, the lyre, must through his own "voluntary power" supply the tune.[31] In Walt Disney's words, we must learn to "whistle while we work."

This disciplinary function of the lyric is wonderfully evident in transformations of the pastoral in poets such as Hannah More. In 1774, More used the inherited lyric feature of repetition to reshape what only later became a standard Romantic variation of the pastoral, the inscription.[32] Deploying repetition of repetition she juxtaposed conditional statements,

> If you love a verdant glade,
> If you love a noontide shade

accumulation of detail,

> Where the bluest violets grow,
> Where the sweetest linnet sings,
> Where the earliest cowslip springs

and direct address

> Come and mark within what bush
> . . . . .
> Come and watch the hallowed bower

into a lyric structure that invites two crucial moves. First, there must be an apostrophic turn to the reader who was so insistently called to that specific place.[33] Second, that apostrophe is necessarily disciplinary—it warns and judges—so as to prevent disruption of what has been naturally accumulated.

The canonical connection here is to the admonition at the end of Wordsworth's "Nutting." More makes the turn doubly disciplinary, as distinctions of kind—mortals versus fairies—give way to distinctions of degree—degrees of relative moral clarity:

> Mortals! Formed of grosser clay,
> From our haunts keep far away,
> Or, if you should dare appear,
> See that you from vice are clear.

Those few who have earned the right degree are finally, at the end of the poem, allowed to open their mouths—but they are, of course, *told* what can come out: "You the mossy banks may press, / You each guardian fay shall bless."

I ask you only to keep this lyrical logic in mind as we turn to the second change in labor I mentioned: from combinations to trade unions—a change in which grouping and group behavior are crucial. Labor historians have puzzled over how to assess that strange sequence of legislation which led from the passing of the Combination Acts (forbidding workers to associate in groups) at the turn into the nineteenth century to their repeal only twenty-five years later. The sequence is strange for a number of reasons. First, there were already many laws on the books prohibiting conspiracy which had already been used against combinations of workers.[34] Second, workers continued to combine, both openly, for the illegal purpose of effecting wages, and clandestinely, as "mutual good and benefit" societies.[35] Third, the Acts were rather infrequently applied and enforced.[36] To assess their passage and removal in terms of immediate need and efficacy, then, fails to give us a strong sense of their historical function.

My alternative is to step back and see the entire sequence together as a classificatory act, one that not only directly affected particular workers and owners, but also recast, within a newly lyricized narrative, their understandings of work. This change is precisely articulated in a text authored by the critic who made a career out of disciplining Wordsworth: Francis "This will never do!" Jeffrey.[37] His periodical, the *Edinburgh Review* (founded in 1802—see Chapter 9) had been a major forum for debate not only over what he called new "systems" (458) of lyric, but also over the Combination Acts. Thus, shortly after their repeal, he was asked to give a toast and speech at a public dinner honoring Joseph Hume, an M.P. who played a key role in achieving that end.

Jeffrey had to reconcile two potentially contradictory aims: celebrating the justness of the repeal and deploring the outbreak of worker violence which immediately accompanied it. His strategy was to employ the disciplinary turn that I shall call the "Freedom, But," after the opening words of his toast to Hume: "Freedom of Labour—But let the Labourer recollect, that in exercising his own rights, he cannot be permitted to violate the rights of others."[38] The turn signaled by the *But* configures Jeffrey's entire argument. He begins by asserting that the laws were "fundamentally Unjust," adds a qualification—"It is but fair however to state, that the *mis-*

chief, in my opinion, was far greater than the *injustice,*" and then qualifies the qualification: "I do not mean, however, to deny, that they were also substantially unjust" (5–6).

These rhetorical tacks reflect the governing logic of the entire speech: the repeal of the laws was "just" not because combinations are just but because they are unnecessary. The government, that is, never should have banned them because the workers themselves should have realized that they were unnecessary; the middle of the speech consists of a list of five reasons why combinations make no economic sense. The problem with the laws forbidding them, then, was not that workers were denied a valid vehicle for forwarding their interests but that the prohibition inflamed the wrong passions: the Acts' "great evil was, not that they kept wages unreasonable low, but that they made every variation in their rate, an occasion of hostility, suspicion, and disorder" (5). Those variations *should* have been viewed, within "the plain and simple doctrines of Political Economy" (12), as the unavoidable consequences of the freedom of the market.

That is the freedom that Jeffrey's toast offers the workers: the "extending" of "the great principle of *free competition* to the great market of Labour" (4). But to accept that freedom was to define one's self within the discourse of individual "rights" and thus individual responsibilities: "the independence or degradation of the lower orders now depends," concludes Jeffrey, "on their own conduct" (20). The choice for workers was simple: discipline themselves and thus return "in safety from the perilous courses on which they have lately adventured," whistling while they work, or fall into "another description of persons" for whom "there should be *no indulgence* and *no toleration*" (16).

The passing and repeal of the Combination Acts discursively configured these new descriptions; they mark a historical distinction between combinations, of those workers who resisted—from the outside—the "Freedom, But" of the new market, and trade unions, composed of those whose very acts of self-interest transpired *within* that disciplinary domain. "Come," wrote Hannah More, "ye happy virtuous few, / Open is my bower to you": the eighteenth-century pastoral retreat was lyricized into a newly valorized Nature, but the price of admission was learning to whistle the right tune. In the words of the magistrate in the second epigraph heading this chapter, men were "open to conviction." Wordsworth called such conviction "resolution," his word, as we saw in Chapter 1, for a properly disciplined mind.

The century that began with this transition from combinations to trade unions culminated, as we have seen, with a trade union for those for whom whistling was more than a preoccupation: the Confederation of Intellectual Workers (1901) was based on the final division of labor with which we will deal—mental as opposed to physical. Within the ideological circle I described—in which work valorized as joyful was made more so by the privilege and high pay attending that valorization—the cliché I invoked earlier became a characteristic expression of male development. "Look Ma, no hands!" celebrates how gaining an expertise that does not require "hands" can take the form of play, producing happiness for one's self and for others.

Quantifying such happiness first became a crucial issue for mental labor within the experimental maneuvers of political economy and the lyric. An essay within the former, for example, published by a William Thompson in 1826, begins with a rather strange apology "To the Industrious Classes":

> I am not what is usually called a laborer. . . . For about the last
> twelve years of my life I have been living on what is called rent, the
> produce of the labor of others. Finding wretchedness in idleness,
> fond of the pleasures of activity and successful effort . . . I have
> endeavoured by voluntary mental labor to raise myself to an equal-
> ity of usefulness with the productive classes.[39]

How strange this endeavor actually was becomes clear only when we discover that it was written in response to another essay in which Thompson found "preposterous claims of mental laborers to an exorbitant portion of the products of physical, or muscular, labor" (2). Both that essay, *Labor Defended Against the Claims of Capital*,[40] and Thompson's *Labor Rewarded* could not, in other words, address the position of labor within capitalism without raising the problem of how to reward and defend their own kind of efforts.

Thompson uses political economy to provide an answer, for its mix of quantification and generalization enabled it to posit a totality—Smith's wealth of the nation—that was understood to be produced and distributed according to a set of generalizable axioms. What Thompson needed to do to establish the usefulness of his mental labor was thus to redefine—in, of course, more mental terms—what made a nation wealthy. "What other good reason," he asks, "can be given that mental labor should be rewarded, except that *it tends to increase the common mass of happiness?*"

This hypothesis—that the value of mental labor, particularly reading and writing, should be assessed according to the quantity of pleasure it can produce for others—should sound very familiar to literary historians. It was a problem that came to permeate the lyric at the turn into the nineteenth century, for poetry was then being lyricized at the same time that the making of it increasingly became an occupation rather than a by-employment. Thus, in its self-critical turns, the lyric characteristically thematizes its own production. Anna Barbauld's poem to Coleridge[41] is one of the most startling examples, mixing lyric description that sounds like, but predates, *Kubla Khan,*

> A grove extends; in tangled mazes wrought,
> And filled with strange enchantment

with explicit turns to the division of knowledge,

> Midway the hill of science

and the division of labor,

> Nor seldom Indolence . . .
> . . . sits
> In dreamy twilight of the vacant mind.

The two divisions connect in the eighteenth-century sense of science as useful knowledge, leaving STC to be disciplined as one who risks losing his own happiness to a "spleen-fed fog" by not directing his mental efforts to increasing the happiness of others: "For friends, for country."

This same concern underlies Wordsworth's declared experiment in *Lyrical Ballads*: his effort to ascertain how far uses of language among certain social groups were adapted to the purposes of "pleasure." The pleasure that we now associate with the "Love of Literature," in other words, figured experimentally not only in the reorganization of knowledge which valorized Literature, but also in the reorganization of work which valorized mental labor. Although we tend to read *experiment* as *experimental* in the sense of innovative and cutting edge—and thus as a cutting off from the past—this experiment was performed and re-performed throughout the eighteenth century with changing materials and altered hypotheses.

Samuel Johnson, for example, writing in a form—"lives" of poets—which proved crucial to the formation of Literature, repeatedly praised Milton for his hard work. Valorizing a crucial component of a canonical Literature—the individual Author—he presented that propensity as a character trait—Milton "was born for whatever is arduous"—and described his "purpose" (in writing *Paradise Lost*) in the same terms: it was "the most useful and the most arduous."[42] That specific religious use was obvious (vindicating the ways of God to man), but of what use is hard work "for *whatever*" (emphasis mine)? The late eighteenth-century shift from Miltonic epic to lyric—initially a lyricizing of the epic, as in Collins inserting Milton into an ode and Wordsworth mixing epic ambitions with autobiography[43]—allowed for new hypotheses such as the social value of mental labor. Other genres, however, also came into pleasurable play, the novel—the subject of the next section—chief among them.

III NOVELISM
LITERATURE IN THE HISTORY OF WRITING

6   Periodicals, Authorship, & the Romantic Rise of the Novel

§● *Things As They Are; or, The Adventures of Caleb Williams*—Title of a novel, 1794

§● Real life can always be dismissed, it seems; fiction has to be dealt with.—Review of the film *Menace II Society*, 1992

Haunting our efforts to understand the "rise" of the novel is one of the stranger twists of literary history: the moment the novel actually did rise—rise literally in quantitative terms—is the moment that we have paid it relatively little attention. The problem is not an inability to count, or a failure to connect genre to history, but rather the power of the connections that already do count. Our associations are firmly fixed: once we rise novelistically past Fielding, Richardson, and Sterne, and the 1780s and 1790s come into view, critical attention shifts to the supposedly lyrical advent of Romanticism. But those were precisely the decades when the novel took off, with publication reaching, in James Raven's words, "unprecedented levels in the late 1780s."[1] Growth until that point in the century had been slow and erratic. From an annual rate of only about four to twenty new titles through the first four decades, and remaining—despite Fielding's and Richardson's popularity—within a range of roughly twenty to forty for the next three, new-novel production peaked briefly near sixty in 1770 before a steep decline to well below forty during the latter half of that decade. Within the next seven years, however, the output jumped—more than doubled—to close to ninety and continued to increase sharply into the next century.

That rise was not, of course, against the grain; Raven's figures clearly show a parallel surge in the overall *English Short Title Catalogue* (*ESTC*) publication totals. We need not look far for possible causes; population was following a similar curve, and, following Raven, we can add: "the expansion of the country distribution network, increased institutional demand, and new productivity based on financial and organizational innovation" (35). The question is not how the novel bucked or solely initiated a trend, but how it joined and furthered it—how it participated, that is, in the increased proliferation and the naturalization of writing.

The quotations that head this chapter mark important moments in the history of that technology, calling attention to its scenario of change as a matter of continuity and discontinuity. What is continuous is the power of the *or* in Godwin's title: how *Things As They Are* can almost silently give way to the fictitious *Adventures* of an individual character. What both fascinated and puzzled even hostile contemporary reviewers was Godwin's presentation of that individuality: "We are somewhat at a loss how to introduce our readers to an acquaintance with this singular narrative. Of incident it presents little, of character and situation much." The quantitative rise of characters who convey "strong feeling" arising *from* the author's "depth of reflection on . . . society"[2] signals the proliferation and valorization of fiction and of the novel-of-character as an effective form for it.

"Things" are still becoming fiction today in works such as *Menace II Society,* which, as the reviewer points out, also subordinates "incident" to "feeling": "You can only absorb its emotional content. The story is relatively simple, to the point of being nonexistent." What is discontinuous, of course, is the form—film rather than novel—but even that discontinuity evokes other continuities. Just as Godwin's novel *is* not only writing but a *thematizing* of it—in particular, writing's efficacy in producing and sustaining a character worth vindicating[3]—so this movie offers itself up as the stuff of character: "although the characters in this startling debut by the twenty-one-year-old twin brothers Allen and Albert Hughes may be sociopathic," reports the reviewer, "the truly disturbing thing is, so is the movie."

My point in emphasizing this mix of continuity and discontinuity is that if Raymond Williams is right about our now entering a "new cultural period," we have more reason—not less—to turn to periods past: knowing how we arrived at the present point of departure may point to where we may be going next.[4] If, for example, the shift from novel to film, from written word to electronic media, furthers the phenomenon that sociologists are now calling *aliteracy*—being able to read and write but choosing not to—then we might want to examine the historical moment in which the choice to use those skills *was* made. Caleb the character wants to read and write; in fact, he becomes a character by doing so. *Caleb* the book is, in important ways, a product of similar longings in its author and audience. As such, it participated in the jump in production and consumption which signaled the quantitative rise of the novel. How, at that moment, did prose fiction become so desirable, and how did the novel become the form of that desire?

This chapter seeks, in part, to establish some of the conditions of possibility for that specific historical event: the seemingly natural surge of desire for writing as novelistic fiction. The conceptual space for such an effort has been opened by recent work on the novel and on Romanticism. At the 1993 conference of the American Society for Eighteenth-Century Studies, for example, a session that spilled into the hotel corridors featured papers that located the English novel in America and in captivity narratives, linked it back to prose fiction from the classical past, and detailed how conflations of genre, gender, and nation produced a novel that was originally English and always on the rise. When, in the ensuing discussion, a member of the audience commented that the cumulative effect of this work was to remake the novel into something that it simply had not been before, heads nodded vigorously throughout the room.[5] A similar moment of consensus—in a sense, a shared acknowledgment of disciplinary change—occurred a few months later at the first annual conference of the North American Society for the Study of Romanticism. As more and more papers were given, more and more participants began talking about how relatively little time was being spent on the six standard male poets, with attention focusing instead on other authors, other genders, and other genres.

I turn now to that otherness in order to follow the novel into its Romantic rise. Each of the next two sections will link a changing function of authorship to the gendered workings of a genre—the genre that mixes with the novel throughout the eighteenth century. In the various forms of the periodical, I argue, these new workings of authorship fostered new kinds of audiences—desiring readers who proved crucial to the quantitative rise of prose fiction.[6] The final section will return to Godwin as an exemplar of that desire, both in his priming and gendering of character and author and in his critical evaluations of history and romance. The argumentative twists and turns of his essay on those genres finally point, I conclude, to the formation of a field into which the novel could rise: Literature.

Author-Before-Work: The Flow of Capital

Living at a historical moment—the last decade of the twentieth century—in which so much seems to be falling—interest rates and employment, walls and governments, university budgets and disciplinary boundaries—the turn to eighteenth- and early nineteenth-century Britain seems strangely like a U-turn. Back then and there, everything appeared to rise: capitalism and the middle class, nationalism and imperialism, population and literacy, the novel and the author. Or did they? With my claim for a Romantic rise of the novel, it appears as if I have only added to the list. My purpose in specifying that particular quantitative event, however, is to provide a perspective from which we can reconsider some of these other narratives. Although most of them have largely maintained their momentum in recent scholarship, some inquiries have managed to touch the brakes, questioning either the uniformity of a particular "rise" or the implications of writing up change in that manner.

Anthony J. Little, for example, in a book entitled *Deceleration in the Eighteenth-Century British Economy*, argues that far from there being sustained, let alone accelerated, economic growth during the early eighteenth century, the second quarter (1720s to 1750s) actually witnessed "stagnation."[7] So marked was this "pause" (10) that "pamphleteers writing in the 1740s," as Phyllis Deane has observed, used estimates

> made half a century or more before, to illustrate their assessments of the current economic situation. So little evidence did they see for economic growth that they were prepared to adopt calculations made in the 1670s or the 1690s to reflect the conditions of the 1740s. Population, prices and productivity could, they judged, fluctuate upwards as readily as downwards and there was no reason to expect them to go in one direction rather than the other.[8]

What little economic expansion there may have been "was along traditional lines with little or no movement towards" the two central elements of an industrialized economy: the "factory system and mass consumption."

The transition toward the latter element, maintains Little, "was hindered by the failure to reduce costs through innovation, by the check to population growth, and the rise in transport costs. The very slow improvement in the infrastructure of the economy despite the increase in commerce is an outstanding feature of the second quarter of the eighteenth century" (101). That quarter, despite some higher real incomes and low agricultural prices, was also characterized by reduced profitability as supply outstripped demand for a wide range of products and wares. In the face of such low profits "and expected low rates of return on long-term investment . . . low and falling interest rates were largely ineffective in stimulating capital expenditure." The result, concludes Little in a most memorable phrase, was a period of "profitless prosperity" (100–101).

That phrase should be etched on the political tombstone of George Bush, a president (whose opponent's catchword was "It's the economy, stupid") done in by a combination of ineffectively lowered interest rates, an unimproved infrastructure, failure to reduce costs through innovation, inadequate long-term investment, and low profit levels. My point is *not*, of course, that we were in the *same* economic situation but that—engaged outside of traditional assumptions about what rose and what is falling—the two situations can, in certain ways, speak to each other. What I have in mind are historical connections between Authorship and economic change. On the one hand, the construction of the Author in Britain coincides with the end of the eighteenth-century deceleration I have just described; on the other, its threatened disappearance today—whether at the hands of theorists or within the new collectivities of the Internet—coincides with the advent of the present period of profitless prosperity. What is at stake in both cases, I will argue, is the efficacy of the forms of professional behavior which Authorship has, until now, so efficiently naturalized.

Authors, of course, unlike the Worshipful Company of Apothecaries, have never joined in a formal association to police their status or govern their market. Instead, writing was professionalized only when it came to be accompanied by the alternative forms of institutional self-control which we know collectively as *criticism*. Through the proliferation of periodicals and reviews during the first half of the century and the spread of the philosophical discourse that became *aesthetics* during the second half, a market of readerly domains was constituted and matched hierarchically to levels of writerly expertise: what came to be called *culture* was divided tastefully into high and low as serious writing and reading was marked off from mere entertainment and what eighteenth-century writers called "Castle-Building,"[9] or, less kindly, novels as "killer drugs."[10]

The historical sequence I am trying to elaborate here—criticism as an enabling condition of Authorial professionalism, and, as I will argue next, professionalism as an enabling condition of economic growth—makes sense only when we open our *rise* narratives to deceleration, a phenomenon that was particularly evident in the business of print. By the 1720s, all of the technological elements necessary for an acceleration in that business appeared to be in place: Britain had opened its first type foundry in 1720, the output of British paper had increased four-fold during the previous decade, and the booksellers were ready with their presses and their shops. But, for the next quarter-century, precisely the opposite happened. Demand for paper dropped precipitously, leaving many papermakers bankrupt and turning many of the mills back to their original uses as fulling and corn mills (Little 73–74). During roughly the same period, the number of London booksellers dropped by more than half—from 151 to 72 between 1735 and 1763. The number of titles printed also fell significantly, from, says Alvin Kernan in *Samuel Johnson and the Impact of Print*, "8,836 in the decade ending 1710 to 7,605 in the decade ending 1750"—a drop of more than 1,200 titles.[11]

For Kernan, these figures suggest a strange conjuncture: the "crucial beginnings and central years" of the writing life of the hero of his rise-of-print tale—Johnson in the 1730s through the 1760s—in fact "corresponded to a period of depression in the book business." Acknowledging "no obvious explanation" for this challenge to "our traditional assumption . . . that growth was continuous," Kernan nevertheless reinvokes the "long-range" upward "trend": "the numbers, therefore, while telling us something extremely interesting about the ups and downs of the book publishing business during that time," do, "in the end," insists Kernan, support the rise-of-print thesis (62).

Since Kernan declines the opportunity to tell us what *is* interesting about the falling numbers, I will take a stab at it. The book business, like many other sectors of the decelerating British economy in the second quarter, suffered not only from such external factors as an apparent demographic downturn (Little 54), but also, to use Little's words, from internal "impediments to growth or bottlenecks" (10). The result was "profitless prosperity" *not* "depression," not a collapse of economic activity but—to sustain the metaphor—a failure to induce the flow of capital. This distinction is crucial, for it helps us to see that it was the activity that prospered *even during the contraction* which helped to produce the means of reversing it.

That activity was the prospering of the periodical press, and the product of its critical efforts was new forms of professional behavior embodied in the Author. The second-quarter deceleration, in other words, embraced precisely the decades (1720s through 1740s) that saw the proliferation of the periodical project that Addison's and Steele's efforts had helped to initiate. That project began with a maneuver that highlights its constitutive role in the history of the Author. Although today we tend to think of periodical work as less author-centered than so-and-so's latest book, that work, in fact, first prospered by highlighting the writer, rather than—as with many of the contemporaneous fictional forms—the tale or subject matter. Volume I of *The Spectator* began with Addison describing his own life and character.

How powerful and habitual that maneuver became for writers and readers by the end of the first quarter of the century is particularly clear in Eliza Haywood's *Female Spectator* (1744). The critical function of such periodicals surfaces immediately in the introduction to Book I: since "it is very much by the Choice we make of Subjects for our Entertainment, that the refined Taste distinguishes itself from the vulgar and more gross," the problem with the particular "Amusement" called "Reading" is how "to single out," from what is "perpetually issuing from the Press," the works that "promise to be most conducive" to the best "Ends." The solution presented by Haywood is naturalized as desire: "I, for my own part, *love* to get as well acquainted as I can with an Author, *before* I run the risque of losing my Time in perusing his *Work*" (emphasis mine). Confident that "most people are of this way of thinking," Haywood initiates her periodical venture "in imitation of my learned Brother of ever precious Memory"—Addison—by giving "some Account of what I am."[12]

The periodical, in other words, in performing its critical task of naturalizing socioeconomic difference as "refine[ments]" of "Taste," established a practice that proved crucial to the formation of modern literary institutions: *Author* "before" *work*. We engage the latter *through* the former; in Foucault's terms, the Author "serves," habitually, "as a means of classification"[13]—so that, for example, professors of English are still asked repeatedly, "What authors do you work with?" Authors—not genres, not issues, not events, not texts.[14] Author-before-work, in other words, reconfigures the very nature of work itself. In the eighteenth century it worked to facilitate and control the flow between print production and knowledge consumption. Authorship became, that is, a means of accelerating economic growth at mid century—and thus ending profitless prosperity—by virtue of its participation in both of the productive processes that characterize capitalism. On the one hand,

the Author performs the function of labor, producing actual commodities—in this case, books. On the other, he or she performs the
function of capital, facilitating the appropriation of surplus value
by relocating it ideologically within the individual. Consider, for
example, the authorial organization of most anthologies of Literature, the revenue generated today by the Stephen King Book Club,
and the attention paid to a poem before and after being attributed
to Shakespeare.

Reader-As-Author: The Flow of Conversation

The Author put before the work did not need, of course, to be a
representation of the actual writer; from the moment early in the
periodical project in which Steele assumed the guise of Bickerstaff,
the eidolon became a standard and very successful practice. The
drawing power of any "real" individual was secondary to the
power of an Author—any Author—as the reader's point of connection to a text. In fact, as Robert Mayo has shown, ventures into
the burgeoning magazine field of the 1760s by writers of reputation, such as Tobias Smollett and Charlotte Lennox, met with little success.[15] Their names, that is, did not ensure a successful negotiation of a central problem of print: what David Kaufer and
Kathleen Carley call "communication at a distance." Calling into
question theories of communication which "start with the supposition that individuals are *already* engaged in transactions with
texts" (emphasis mine), they focus on the ways in which contact—
over the spatial, temporal, and social distances opened by print—
is initially established (12–13).

   In the eighteenth century that negotiation was conducted in
terms of the distinction between public and private and the notion
of *conversation*. Habermas's concept of the public sphere is useful in
understanding the pervasiveness of that distinction across the genres, from title pages through prefaces and into the works themselves. What is crucial to his argument, but often overlooked, is
that he describes not a single public/private binary, but a double
one—a doubleness that he presents as historically constituted. The
eighteenth century, he argues, inherited a "fundamental" distinc-

tion between the state, as the sphere of public authority, and society, as the private realm, and then differentiated the latter into a political and cultural public sphere versus the privacy of the family and civil society. "Included in the private realm," Habermas explains rather cryptically, "was the authentic 'public sphere,' for it was a public sphere constituted by private people."[16] His meaning becomes clearer, as does the role of writing in that differentiation, when we read Anne Dutton's defense of "PRINTING any Thing written by a Woman," 1743:

> communicating ones Mind in *Print*, is as *private*, with respect to particular *Persons*, as if one did it particularly unto every one by *himself* in ones *own House*. There is only this *Difference*: The one is communicating ones Mind by *Speech*, in ones *own* private House: The other is doing it by *Writing*, in the private house of *another* Person. Both are still *private*.[17]

Print, in Dutton's reading, overwrites the category of public-as-state, by instituting, within the private realm of society, a new kind of publicness—one that is accessed and thus produced in private terms.

In this mode of access, the "distance" of print does dislocate, requiring movement from house to house; however, that dislocation is precisely what recuperates both the private—in enabling one-to-one speech acts—and a new kind of public—in the reproducibility and dispersal of those acts. *Conversation* became a crucial term in the eighteenth century for describing not just the private individual exchanges, nor the public ones generated out of their multiplicity, but the flow *across* those newly reconstituted fields. That flow of conversation was seen as so crucial to the health of both the private and public—to the growth of individuals and of nations—that it was often cast in terms we associate with the flow of capital it facilitated. Hume, for example, fixed on *conversation* as a key term, using it, as Graham Burchell points out, "to describe the form ideally taken by the 'commerce' of . . . [the political culture] of opinion, the appropriate cultural form of exchanges between individuals of the 'middling rank' immersed in 'common life.'"[18]

With such high individual, social, and commercial stakes, writers vied generically to produce the kind of writing most suitable to the demands of conversation. Note carefully, for example, how Wordsworth describes his experiment in *Lyrical Ballads*: "The majority of the following poems are to be considered as experiments. They were written chiefly with a view to ascertain how far the language of conversation in the middle and lower classes of society is adapted to the purposes of poetic pleasure" (*Prose* I.116). The two terms of this experiment—aside from "experiment" itself—which have drawn relatively little critical attention—"conversation" and "poetic"—are precisely the ones that pin down its historicity. Faced with the quantitative rise of what he called "frantic novels" (*Prose* I.128), Wordsworth offered up his new kind of verse as the genre that can carry on conversation. He thus ended up in competition with writers in other genres, such as Jane Austen, who, as Robert Kiely points out, sought to adapt to the novel her sense of "polite conversation."[19]

In 1797 the *Edinburgh Magazine* published an entire issue "On Conversation." Its admonition to young women not to shine in conversation,[20] like Wordsworth's turn to "class" and Dutton's defense of writing by a "woman," demonstrated how conversation in print was always an occasion for reproducing, and possibly altering, hierarchical differences. As the genre that had initiated and sustained conversation throughout the eighteenth century, however, the periodical was particularly well suited to that task. It had from its start engaged women and issues of gender, both through periodicals written by and for women, such as *Records of Love or Weekly Amusements for the Fair Sex* (1710), and through Addison's and Steele's decisions to, in Swift's words, "fair-sex" it in the *Spectator* and the *Tatler*.[21] It also helped to articulate class, as well as gender differences, by inducing what was then a multiplicity of middle orders into an increasingly univocal conversation.

In both cases, the key inducement was the Author. As we have seen, not only was the Author put before the work as a point of contact, periodicals also gave the Author a more or less fictive voice to make conversational contact desirable. Whether tattling to female readers, or, for the benefit of those seeking improvement, assuming a "courtly and deferential air associated with the genteel tradition" (Mayo 232) the Author-Editors were always to some extent a fiction, as were their "correspondents." For actual readers, then, conversation with periodicals was about how to converse. Such self-reflexivity was, of course, a part of the effort of every genre to close the communicative distance of print. The periodical, however, malleable because accessible both in terms of frequency and price, became an important site for literary and social change. Its self-reflexivity altered its audience, itself, and the forms with which it mixed: the centering of the Author as a desirable fiction early in the century, led, by its end, to the centering of fiction as that which was desirable.

Haywood's *Female Spectator* encapsulates, in two years (1744–46) near the end of the quarter of "profitless prosperity," some of the most significant changes. Initially a single-essay periodical, as were many of the imitators of Addison and Steele during the first half of the century, its centered Author quickly induced flows of both conversation and capital. A volume reprint was issued in 1745, to be followed by six more editions over the next twenty-six years. After only the first four numbers, Haywood expanded into what was then becoming an increasingly popular form of the periodical, the miscellany. This changed the function of fiction in the *Female Spectator* in two ways. First, it extended the fiction of Author-in-conversation by presenting the new miscellaneous pieces as letters from correspondents, although, as Deborah and John Sitter point out, "it is likely" they were Haywood's own. Second, some of those pieces were themselves fiction, including tales as long as twenty pages with titles such as "The Lady's Revenge" (Sullivan 120–26).

These changes in periodical form and in its fictions had been accelerating since Edward Cave founded the highly successful *Gentleman's Magazine* in 1731. But, unlike Haywood, Cave and his imitators did not expand from the single-essay format into the miscellany by presenting more of their own, or any single Author's work, under different guises; rather, Cave saw the "magazine" as just that, a "storehouse" of material most often printed elsewhere first. He did maintain, however, as Walter Graham observes, the Authorial fiction in the form of an editor conversing, in genteel fashion, with a society of readers. The combination of that pose and more material proved so successful that it quickly became subject to parody, as in John Hill's *British Magazine*, and increasingly extreme forms of imitation. *The Magazine of Magazines* appeared in 1750 followed by the *Grand Magazine of Magazines* in 1758.[22]

As the limits of condensation, summary, and reprinting were tested at mid century, a new form of production which provided much-needed original material arose: readers who had, in a sense, been "fiction-ed" into conversations with Authors became real authors themselves. In Robert Mayo's words:

> The handful of learned correspondents and poetasters who
> addressed letters and verses to Mr. Sylvanus Urban in the 1730s and
> 1740s became three decades later a legion of eager volunteers, over-
> whelming grateful magazine publishers with mountains of verses,
> essays, and sketches, biographical articles, sermons, allegories, news
> items and extracts from books and other magazines, drawings,
> musical compositions, recipes and specifics, maxims, riddles, re-
> buses, charades, acrostics, short stories, and novels. (306)

This flow of conversation from Readers-as-Authors induced the flow of capital, for this was the appropriation of surplus value in its purest form: almost all of this material was provided (and could be reprinted) for free. New periodicals could thus be launched and sustained with very little capital, making them a primary engine for the takeoff in overall publication levels in the final decades of the century.[23]

The changes in the role of fiction in the periodical which we saw on a small scale in Haywood were magnified enormously by this new kind of productivity—magnified in ways that ensured fiction's participation in the takeoff. The extension of the Authorial fiction to readers not only increased the number of authors; it also confirmed them as readers desiring at the very least to read the *kind* of material which they themselves wrote or which appeared in the periodicals for which they wrote. To the extent that these readers fiction-ed themselves into the fictional guise of the Author, whatever kind they wrote was at least partly an experience in fiction, making it an increasingly natural category for their growing reading habit. But in the stricter formal sense of fiction as tales, romances, and particularly novels, we can also point to an extraordinary increase. Like the *Female Spectator*, more and more periodicals included more and more fiction during the second half of the century; Mayo claims that "fiction of some sort was found in four hundred and seventy different periodicals published between 1740 and 1815" (2). He catalogues from that material 1,375 works of novel (twelve thousand or more words) and novelette (five to twelve thousand words) length.

The workings of the Author function in periodicals—both Author-before-work and Reader-as-Author—thus contributed to the proliferation of print *and* to making fiction, particularly the novel, an apparently desirable part of that proliferation. Raven's figures juxtaposed with Mayo's illuminate two important aspects of the growth of that desire. First, although the initial increases in magazine novels in the early and mid 1760s and early 1770s correspond to some growth in new novel titles, the most striking rise— not surprisingly, given the availability of texts and the likelihood of profit—was in reprints. In fact, the gap between the number of new titles and total novel production widens during those decades. Second, after 1775, Raven's new title numbers, in his words, show "striking similarities" (34, 40) to Mayo's magazine counts, their mutual strong growth both closing the gap I have just described and confirming the advent of a two-tier market—one in which the popularity of one product supports rather than cannibalizes the sales of the other.

Mayo attributes a "slacken[ing]" of the magazine figures after 1792 to "the gradual concentration of this activity in fewer, more widely circulated magazines, which placed more emphasis upon originals, and upon stories of greater length" (648). However, as Jon Klancher has argued, the early 1790s also brought other changes to the periodical market:

> Eighteenth-century journals had organized English audiences by forming the "reading habit," but after 1790 that habit became the scene of a cultural struggle demanding a new mental map of the complex public and its textual desires, a new way to organize audi-

ences according to their ideological dispositions, their social distances, and the paradoxically intense pressure of their proximity as
audiences.[24]

Klancher is careful to acknowledge that the eighteenth century is
also complex, its "public sphere" "qualified" and "dualistic" in its
efforts to engage specific readerships within the "'widening circle'"
of an "ideally transparent language." However, he argues, "in the
1790s, when such a sphere could no longer be assumed, writers
renounced the 'widening circle' and everything it implied" (26).

That renunciation, of course, could have been no more univocal than the circle it denied. Different writers did it in different ways
for different purposes, resulting in some of the audiences (middle-
class, mass, radical, institutional) that Klancher productively pur-
sues (4). As an act of writing, it was also done—or, perhaps, not
done—in particular places, that is, genres; and, as a change in the
history of writing, it needs to be engaged, as I suggested earlier, as
a matter of continuity as well as discontinuity. Where, in writing,
did the "habit" and its "desires" go? Where and how was the circle
refigured, perhaps on a different scale? What about the genre that
was rising, quantitatively, at the moment that the audience of its
close ally—the periodical—appeared to fracture? I am not suggesting that another sphere—one embracing *all* of the politically and
socioeconomically diverse audiences of the newly complex public—
coalesced around the novel. But I do want to point toward the need
to investigate how generically configured audiences can overlay not
only each other, but audiences configured along other lines as well.

The periodicals themselves, despite—actually, because—of
their diversification, evidence the increasing consolidation of the
cultural power of the novel. At the moment of audience remapping,
as Ioan Williams points out, the established journals were reviewing fiction more frequently, and new ones arose for which "novel-
reviewing was an important activity" (22). The two that Williams
singles out were both very much the products of Britain's end-of-
century "cultural struggle." Joseph Johnson's *Analytical Review* was
one of the most important forums for liberals and dissenters during the 1790s until Johnson's arrest for sedition in 1798. *The British*

Critic, on the other hand, was initially funded by Secret Service money from William Pitt.[25] Both periodicals joined with each other and—across political lines of another kind—with the many new entries for women, in attending to the novel. In fact, so well was the conversation flowing that, in one of the new titles, the novel attended them: in 1791, William Lane founded the *Novelist, or Amusing Companion.*[26] Writing in the form of the novel, with its family of characters, began to feel—as we shall see in greater detail in the next chapter—comfortable.

Reader-Author-Character: The Flow of Literature

It was in the context of this rise not only in the number of novels but also in the attention paid to them, that Godwin could slip so quickly and easily into fiction. Three years later, in fact, he explicitly cast the move from *things* to *character* as a generic issue. His essay "Of History and Romance," in which he uses *romance* interchangeably with *novel,*[27] argues that the best type of history, even social history, requires "knowledge of the individual" (363). However, since a historian cannot possibly "know any man's character," he is inferior to the "writer of romance," who, "we should naturally suppose," can "understand the character which is the creature of his own fancy." The romance writer is thus the "writer of real history," for "true history consists in a delineation of consistent, human character" (371–72).

Notice that the Author is put before the genre; by emphasizing not that romance is better than history but that the "writer" of romance is the best historian, Godwin is able to distance himself from the bad reputation of the genre—in a sense, he is not so much writing romance as writing better history. But genre is not the only problem here, for Godwin blames that reputation on the need to supply romances for "women and boys." Critics have made the mistake, he argues, of judging romance according to the "speculations of trade"—judging it, that is, as if *every* romance must count in the weighing; instead, he writes, we should do it the way "literature" already does it for "poetry": throw out the "scum and surcharge" first. What is also being thrown out, in a sense, is the connection of the genre to the gender with which it was linked throughout the eighteenth century: the women whose "continual" need had elicited the scum (369). Real romance can then be written—romance that is really history—history that treats "the development of great genius, or the exhibition of bold and *masculine* virtues" (364).

The flow of conversation is being rechanneled here, as hierarchical differences are being reproduced within a new context. Godwin's essay points to the way in which the Romantic rise of the novel was not only quantitative but qualitative as well: *literature,* previously a term for all writing, once put into opposition to the indiscriminate workings of *trade,* became a newly restricted and hierarchical category. The restrictions apply to gender, genre, and even writing itself, as is evident in the apparently strange twist with which Godwin ends his essay. After going to such great lengths to establish the superiority of the romance writer, he suddenly announces in the penultimate paragraph that "to write romance is a task too great for the powers of man."

Why this extraordinary reversal? The reason Godwin offers is that even though the character he exhibits is his own "creature," the romance writer "does not understand the character he exhibits" and is thus "continually straining at a foresight to which his faculties are incompetent." He cannot, that is, fully comprehend his own fiction, a claim that seems bizarre—*until* we remember what readers came to demand aesthetically of a successful character in a "new" novel; a character who could be completely comprehended—in the etymological sense, encircled—by writer or by reader, must not be "round" enough. The very best writing, in a sense because it is the best writing, can never fully capture a character who, in Godwin's words, always "increases and assimilates." The price—for writing—of the novel's Romantic rise was always to admit its final subordination to the new kind of self it constructed. That central social concern of eighteenth-century periodical conversation—whether the self would be changed by this new power of writing—became a celebration of writing undone by a self. Overwritten by the risings of what I shall call *novelism,* writing became Literature.

7   The Novel, the Nation, &
the Naturalization of Writing

§☛   The thirst for this species of composition is inconceivably ardent and extensive. All classes of persons in society, from the dignified professional character to the lowest grades of labouring indigence, seek and devour novels.—Samuel Miller, *A Brief Retrospect of the Eighteenth Century*, 1803

§☛   "In order to find the courage to write this book, it helped me to find a label that allowed me to go over the top," she explains. "The word 'romance' was like a smile. Also, the novel becomes such a self-conscious enterprise for people who read a lot. You want to do something that takes into account all the options you have in fiction. Yet you don't want to be writing about fiction, but making fiction. So I sprang myself from fictional self-consciousness by saying, 'It's a novel—its more than a novel—it's a romance!'" She opens her arms and laughs un-self-consciously. "And I fell into the book like Alice in Wonderland. For three years, I worked 12 hours a day in a delirium of pleasure. This novel is really a turning point for me."—Account of Susan Sontag's efforts to describe the genre of her recent book, *The Volcano Lover*, 1992

By *novelism*, I mean the now habitual subordination of writing to the novel. When Susan Sontag, for example, sought to "go over the top" of the novel, she clearly found it no easy task. Even as she seeks to spring beyond the self-consciousness of that genre, her own simile brings her back down to novelistic earth: she "fell . . . like Alice in Wonderland." And, her supposedly transcendent act of labeling—"it's a romance!"—is but a brief blip on the generic sonar as her final sentence about what the book "really is" relabels it a "novel."

One might argue that in this final usage Sontag simply means *book* or *piece of writing,* but that is my point: we have so thoroughly conflated the novel with writing that even when we want to separate the two—as Sontag so passionately intends—we have trouble pulling them apart. Our habitual behaviors make them stick, from the common assumption that a would-be "writer" is an aspiring "novelist" to the professional celebration of the novel as the aesthetic (Great Tradition) or heteroglossic (Bakhtin) aspiration of writing itself. Stickiness, of course, can be quite pleasurable, as Sontag's three-year delirium suggests. With the novel securely in place, we can more easily, like her, use it to mark "turning point[s]" or simply enjoy what novels make and keep familiar: the flow from work to play as we reach for the bedside paperback; the pedagogical comfort of novels in multicultural syllabi. By ordering our experiences with and understanding of writing, novelism—as the discourse of and about novels—produces and reproduces private, public, and professional norms.

My focus in this chapter is on how that work first came to be performed; I am exploring not "the rise of the novel," but the advent of novelism. In fact, one of my primary tasks is to recover, from the histories of the novel which have metonymically displaced it, a history of writing. That recovery is a pressing problem for us now, since, as I discussed in the Argument, the particular configuration of writing, print, and silent reading with which we are familiar is presently undergoing change. "In the new cultural period we have . . . entered," argues Raymond Williams, "print and silent reading are again only one of several cultural forms, only one even of the forms of writing."[1] The "again" turns us back to the eighteenth century when the familiar form of writing first became, in Williams's word, "naturalized."

By "us" I mean critics, novelists, and readers alike, for at the same time that the work of Armstrong, Bender, McKeon, Warner, and others has helped critics to rethink the history of the novel,[2] writers such as Sontag have taken the novel back into history. Not only was her turn to romance a turn to the eighteenth century, but *The Volcano Lover* was succeeded on the best-seller lists by a novel whose title points explicitly to the same historical moment. By calling her work *The Secret History*,[3] Donna Tartt echoed one of the most popular phrases in late seventeenth- and early eighteenth-century fiction; in 1729, for example, Eliza Haywood sought in a preface to distinguish her work from "so many Things . . . which have been published under the Title of SECRET HISTORIES."[4] The return to such "things" now—Deborah Ross labeled her recent study of the romance and novel "A Secret History"[5]—points to my specific concern in this essay. Their appearance as Williams's period of naturalization opened, and their reappearance at its apparent close, point to the ongoing correlation of novelism and the history of writing. To explore that correlation—What did the novel do to writing? What would writing be without it?—I will turn to the act that not only enables these returns to the eighteenth century, but is, itself, a feature of that time—one to which we are now strangely returning: imitation.

Discussion of imitation in eighteenth-century studies has been fixed generically upon poetry, feeding upon Augustan poetic practice at the start of the century and Romantic mirror-and-lamp arguments at its end. Within novel criticism, however, when issues of imitation arise at all, they appear in a different terminological guise, primarily, because of the hegemonic power of Watt's formal realism, as the problem of verisimilitude. Rethinking imitation in regard to the novel must thus be an act of recovery—of re-placing that issue of adherence to the real under a rubric that can link it to other concerns. To make those connections we must shift our attention outward from *the* novel as an object fated to "rise" to the discursive space I am calling *novelism*. With our teleological blinders removed, we can then opt not to subordinate the history of writing to tales of aesthetic improvement. To that end, I offer the following arguments:

- First, *novelism is the discursive site in which the naturalization of writing is negotiated*, in large part through the rubric of imitation. I will show how attending to the fate of imitation allows for a new understanding of what *rose* in the eighteenth century. *Rise* narratives, that is, are themselves a part of my generic history of novelism—a history in which neo-Classical tales of imitative decline from past masters give way to Romantic tales of developmental innovation.

- Second, from the perspective of that shift, *Fielding and Richardson largely function as dead ends*; what William Warner calls their "programs" (579) for the novel had, in important ways, to be written off before the novel as we know it rose up.

- Third, what rose was "English" because *novelism helped to institute the form of nationalism peculiar to a newly united kingdom*. Rather than the standard scenario of a group aiming at political sovereignty, Great Britain, as we have seen, was a sovereign state aiming to form a group. The success of that formation depended, in important ways, on the technology deployed to articulate it. Its foreign parts cohered into a newly domestic whole as that technology itself was—under the rubric of novelism—domesticated.

- Fourth, what we know as the English novel is tied to a particular way of knowing: *novelism is linked inextricably to modern disciplinarity, and that link is an important basis for the ongoing institutional power of the novel*. This is why Sontag's discomfort with the novel—the need to "top" it—is occurring at the same moment that discomfort with disciplinary "limits" has led to widespread calls for interdisciplinarity. Novelism entails ways of behaving in writing which, like scientificity, become crucial to the making of modern knowledge—and thus the current rethinking of what we have made.

Writing and Imitation

For those experiencing the specific historical changes I have been describing in this book—both the initial proliferation of writing and their innovatively transformative roles within it—a central concern became who and what else would be changed and in what ways? They had to come to terms, that is, with the particular way that Britain experienced what Michel de Certeau calls the *scriptural economy,* his term for the workings of writing in the West in the "modern age." For de Certeau, writing—a "concrete activity" in which a "text" is "constructed" on the "blank page" that "delimits a place of production for the subject"—is necessarily transformative: as "the production of a system, a space of formalization," it "refers to the reality from which it has been distinguished *in order to change it."*[6]

That concern *with* writing, I have been emphasizing, was articulated repeatedly during the eighteenth century *in* writing, making writing as much an object of inquiry as a means: writing about writing produced more writing in a self-reflexive proliferation. All writing became, in that sense, critical. To see criticism only as a separate kind is thus to miss the historical point: as I suggested in the Argument, it was a condition and product of the act of writing itself, as long as that act was still experienced as new.[7] That is why, as Habermas observes of the eighteenth century, "philosophy was no longer possible except as critical philosophy, literature and art no longer except in connection with literary and art criticism" (42).

The connections to the critical were both internal (e.g., digressions, tone) and external (e.g., prefaces, reviews), affecting every literary kind. An important manifestation in poetry was the spread of the lyric, which, as I argued in Chapter 5, was historically well suited to be a site for experimental mixing of creative and critical features. The comparable location in prose at the turn into the eighteenth century was in fiction. By seeing the critical as not just a supplement to, but a constituent part of, that Authorial output we can begin to distinguish between the *novel,* as an autonomous aesthetic object in the category of Literature, and *novelism,* as the discourse of and about novels.

There, critical self-reflexivity permeated and accompanied the competing forms of romance, history, and novel. In Aphra Behn's *Oroonoko* (1688), for example, writing is itself written up as the contractual tool of the white man, allowing the spoken word to function dishonorably as a weapon of deceit.[8] The tale as a whole is itself a mix of various kinds of writing, from travel literature (115–17) to heroic myth (118–20). Behn's frame for these diverse parts is explicitly critical: she repeatedly raises the self-reflexive question of whose pen—with gender the central issue—can "write" *Oroonoko*'s "praise" most effectively (108, 140).

A more startling example is Delarivier Manley's *The New Atalantis* (1709), a work that reads so strangely to us today precisely because, when we expect characterological depth and agency, we find instead writing that relentlessly thematizes itself. In this supposedly amorous intrigue, the seducers are "airy romances, plays, dangerous novels, loose and insinuating poetry."[9] Charlot can effectively act only as an actress; the Duke is indifferent to her until "One evening at a representation" (32). He is aroused, but the work of arousing her remains the work of representation; in the actual seduction it is writing that works: "She took the book [Ovid] and placed herself by the Duke; his eyes feasted themselves upon her face, thence wandered over her snowy bosom and saw the young swelling breasts just beginning to distinguish themselves and which were gently heaved at the impression Myrra's sufferings made upon her heart" (35).

Writing turns critically upon itself not only as a feature within these texts, but also in one of the most prolific venues of novelism: the wide range of extratextual materials, from prefaces and introductions to footnotes and afterwords. In the Preface to *The Secret History of Queen Zarah and the Zarazians* (1705), Manley's writing about writing is again representative as she makes comparisons with France, defines history, and theorizes the probable.[10] But, for us, that is only the first layer of self-reflexivity; we now know, thanks to John L. Sutton, Jr., that the Preface is a translation of part of an essay published three years earlier, which is itself a paraphrase of a work that first appeared in 1683.[11] Considered within the critically inclusive rubric of novelism, this (unacknowledged) act can be seen as a variation of the same strategy that led Manley to acknowledge (falsely) *The New Atalantis* as a translation of a French translation of the Italian original (3). In both cases, she shares with writers of all forms at that time—Joseph Bartolomeo is right in calling the purloined preface "as prospective as it is retrospective" (23)—an overriding concern to contextualize and thus control the power of writing.

Three areas of inquiry dominate discussions of that power:

- What can writing do?
- With what consequences?
- In whose hands?

How the questions were posed, the mode of pursuing them, and the kinds of answers varied from one sort of writing to the next. The shift within poetry to the lyric I noted earlier, led, through psychologizing strategies, to answers made familiar in works such as *Lyrical Ballads*: the capacity of writing to induce sympathetic "pleasure"—that is what writing does—could cure individuals and societies of their "savage torpor"—that is the result—when exercised by "a man speaking to men"—when put in his hands.

As poetry was lyricized, prose was novelized, with the competition among the forms of fiction adding a characteristic slant to the questioning of writing. Since, as Shaftesbury put it in 1711, the problem of "Human Fiction," was the problem of "Imitative Art,"[12] the queries cited above were posed within novelism as issues of imitation: "What can writing do?" became "Can the novel imitate real life?"; "With what consequences?" became, reversing the previous question, "Does real life imitate the novel?"; and "In whose hands?" became "Whom should novelists imitate?" The texts that directly address—or are configured by—these questions do resemble, as many recent critics have noted, conduct books; matters of imitation, particularly under the imperative of pleasurable instruction, prescribe behavior. But whether we read Manley's novels, peopled by "dangerous Books" (*New Atalantis* 37), or her prefaces, addressed to "a *reader* who has any sense" (24; emphasis mine), we realize that the behaviors at stake are all either behaviors toward, generated by, or mediated through, writing. The results—the early products of novelism—are less conduct books than users' guides to that new technology.

Fielding and Richardson wrote the definitive guides for the eighteenth century. Actually, it was one comprehensive guide, since, as they responded to each other's efforts, they quickly constituted an inclusive binary. Samuel Miller could still use it in 1803, fifty years later, to summarize the fate of the novel during the previous century:

> FIELDING is humorous and comic; RICHARDSON more grave and dignified. They both paint with a masterly hand; but FIELDING is perhaps more true to nature than his rival. The former succeeds better in describing *manners*; the latter in developing and displaying the *heart*. (II.159–60)

And so on. Like users' guides today, however, the shelf life even — or perhaps especially — of such an apparently comprehensive effort was determined both by its conceptual apparatus — the particular way it makes the technology make sense — and by changes in that technology.

That apparatus was imitation. The "contingent decision" (Warner 578) in favor of their work over that of Behn, Manley, and Haywood was so quick and definitive not because they offered a thoroughly innovative *departure* from their predecessors, but because they so systematically foregrounded the *same* imitative concerns regarding writing. Although they introduced some innovative features, and some innovative functions for inherited features, their work was, in that important way, a culmination. Together, for example, they standardized the self-reflexive turns of writing. Fielding, on the one hand, as Charles Jenner dutifully noted decades later (1770), made them regularly discrete parts of the novels themselves, declaring "introductory chapters" — of "observation and reflection" — "one of which he has prefixed to each book of his history of a Foundling, to be essentially necessary to this species of writing."[13] Richardson, on the other hand, set standards for the extratextual turns of novelism, critically contextualizing his novels by precirculating the manuscripts, gathering critiques, writing replies, and carefully assembling all of the materials in extended prefaces.

Both the embedded and juxtaposed material used imitation arguments to tame the technology, and it is in that act of taming, domesticating, finding a home, making writing feel at home, that a home was made. The critical self-reflexivity in the discourse of and about novels turned relentlessly on the nation. The claims of Fielding and Richardson to be doing something "new" were not modern assertions of radical and unfamiliar difference; this newness was intended to make writing seem less strange, more acceptable, natural—in other words, in what became the critical shorthand of the day—English. Like Behn, Manley, and Haywood before them, Fielding and Richardson critically represented earlier and other forms of writing as foreign, particularly French, and warned against the foreign as uncontrolled—for example, the romance—and, therefore, potentially uncontrollable—it might induce romantic behavior—behavior, that is, coded as not-English.

Novelism and Nationalism

To suggest that British nationalism functioned, in part, as a domesticating solution to the uncomfortable threat of writing is not to trivialize it. Doing so does not preclude the more conventional links to political issues of liberty, the conditions of war, or the state of the economy, but offers up new angles from which to approach them. In regard to the economy, for example, James Raven has documented, with a particular focus on the place of novels in "the productive and distributive capacity of the book trades," how a "competitive literature industry" played a major role in "legitimiz[ing] specific modes of economic and social behaviour by upwardly mobile groups"; it "defined in practical terms," he argues, "acceptable and unacceptable methods of gaining, retaining, and deploying wealth during a period of often bewildering change and instability."[14] Wallace Flanders uses the novel to focus particularly on gender instability, seeing the critical transformations of that form in eighteenth-century Britain as crucial to working out the "severe contradiction between the dictates of egalitarian enlightenment thought on the status of the individual in society and the position of women."[15]

But the most important reason for putting British nationalism *in* the history of writing and *in* novelism is that it helps us understand the particular form that nationalism assumes in Britain. As I argued in Chapter 3, in eighteenth-century Britain, political sovereignty came first; a group did not aim at political sovereignty, but a sovereign state aimed at forming a group. This process of group formation within a political frame was thus necessarily a process of self-critical accommodation. The union with Scotland exemplified this difference, for it was a political union of parliaments which left, as we saw, group cultural features of law, religion, and education initially untouched. They were then, however, as detailed by Wuthnow,[16] uncomfortably subject to ongoing revision to make the new form of sovereignty work. As the outpouring we call the Scottish Enlightenment makes particularly clear, the technology that lent itself—at that historical moment—to such self-critically productive work was writing. The discourse of nationalism, in turn, I am arguing, lent itself to the society's accommodation with that technology.

This mutual accommodation was completed[17] in the late eighteenth and early nineteenth centuries. In the words of Gerald Newman: "It should be obvious, to begin with, that the so-called 'first generation of Romantic poets,' the Lake Poets—Wordsworth, Coleridge, Southey—were the chief carriers in this era, indeed the last great theoreticians, of the English nationalist aesthetics."[18] With the newly obvious in sight, Newman can challenge much of what has previously seemed obvious to literary critics less familiar with nationalist ideology. Standard judgments about first-generation Wordsworthian reaction and second-generation Byronic radicalism, for example, are grounded, he claims, in a historically incorrect identification of patriotism with conservatism. If we turn from *"debates over civil liberties"* to the *"social,"* we see that "it was Wordsworth and his friends who were the true radicals, and Byron and his who were the aristocratic reactionaries of contemporary letters . . . sustain[ing] . . . the intellectual and social internationalism—in a word, the mental, moral, and social divisions—of traditional and hierarchical society, the aristocratic society of eighteenth-century Europe" (241–42).

David Simpson also turns to nationalism to help us rethink the standard constitutive binaries of Romanticism. What has appeared to be a straightforward epistemological and philosophical difference between theory and method, on the one hand, and empiricism and common sense, on the other, is shown by Simpson to have been

configured Romantically along national lines: French system building versus English practicality. By following those lines into our
contemporary theory wars—where the English disdainfully dismiss
"French" theory—Simpson can focus on "the considerable coherence between past and present"—the seeming replication today of
the eighteenth-century discourses of Romanticism and nationalism
and of their relationship to each other.[19]

One of the most influential current works on nationalism, for
example, even takes as its premise and title the operations of Romanticism's chief construct: nations are communities that must be
"imagined," says Benedict Anderson in *Imagined Communities*;
they require imagi*nation*. These discourses have become so thoroughly mixed because they thematize the same technology: Romanticism is, of course, particularly in regard to Britain, a period
of writing, and nationalism both explicitly invokes writing—for
example, Shakespeare's superiority—and, according to a growing
consensus of historians, sociologists, political scientists, philosophers, and literary critics, has been instituted by it. Newman calls
nationalism a "creation of writers," Anderson credits "print capitalism," and Ernest Gellner centers mass communications.[20]

There is considerable agreement, in other words, that writing
matters in making the nation—but not on how. For Newman,
writing matters in terms of *what* was written, particularly diatribes
against France and histories and compilations of what was British.
For Gellner, however, emphasis on content misses the point because it is the means of communication itself which is crucial: "the
pervasiveness and importance of abstract, centralized, standardized, one to many communication, which itself automatically en-
genders the core idea of nationalism, quite irrespective of what in
particular is being put into the specific messages transmitted"
(127).

What Gellner's formulation does not dwell on are the problems of which "one" and how "many"—problems that turn upon
the particular form of connection. Newman's statements regarding
Romanticism as the moment of the "*mental unification, moral reformation, and social reorganization of the country*" (242) focus on it, in
standard fashion, as an age of poetry.[21] However, it is also, from

the perspective offered by the history of writing in Britain, a crucial moment for novelism. In fact, it saw the start of what I have
termed the metonymic displacement of the former by the latter as
two crucial events took place:

1. The *statistical* rise of the novel. As detailed in the previous
   chapter, growth until the 1780s had been slow and erratic.
   During that decade, however, the output jumped—more than
   doubled—and continued to increase sharply into the next century.
2. The *generic* rise of the novel. The novel was a low form in the
   generic hierarchy until roughly the 1820s, when critics self-
   consciously noted a new attitude toward what was being described as the "new" novel.[22] This was not simply a matter of
   shifting opinions, but, I shall suggest, a change in the narrative
   form of literary history.

To grasp what is at stake in these claims to being "new," particularly in regard to nationalism, we need to examine how the
claims of Fielding and Richardson to "new"-ness became old. To
make writing "new," in their sense, was, as we have seen, to domesticate it by containing it within the criteria of imitation; by bringing it into proximity with real life as something it could and should
imitate, writing, they thought, could be held accountable for lives
that imitated it. In Manley's borrowed words from the Preface
to *Queen Zarah,* the writer ought "to observe the probability of
truth, which consists in saying nothing but what may morally be
believed" (23).

That scenario of imitation, in which the novel negotiates the
relationship between "truth" and "what may morally be believed,"
was what generated the normative binary of *Pamela/Shamela*. That
was why statements about how good Fielding and Richardson
were as novelists turned throughout the century on assumptions
about the novel's imitative relationship to moral good-ness. Such
statements were themselves features of the particular *kind* of historical narrative generated by the imitative imperative. Here, again,
is Miller: "The earliest productions of Great-Britain in this department of writing may be considered as her best. FIELDING

and RICHARDSON have never been exceeded, and probably not equalled, by any novelists since their day" (II.159).

The shape of the argument is, of course, a familiar one: an Ancient/Modern story of imitative decline transposed into, and reduced to fit, the second half of the eighteenth century. The program of Fielding and Richardson to "elevate" the novel was, as Warner and others insist, "countersigned" by the public, but *not* as a "rise of the novel" as we now know it; the narrative had no upward curve, but rather a sudden apotheosis and then a flattening failure to measure up. In fact, I should add, that flattening was preserved within the later developmental narrative of The Great Tradition as a temporary lack of genius during the late eighteenth century. Its imitative function, however, was, once again, to domesticate writing; the narrative was invoked to demand more formal and moral discipline from those who were always already falling short of the Ancient heights.

The success of that tactic was, of course, its demise. As writing was made more familiar, it no longer had to be handled in imitative terms; in fact, imitative caution toward the end of the century seemed increasingly out of place. In 1778, for example, Clara Reeve introduced *The Old English Baron* in imitative terms as "the literary offspring of the *Castle of Otranto*"; however, the subsequent argument demonstrates how—as more writing produced more models—efforts to reconcile imitation of other novelists with imitation of the real produced almost disabling levels of distinction. Only by arguing, as we saw in Chapter 2, that ghosts are okay, but helmets over a certain size are not, can Reeve press forward with her plan to preserve and reform Walpole, fearing, even then, that "it might happen to me as to certain translators, and imitators of Shakespeare; the unities may be preserved, while the spirit is evaporated."[23]

Charles Jenner, a bit earlier in the decade (1770), turned to the same figure to articulate the difficulties of imitation, citing "what Swift said of Rowe's Jane Shore: 'I have seen,' says he, 'a play written in professed imitation of Shakespear, wherein the whole likeness consisted in one line, "And so good morning to you, good Mr. Lieutenant"'" (126). Unlike Swift earlier in the century, however,

Jenner had another alternative to offer other than better imitations. Although his argument was itself part of an explicit imitation of Fielding—it is in an introductory chapter of "observation and reflection" in a novel entitled *The Placid Man*—it proposes a hierarchical distinction between those writers qualified for "original composition" and those, "in the next place," qualified "for imitation" (126). With the demotion of imitation, came, as well, a reappraisal of the moral imperative of the novel. Observing that "Life is full of cares and anxieties" requiring "many expedients to make it pass on," Jenner argues that man applies various schemes

> for that purpose: one hunts, one shoots, one plays, one reads, one writes. Scarce anyone expects his mind to be made better by every one of them; happy if it is made no worse; and in this light what more pleasant, what more innocent than that amusement which is commonly called Castle-building? . . . For which species of amusement nothing affords so good materials as a novel. (127–28)

This increased emphasis on the positive entertainment value of the novel was accompanied by a reformulation of its dangers. Writing in 1785, Henry Mackenzie shares the imitative concern that real life can follow novels, but he claims not to be "disposed to carry the idea of the dangerous tendency of all novels quite so far as some rigid moralists have done." The issue for him is no longer the violation of absolute standards of behavior induced by wayward texts, for he brings additional terms into the equation: in judging novels, we need to "attend to the period of society which produces them. The code of morality must necessarily be enlarged in proportion to that state of manners to which cultivated eras give birth."[24] With society and history in play, real life and morality are subject to change in which the novel naturally—but no longer dangerously—participates.

This naturalization is one of the most important effects of novelism. When writing becomes just like hunting and shooting, then novels may still be dangerous, but we know how to handle them. As the technology is contextualized in other concerns—society, history, the original mind of the author, the personal architecture of castle-building—the old users' guide gathers dust on the shelf.

Imitative imperatives—and fears—are qualified; epistolary novels wane after the 1780s, and, as Jenner indicates, imitators of Fielding's mixing strategies dwindle. What ensues is not so much a new chapter in the history of *the* novel, but a new type of history, as the tales of imitative decline give way, early in the next century, to now familiar tales of ongoing improvement: the "rise" of the creatively autonomous aesthetic object called the *English* novel.

This sense of Englishness built upon, but was different from, the largely oppositional writing of the nation earlier in the eighteenth century. Whereas the initial role of novelism in instituting nationalism in Britain turned upon the generic identification of France with the older form of romance the novel claimed to supersede, this later stage depended upon a different generic link—one that constructed national identity no longer as self versus other but as whole embracing parts. To be specific, the quantitative rise of the novel at the end of the century occurred at precisely the moment that the audience of its close ally—the periodical—began to fracture. The politically and socioeconomically diverse audiences of this newly "complex" public appear, as I suggested in the last chapter, to have coalesced around the novel. In fact, the periodicals themselves, despite—actually, because—of their diversification, point to this increasing consolidation of the cultural power of the novel. At the moment of audience remapping, as Ioan Williams points out, not only were the established journals reviewing fiction more frequently, but new journals arose for which "novel-reviewing was an important activity."[25]

Novelism, embracing both the novels and the reviewing of them, was thus a primary arena for what Marilyn Butler calls the "war of ideas."[26] What emerged was an Englishness that did not resolve but regulated difference, which in the 1790s accommodated both Godwin and Austen under the shared rubric of writing the regular: "things as they are," "bits" of the "ordinary." For the reviewers, these efforts were "singular" and "new," their detailings of "character and situation"[27] unlike their predecessors. And, when Walter Scott and Richard Whately wrote up Austen's new-ness, they did so in a new way: not as a return to the Ancient heights of

Fielding and Richardson, but as an emerging "style," one that "has arisen."[28]

Novelism now featured, in other words, developmental narratives[29] within both the tales themselves (Emma's "unit[ing]" the "best blessings of existence") *and* the critical turns upon them (the novel's "rise"). The mix of the imperative of progress in development with the stress upon the "common" which Scott praised in Austen—common not as low but as that which was ordinarily and locally shared by all—enabled the portrayal of Britain as a land that was itself united and rising. But, as Scott's celebration of Austen's individual achievement, as well as Scott's own apotheosis as Author, shifted attention and concern from writing to the writer, the technology itself was represented increasingly as tamed. It came to be treated as a primarily reflective, rather than inherently productive, tool—a tool that in Austen's hand, for example, was understood increasingly to depict, not construct or change, the details of British life (see Chapter 8). Under the rubric of the newly triumphant novel, writing was domesticated at the same time as that society whose coherence was, in important ways, dependent upon it.

Novelism, Fiction, and Disciplinarity

To emphasize the historical specificity and materiality of novelism, I would like to conclude this chapter by identifying yet another institutional edge. Having connected it to the organization of the state, I want now to connect it to the organization of knowledge. Those formations are themselves, of course, connected; we still, for example, study novels primarily within the disciplinary bounds of *English* Literature and other nation-specific groupings. That is, in fact, the most obvious connection of novels to disciplinarity: they make up a significant part of the subject matter of particular disciplines.

Novelism, however, opens up historical and conceptual avenues of a different kind. By turning our attention from creative/critical distinctions to the hierarchical functions of competing categories of writing, it can help us make sense of shifting categorizations of knowledge. The most recent shift left us with the modern disciplinary divisions of sciences, social sciences, and humanities—divisions rationalized by seemingly natural discursive behaviors—behaviors that, since the eighteenth century, have been grounded in writing. Events in the history of writing, as I have been arguing, were thus instrumental in the institutionalization of these divisions. Given the central role of novelism in that history—and in obscuring that history—we should now be able to gauge its impact on disciplinarity.

The common ground linking novelism and disciplinarity is *fiction*. On the one hand, the discourse of and about novels has been, in a sense, the workshop in which the various activities associated with fiction have been enacted, particularly those concerned with the problem of imitation. On the other hand, fiction has played a generative role in modern disciplines. As Michel de Certeau has pointed out, fiction figures both in terms of the boundaries it sets (as that which each discipline "constitutes as erroneous," fiction "delimits" its "proper territory," as in "fact versus fiction") and, more importantly, in terms of the boundaries it opens: by "render[ing] possible," fiction generates possibilities "for producing or transforming reality" which distinguish disciplinary knowledge as that which is inherently progressive[30]—thus physicists advance knowledge by first making up a subatomic particle and then trying to prove that it exists.

When certain disciplines *"fiction" in writing*—and thus enact the imperative of improvement as the transformative discovery of "truth"—we call it *scientificity*. But what do we call it when other disciplines *write fiction*—and thus enact that imperative of improvement as (remember Jenner) amusing occasions for self development? *Novelism,* I am suggesting, is a term that can help us come to terms with our disciplinary fates. By paralleling it to *scientificity,* we can see that just as, within the sciences, the "fiction" has been subsumed within the "writing," making the scientific disciplines appear as simply hard and factual, and thus consequential, so, within the humanities, "writing" has been subsumed within the "fiction," casting those disciplines as soft and ambiguous, and thus less relevant to the "real" world. As historians of science and literary historians rewrite their respective pasts, recovering—à la Kuhn—the fictive features of science, on the one hand, and the constitutive power of writing, on the other, these parallels will bear additional explanatory weight. Scientificity's valorization of "objectivity," for example, has its humanistic counterpart not in "subjectivity" (they constitute only a self-validating binary), but in the heteroglossia of novelism: while objectivity posits all investigators always arriving at the same answer, and thus speaking with one voice, heteroglossia enacts truth as a multiplicity of voices.

That multiplicity has been one of the ways in which novelism has empowered the naturalized category of writing which we call Literature. The price, however, has nowhere been more evident than in the voices that have been left out. Why, I ask in Chapters 8 and 9, has an author such as Jane Austen been remembered while so many other women writers have not? Having recovered, in this chapter, another chapter in the history of writing from the standard histories of the novel, I end again with the historicity of Literature itself—its formation marked by the naturalizing transformation of imitation I have just detailed, and its current fate, in this moment of technological change, turning upon yet another outbreak of imitation in both the old technology and the new. What is happening in writing in Sontag's nostalgic return to romance and in the vogue for secret histories is also happening on the screen. Is Emma Thompson's adaptation of Austen an imperialistic extension of novelism into the new media or a step in its decomposition under the withering gaze of the camera? Will all the viewers—as breathlessly asserted by a clearly worried writer in the *Sunday Times Culture* magazine[31]—confirm the generic servility of film by running from the theaters to read the novels?

If all of this sounds like another Death-of-the-Novel debate—note the rise of such debates during the latter half of this century—then I hope I have helped to clarify the stakes. At issue is not whether novels will continue to be written and read—here's a tip: you won't go broke betting against extinction, given the size of the market and the means of reproduction.[32] Nor is the debate simply about aesthetic decline, for as we have seen, such "rising" and "fall-

ing" are themselves features of the narratives novelism has authorized. What is at stake is the viability of the historical links between
a kind of writing in *all* of its manifestations—whether branded critical or creative, thus novel*ism*—and the formations it has helped
to articulate, from the political formation of the nation to the disciplinary formation of Literature. If the novel that puts you to
sleep tonight (after finishing this book), the group violence you
glimpse on television in the morning, and the interdisciplinary lecture you hear in the afternoon, all seem, by this time tomorrow, a
little harder to separate, then I will have made my point.

IV GENDER

THE GREAT FORGETTING

8 What We Remember

THE CASE OF AUSTEN

§◦ The fact of the matter is that Jane Austen is safe.—Faye Weldon,
New York Times, 1995

§◦ This Summer, Cupid Is Armed and Dangerous.—Advertisement for
the movie *Emma*, 1996

Is there a disagreement here? Or is the second epigraph merely
Hollywood hype in a summer that began with aliens smashing all
of the world's major cities and box office records?[1] Even if that is
the case, the juxtaposition is not hard to find and reproduce in
other contexts. "You can spend a lifetime reading Jane Austen,"
writes Anthony Lane, "and still be unable to place her: Is she affec-
tionate or flinty? Does her tolerance float free, or does it exist to
peg back her anger?"[2] Lane's formulation is typical in suggesting
that the issue turns on a psychological entity—"she"—who may or
may not be angry inside and who thus produces correspondingly
ambiguous content. But what if we took the safety issue outside?
Rather than pinning down an individual personality or adjudicat-
ing proper responses to the texts, I want to consider Austen's work
as part of the work of writing; in the history of that work, as we
have seen, *safety* surfaces as an issue of technology—what will it do
to its users? Austen's initial reception was, in fact, a chorus of responses to that concern. Given the switch in technologies today, it
is not surprising to hear a reprise in a different key.

Austen and Literature—Why Then? Why Now? So What?

So what? may sound off-key, but the referent for that question when I first heard it was not really Austen, but a conference panel *about* Austen. To be more precise, I was asked to be on a panel belonging to what I call the *So-what?* genre—an increasingly popular and important scholarly genre in literary studies, one that attempts to take stock of the past decade or two of theoretical, historical, and cultural critiques. *So what?* is thus a variation of the safety question: at this moment of technological change, literary scholars are asking if what they have done has been in some way effective, perhaps even dangerous. In its more pessimistic versions, the *So what?* carries overtones of *Enough already;* the more optimistic ones ask *What's next?* The difference turns upon the sense of difference—how much have these efforts changed the study of literature?—and thus a feature of the *So-what?* genre is the centering of an apparently continuous object, such as an author, to measure the discontinuity. "Despite the prolonged and earnest application of ideological approaches to Austen's work," wrote the shrewd organizer of my Austen panel in a strategically successful appeal for inclusion to the Conference's Program Committee, "she *remains* as enigmatic as ever."[3] Our specific charge in that session was to figure out how Austen "can be used to examine, interrogate, and revise certain premises and practices of feminist and cultural criticism."

Unless "enigmatic" meant impenetrable genius—in which case the only choice was, and is, to bow and withdraw—this was a call not to abandon but to recontextualize earlier inquiries. At least I took it that way, since the considerable time and effort I had spent on Austen in the past in an attempt to place her within Romanticism can easily be pushed to the *So-what?* abyss: "So what if Austen was a Romantic?"[4] To a critic such as Claudia Johnson, one might similarly ask, "So what if Austen was a feminist?"[5] Because critics have provided such different answers, what these questions often question is not so much the integrity of the key terms—*Romantic* and *feminist*—but the agendas of those who insist on employing them. The term *ideology* sometimes surfaces as shorthand for the suspicion that Austen is being used to make a political power play that she has been enigmatically able to resist. As the title of that panel—"Out of Bounds"—may at first seem to suggest, should we, or can we, contain Austen within ideological boundaries?

Let me repose that question so as to spread the politics around a bit; after all, we should not reproduce what Janet Todd identifies as a "device" of the 1790s[6]: "if one held radical or liberal views, this was a political stance, but if one expressed proper conservative ones, this was a moral," or common sense, "position."[7] Within what bounds, I would ask, does Austen continue to function ideologically as an enigma? She remains a puzzle, that is, only in relationship to the particular context in which we try to understand her. That context, I will argue, is the discipline of Literature. The acts of labeling her in regard to period and gender have transpired within efforts to produce *literary* knowledge; whatever the results of those acts, we need to address Austen's enigmatic status as a problem within that field. My hypothesis, in other words, is that she poses not just an individual enigma but a disciplinary one.

Let me paint the problem with broad brushstrokes. As we have seen, during the late eighteenth and early nineteenth centuries many women wrote in many different genres with a considerable degree of popular and often critical success. On the other hand, we have also examined the narrowing of the notion of *literature* in Britain, showing how a term that had once embraced all kinds of writing came, during this same period of time, to refer more narrowly to only certain texts within certain genres. This means that these acts of narrowing were also acts of gendering; in Felix Schelling's words (see Chapter 5), they took writing out of the "hands" of women. The discipline that, during the next century, took this newly restricted category of literature as its field of knowledge was thus founded in an extraordinary act—in scope and in speed—of gendered exclusion and forgetting.

Within this Great Forgetting[8] that became The Great Tradition, Austen appeared as a very rare turn to the worlds and concerns of women and women writing and became the subject of aesthetic appreciations. In recent years, however, she has attracted—as evidenced by the current *So what(s)?*—more and more efforts to label her in terms of history and gender. But as those same *kinds* of inquiries helped restore our disciplinary memory, Austen has become a different type of object: "she who was celebrated for being one of the few who wrote and was remembered" has a different spin than "she who, for some reason, was not forgotten *when all the others who wrote were.*"

The critical stakes regarding these different Austens have been raised even higher by recent work on the eighteenth-century novel which suggests that the relationship between that genre and the gender category of *women* was more complex—in fact, basic—than had been thought. Wallace Flanders, for example, acknowledges links based on "the increasing literacy of women," but also, as noted in the last chapter, he identifies what he sees as a more fundamental connection in content: the novel is *about* women. "The characteristic modern consciousness of the 'woman problem,'" he argues, "forms one of the underlying strata of the novel from its beginnings."9 Peter Danahy constructs the same linkage in other ways. Arguing that "discourse about the novel [is] a disguised form of prescriptive discourse about women," he locates the novel "both vertically, as part of an ascending order or hierarchy of genres in which the novel is invariably assigned woman's place in a man's world, and horizontally, as part of a synchronous system of binary oppositions once again equating it with women."10

For Deborah Ross, this equating of women and the novel proceeds by appropriating the terms of older, masculinist literary histories. Arguing that "it was not at all clear to women readers that romances were any less true than what was normally called reality," she reconceives Watt's notion of *realism* to include the adventures of romance, since, as she wryly notes, "'Adventure' literally denotes events that come to one from without, and therefore the lives of the unempowered [i.e., women] are full of it."11

If these eighteenth-century connections between gender and genre are accurate, then Austen's canonical early nineteenth-century fit between the Founding Fathers, Fielding and Richardson, and the Romantic and Victorian heroics of Scott and Dickens may not simply signal a positive, if momentary, turn *to* women. In fact, the almost immediate welcome accorded her by Scott and other male critics could be construed as signaling a crucial moment in

The Great Forgetting: the moment that some of the fundamental links between women and the novel—links that we are only now recovering—were first detached, or at least obscured.

I want to begin now to sort through these possibilities, for here is where Austen functions as a disciplinary enigma. The problems with attempts to classify her in *individual* terms—as a Romantic or as a feminist—point to the problematic nature of the classification system itself: what we think of as, and what we do with, Literature. What is finally at stake in the *So what(s)?*, after all, is the disciplinary identity of those who pose and engage the questions. Austen, I shall argue, has been a figure of such confused concern to us—and is especially so now as literary study confronts budget deficits and technological change—because of her (ongoing) role in the engendering of modern disciplines such as literature. To return to my section title: *Why then?*—because Austen, for very specific reasons I shall try to detail, played an important role in the early nineteenth-century formation of the category of Literature. *Why now?*—because that category is now in crisis, threatening some of our most powerful forms of cultural capital at the very moment that more cable channels and more theaters demand more content. The response of capitalism is, predictably, to bring its full reproductive weight to bear on the threatened market: Austen gets an Oscar.

My point is neither to berate Emma Thompson nor add to the hype; I am trying, instead, to put that hype into history, responding to the *So what(s)?* with specific assertions about what has changed, or is changing, in literary study. Let us see what would happen, for example, if we took Austen out of the standard "rise-of-the-novel" narratives that bind her to Fielding and Richardson within essentialistic assumptions about *the* novel. In *The Historicity of Romantic Discourse* I differentiated her work from theirs by isolating the innovative feature of *development* (125–47), but I see now that other kinds of ruptures—both generic and statistical—can be recovered. In regard to the continuity of form, I argued in the last chapter that epistolary novels like Richardson's began to wane after the 1780s, as did imitators of Fielding's formal strategy of authorial interruptions; as models to imitate, in other words, their works turned out, by the end of the century, to be dead ends. But—and this is why the "rise" narratives, and the system of Literature they inhabit and perpetuate, produce enigmas—that was precisely the moment when, as James Raven's figures show, the novel actually did rise—rise literally in quantitative terms.

Was Austen a Romantic? becomes a newly compelling question in this light—where Fielding and Richardson are not the rise, and Romanticism is not simply lyrical. Scott, Richard Whately,[12] and others brought the category of *new* to their judgments of Austen because her work participated in this new wave of novel writing— a wave that transformed both the market for, and the status of, that genre. Similarly, *Was Austen a feminist?* becomes a newly compelling question when we recognize that this altered market for the novel—and its shift in status—signaled the disciplinary advent of Literature and thus the start of The Great Forgetting. Categorizing Austen's beliefs about, and representations of, women remains an important task in considering her link to feminism, but this new context points to other work to be done. My focus here will be both on market and on genre: the mode of publication, on the one hand, and the mode of writing, on the other.

Where To Publish?

Explanations of Austen's strange publication history—prolific writing in the 1790s but no publishing until the second decade of the nineteenth century—have provided us with often fascinating biographical, psychological, and sociological insights. They have failed, however, to engage the one market option that was both crucial to the Romantic rise of the novel and which was itself reconfigured by that rise. Even Jan Fergus's groundbreaking study of Austen's literary life[13] largely ignores the activity that fueled the takeoff in publication rates which made such a life possible: writing in periodicals worked to make a "Jane Austen," both by giving new value to the position of Author and by making that position more accessible to more people. As we have seen, the proliferation of that genre—fueled by the late eighteenth-century phenomenon of readers becoming authors—led to a two-tier market for fiction in which standalone and magazine sales reinforced each other.

Although, as Janet Todd observes, "women writing in magazines and reviews for the general public became relatively common" by the end of the century (220), Austen did not contribute fiction—or any other kind of writing—to the periodicals. She did send out letters regarding publication under assumed names, but not, like so many other aspiring writers of fiction, to magazine editors. Having sold *Susan*, later retitled *Northanger Abbey*, to a publisher who refused to bring it out, Austen resorted after six years (1803–9) to sending him letters from a Mrs. Ashton Dennis signed M. A. D.[14] Despite her anger, her clear desire to get into print, and her production of a considerable quantity of new and revised fiction, she remained unpublished until 1811, with *Northanger* not even appearing until after her death in 1817.

Why the long wait for publication when Austen was not only aware of, but intimately familiar with, the opportunities opened up by the proliferation of periodicals? When she was thirteen, in fact, her brothers launched their own weekly periodical *The Loiterer*, which lasted through the sixtieth number. Fergus does argue that "*The Loiterer* conclusively demonstrated" to Austen "that publication was a real, available goal for a writer," particularly since the first issue offered itself as evidence: "from reading to writing," wrote James Austen, "is but one step, from writing to publishing it is less." If, as Fergus suggests, Jane "took these words as a challenge," then why did she not meet it in the form it was issued?[15] Doing so did not preclude additional publication in other forms, anonymity was the norm, and Austen was writing pieces (e.g., *Love and Friendship*, *Catherine*) of precisely the length—more than twelve thousand words—that Mayo identifies as the normal range for a magazine novel. The desire to be paid was certainly an issue for Austen, but these shorter pieces were never offered for sale, and the copyright for *Susan* was sold for only £10.

Austen's turn from periodicals is even thematized in the revised version of that work, in the famous defense of the novel at the end of Chapter 5 of *Northanger Abbey*. Her praise of that form has drawn the most critical attention, but it is, in fact, buttressed by a concluding denunciation not of romances or of inferior novels but of the *Spectator* as a "coarse" object of "disgust."[16] What this comparative judgment and her publication decisions—whatever the other factors that influenced them—point to is Austen's apparent participation in the historical transformation of the two-tier market into a hierarchical system of what we now know as high versus low culture—a hierarchization that in narrowing the range of proper writing ushered in the disciplinary advent of the new category of Literature. I say *apparent participation* because the historical point finally is not her intention but the fact that her novels were received and have functioned in what were then newly exclusionary terms.[17] They were celebrated as "new" because they were not just different but better, and better for what they left out: those "things," as *The Quarterly Review* put it, "that should now be left to ladies' maids and sentimental washerwomen."[18]

But there is a twist to this problem of intention which only becomes visible when we respond to the *Was Austen a feminist?* dispute with more than a *So what?* Claudia Johnson's significant contribution to that debate was to show that Austen's participation in the war of ideas was not to depoliticize but to depolemicize. But polemicization was exactly what happened to the periodicals at the moment when Austen began to write: the 1790s, as Jon Klancher has argued, saw a realignment of periodicals and their audiences according to new "ideological dispositions" and "social distances."[19] Could Austen, in employing a depolemicizing strategy that Johnson cannily identifies as the mark of her feminism, have made publication decisions that have allowed her and her novels to play an unexpected role in the disciplinary exclusion of women and women's writing?

Again, we do not know intentions with certainty, so I pose this scenario of historical indirection as question rather than fact. But, by acknowledging that there were publication options and that the option taken affected Austen's visibility, we can begin to grasp the complexity of her role in The Great Forgetting—a forgetting that left her both remembered *and* an enigma. An important early boost to visibility and remembrance, for example, was the direct result of her turn to John Murray to publish *Emma*. As Walter Scott's publisher, Murray made it his business to ask Scott to review the novel for the journal Murray himself had founded, *The Quarterly Review*. Although unsigned, as David Lodge points out, "the extensive and generally favourable discussion of her work in the *Quarterly* was an important milestone in Jane Austen's literary career, the first significant recognition that she was a novelist of unusual distinction."[20]

Applied to Austen, *unusual* means not only *particular* or *special*, but *different* or *strange*, for Scott's review helped to institute a tradition of negative appreciation: Austen's virtues came to be articulated habitually in terms of what she lacks—Shakespearean in some ways, but *not* Shakespeare. Scott's recurrent focus is on the "ordinary" nature of her subject matter, the degree to which she attends to the "daily," "common," and "middling." But he compliments the "tact with which she presents characters that the reader cannot fail to recognize" with the telling word "peculiar," setting the negative tone for the praise that follows: "The subjects are not often elegant, and certainly never grand; but they are finished up to nature, and with a precision which delights the reader."[21]

The reputation that emerged from such negativity was, not surprisingly, similarly qualified: "though not destined to be a popular author," writes F. B. Pinion in language that itself, after 150 years, still enacted Scott's structural negativity, "Jane Austen was soon marked for distinction; and such has in the main been the tenor of her success ever since" (180). Austen's success certainly has been qualified, but the binary of popularity versus distinction can be misleading. If we assume that *distinction* signals a complexity or high seriousness that makes for difficulty or inaccessibility, as opposed to the simpler pleasures of the *popular*, we will have trouble grasping the truly enigmatic tenor of Austen's early reception and its connection to disciplinarity.

On the one hand, Scott does distinguish Austen's novels from the "ephemeral productions which supply the regular demand of watering-places and circulating libraries" (59). On the other hand, however, he stresses as a feature of "some importance" that the reader of *Emma* "may return from his promenade to the ordinary business of life, without any chance of having his head turned" (68). Here, then, was the initial chorus: this sense of *safety* echoes throughout the remarkably repetitive vocabulary of the other initial reviews of the novel: "amusing, inoffensive" (*British Critic*); "harmless amusement" (*Monthly Review*); "an agreeable relaxation . . . amusing" (*Gentleman's Magazine*). Distinction here—the *Gentleman's Magazine* grants *Emma* a "distinguished degree of eminence" among novels—is the reward for being nonthreatening entertainment. Austen's work, that is, was received not only as pleasurable, but as *comfortable*. This was not, let me stress, primarily a matter of patriarchal condescension to domestic subject matter, since Austen's work was being compared with other novels of love and marriage; in fact one point of comparison, according to the *Gentleman's Magazine*, was the "tendency" of Austen's competition "to deteriorate the heart."[22]

To make sense of this sense of *comfort* we need to historicize it: what was so disagreeable, so offensive, so harmful that readers equated its absence with literary merit? What was the threat, and what was the solution? In her bold speculations on Austen's early writings, Margaret Doody suggests that the published novels were their author's toned-down retreat from the brilliantly "disturbing" comedic power of the earlier—but by no means childish—works. Chastened, argues Doody, by Cadell's rejection of *First Impressions* and Crosby's refusal to release *Susan*,

> Jane Austen in maturity made a choice and went in another direction. At the crossroads, she had to choose, and she then wrote the realistic novel of courtship, closely and apparently even modestly related to the style of novel that had frightened her, stimulated her, and made her laugh. She could not laugh so loudly in the later works.[23]

Rather than contrast Austen, as Claudia Johnson does, to "her more conspicuously political sister-novelists" (xxiv), Doody's strategy here is to turn Austen back upon herself—to what she had been and might have become. Thus Johnson arrives at depolemicizing as Austen's mature achievement, whereas maturity, for Doody, is the moment Austen compromised what her "genius" had already achieved.

To see the six novels as not only domestic but domesticated—in the terms still with us today, a *safe* solution—is to begin to unravel the enigma of Austen's reception. The problem that invited that solution, however, still needs to be articulated, for Doody's focus, whatever the merits of her valorizing of the juvenilia,[24] is on what threatens the author and not the readers. Even the threat of rejection she specifies must be qualified, for Austen herself, as we have seen, also did some rejecting, turning from the periodical option that—with its many variations—might well have accommodated her "laughter." Certainly the readers could not have been threatened by what remained unpublished and thus unread, so the threat must have originated in other writing—in fact, I would argue, in writing itself. Without the proliferation of writing—in quantity and in kinds—which occurred throughout the eighteenth century and accelerated at its close, Austen could not have had choices to make or readers to comfort. Her actions, and their reactions, make sense only when we broaden the historical context from a single career to the sphere of activity which enabled it.

What's New?

Fiction, in the forms of romance and novel, served as a particularly charged locus of concern about the power of writing throughout the century. Early efforts to assuage that concern, led by Richardson and Fielding, focused on the morality of the tale: if writing provided the proper models, then any changes it induced would not be cause for alarm. Such strict propriety, however, as Johnson's mid century *Rambler* essay on fiction made quite clear, is not so easily maintained when realism is a priority. Not only is there a greater chance that, "for the sake of following nature," novelists will "mingle good and bad qualities," but "susceptible" readers will be more inclined, argued Johnson, to "follow the current" when the world on the page more closely resembles their own. Thus the more the novel centered on real life, the more suspect a form it became.[25]

The threat, then, was writing, and the solution was—for some reason—Austen's "new" kind of novels. What was so extraordinary about their reception was the lack of suspicion. Reviewers were so relaxed, so unalarmed by Austen's work—even as they complimented her on realistic characters that come "home to the heart," but, "agreeabl[y]" enough, do not "deteriorate" it (*Gentleman's Magazine*). What reassured them was not a more stringent morality; their admiration for her "accuracy" appears to have displaced rather than aggravated the concern for propriety. In fact, as thematized by Austen in *Northanger Abbey,* that concern was displaced right out of the text; the narrator concludes by "leav[ing] it to be settled by whomsoever it may concern, whether the tendency of this work be altogether to recommend parental tyranny, or reward filial disobedience" (252).

Despite the flippant tone, Austen makes it quite clear that this gesture is not meant to trivialize moral judgments but to mark them as complex—more specifically, as resistant to simplistic cause-and-effect analysis. In fact, the gesture is made in response to an example of such complexity: the cause—the General's "unjust interference" in Catherine and Henry's affairs—does not produce the expected effect—"injur[y]"—but rather the opposite—it "improv[es]" their relationship. Only when "convinced" by this turnabout, does the narrator "leave" "recommend[ing]" to others. What is being abandoned, then, is not morality, but the mode of moralizing.

Calling that mode into question, however, is not just a device to end *Northanger*; the cause-and-effect linkage surfaces throughout the novel in Austen's focus on what writing does to those who read it. The threat of writing which the novel enacts is premised on linking, in that manner, behavior on the page to the behavior of readers. The discomforting question is whether we become what we read. Austen's answer—an answer that I would argue signals a change in the status of writing from a worrisome new technology to a more trusted tool—is "Yes and no, but don't worry." Catherine Morland does—at times—behave somewhat like the Gothic heroines she reads about, but she is neither "born" (13) to be such a heroine nor doomed to become one. The linkage is too complex to be predictable, in terms of both what behaviors are enacted and their consequences. As with the General's villainous "interference," even the most threatening experiences contribute, finally, to the "improv[ement]" of "knowledge" (252) which fuels development.

I am not arguing that Austen solved the threat of writing simply by writing it off. This type of overt thematizing certainly played a role in altering perceptions of the power of writing—and, to the extent that it did so, exemplified it—but the fate of writing also depended, and depends, both on matters of publication, including access and circulation, and of mode, including kind and institution. Austen's enigmatic "new"-ness—and thus her role in The Great Forgetting—derives from her inhabiting a crucial historical intersection of all of these concerns. There, the "taming" of her writing, as Doody describes the changes occurring on the micro level of the individual career, corresponds with and participates in, the taming, on the macro level of her society, of writing itself.

I want to be very precise about the kind of claim I am making here. By linking Austen to such a weighty phenomenon as the taming of writing, I am not trying to repeat, but to explain in a different key, the standard story of her important position within a developing Great Tradition. The problem, that is, is not whether, in aesthetic or other terms, she deserves to be valorized within the "rise" of the novel and of Literature, but the fact that *she has been* and continues to be. Both the "rise" and the reasons she is in it are matters I am locating within a history of disciplinarity—of the engendering of the modern organization of knowledge. My purpose is not to revalidate established disciplinary knowledge—the category of Literature in which Austen is comfortably remembered— but to put it into history—a history of writing which invites other forms of knowledge and other acts of remembrance. In doing so, I am trying to identify some of the features in Austen—the *hooks* into a newly forming disciplinarity—which can help explain how she gained and maintained such a privileged position. I am putting, that is, the hype into history.

The issue of periodical publication, for example, exemplifies the connection between the comfortable and the memorable which served Austen so well. One way to contain writing comfortably is to divide it up, valorizing certain kinds and targeting them to specific audiences for specific purposes. In describing the late-century take-off in publication rates, the formation of the two-tier market for fiction, the polemicization of the periodicals, and Austen's refusal to publish in them, I have been attempting to locate her in the marketing changes that made writing more manageable—more like the still titillating and perhaps useful, but ultimately benign amusement thematized in *Northanger*. Staying out of the periodicals and not publishing the early works were exclusionary practices that resonated on both the micro and the macro levels: the six novels have, of course, dominated their author's individual oeuvre—a canonical formation Doody is trying to break—and, as markers of the new and comfortable, they have helped to enable and sustain the narrowing and hierarchizing that underwrite the discipline we now call Literature.

Who's Left?

Austen, in other words, in disciplining the threat of writing, helped to turn writing into a discipline. When writing's threat is subordinated—when it appears to function more as a medium than as an object of attention—other subjects can come into view. Disciplinarity, then, can be seen, historically, as an organizational form of comfort with writing—a form in which a narrowing—and thus more easily mastered and monitored—range of inquiry is supposed to ensure a greater depth of understanding. Literature, as the particular discipline that takes writing as its subject, may—I mean no offense to colleagues—be said to take this comfort particularly seriously—thus the assessment by the *Gentleman's Magazine* of Austen's novel as an "agreeable relaxation from severer studies."

The price of that comfort was The Great Forgetting. What Austen's "new" narrowing left out were not just those *things* that made writing uncomfortable, but, as we saw in the *Quarterly Review*, the "ladies' maids and sentimental washerwomen" they were "left to."[26] The historical connection was, once again, indirect, for Austen's immediate target was not gender but genre. Those *things* were features of the particular kind of fiction—the sentimental—which was most closely identified with the problem of the constitutive power of writing—its capacity, as Janet Todd describes the sentimental, to bypass the mimetic and "force" response by linking the "literary" experience with the "living one."[27] But that kind of writing, in turn, was most closely identified with women, so that the taming of writing, through the subsuming of the sentimental within newly comfortable forms, inevitably entailed the disciplinary disappearance of many women writers.

Austen has been read consistently—Richard Simpson called her the "ironical censurer of her contemporaries" in 1870[28]—as a source of important models for that subsuming. It is not surprising, then, that the discipline those models enabled has remembered her while forgetting so many others. Simpson did not intend, nor do I, to suggest that an ambitious and/or mean-spirited Austen deliberately managed to depose her rivals. Rather, I am arguing that her mode of censuring—the ironic containment of inherited features—functioned, like the mode of publication, as another hook by which she could be taken up by the very literary histories (e.g., Scott, Whately, Simpson) which left them out.[29]

The abstract-sounding issues of *taming* and *comfort* materialized in those hooks—in matters of where writing appeared and of how familiar features were transformed. As we have just seen, the standard moral didacticism of sentimental fiction was contained in *Northanger Abbey* by Austen's portrayal of the ironic insufficiency of cause and effect. Such maneuvers increasingly differentiated the fiction in the magazines from the fiction in standalone volumes, especially as critics valorized those acts as evidence of something new subsuming the old. That subsuming—despite the seemingly substantial gender differences between Austen's "bit[s] . . . of Ivory" and Scott's "Big Bow-wow,"[30]—was what he and other (male) critics could claim to find in, and, to a certain extent, share with, Austen.

What they saw as shared typically followed the two-part pattern of *Northanger*'s conclusion: a narrowing (e.g., the refusal to moralize) for the sake of depth (e.g., the developmental "improv[ement]" of "knowledge"). Thus Scott argued that Austen's work "bears the same relation to that of the sentimental and romantic cast, that cornfields and cottages and meadows bear to the highly adorned grounds of a show mansion, or the rugged sub-limities of a mountain landscape" (68). The sublime is subsumed in Austen, according to Scott, as the turn from the "excitements" of older forms of writing enables a "depth of knowledge" which marks the more comfortable "new" (63). For Scott himself, of course, the subsuming of romance was also crucial, though, in his case, more Romantic features remained, and the newly deep knowledge was less of "ordinary walks of life" than of "national character."[31]

Austen was thus inserted—enigmatically—into literary history as particularly narrow but thus admirably deep. On the one hand, the narrow-but-deep formulation was a crucial disciplinary link to her future in Literature. The concluding gesture of *Northanger*'s narrator—"I leave it to [others]"—is what disciplines do in order to go about their own work. On the other hand, the degree of nar-rowness (domesticity) and the kind of depth (female develop-ment) invited the tradition of negative appreciation. Austen was thus a site for the engendering of disciplinarity: where she pub-lished, what she wrote, and the ways in which she has been valued and devalued demonstrate how the new divisions of knowledge were informed by divisions of gender. From its inception, as I ar-gued in Chapter 2, that system of knowledge has functioned to articulate and enact those divisions.

Just think of how they are being enacted now in the Holly-wood frenzy over Austen. The newly threatening technology now is not writing, but the electronic media, and, once again, the pro-fessional status of women is at stake. Many of the same critics who are celebrating the Austen ascendancy as a breakthrough for women characters, actors, directors, and screenwriters are also prais-ing and explaining the results in terms of the taming of movie vio-lence by the supposedly timeless nature of these domestic tales—a timelessness in which what women know is the heart, and what they want is a husband. That is yet another context of the opening epigraph of this chapter: "The fact of the matter is that Jane Austen is safe."

Neither the current Austen craze nor her survivor role in the early nineteenth-century remasculinization of writing[32] is a matter to be adjudicated solely in terms of our aesthetic judgments or her individual beliefs or behaviors. Each is, importantly, a problem in the historicity of the category of Literature. Current concerns over the stability of that category—and of the organization of knowledge that category stabilizes—have helped to generate the *So-what?* genre I cited at the start of this essay. As a moment troubled by newly disturbing technologies and signs of another remasculinization,[33] the present invites, even demands, a better understanding of the past—of the forms of comfort secured in Austen's time and of the price.

9 How We Forgot

REPRODUCTION AND REVERSE
VICARIOUSNESS

§◈ Writing itself feels largely unmoored, these days, from a literary
past. . . . Decades beyond the end of Empire, long after the "dark Satanic
Mills" of industry have come and gone, the nation seems to grope
around, in search of the outline of itself.—Kennedy Fraser, "Piper Pipe
That Song Again," 1996

I end by trying to remember, and therefore with an overwhelming
sense of irony: if, as Fraser suggests, the very discipline that arose
by forgetting is now adrift—the technology and nation seemingly
sundered—then its best bet is to remember everything it can. The
study of women writers is, in fact, becoming at least a temporary
mainstay of English Literature departments. That is not to say, of
course, that anyone or anything can be made "safe" again—no
matter how many Austen movies we make and view. All of our
efforts are, as I put it at the start of the book, haunted by technological change.

　　Such language sounds threatening—or certainly melodramatic
for a scholarly book—but my point is not that the future is lost but
that the past may be recoverable. What I want to recover are not
only texts and writers but some sense of what happened to them
and how. Since I have been describing past change in terms of the
mixing of kinds, that is the procedure I will experiment with here.
To a brief reading of a passage by Bishop Percy I will add statistical
information on population and the economy mixed with features
from communication theory, all within a literary historical frame.[1]

I am not proposing this mix, or those found in my other chapters, as standard formulas for future recovery efforts. They are not, however, haphazard combinations, and there is an informal test of their effectiveness: do they help make sense of the current proliferation of descriptions of contemporary change—many of which also seem like haphazard mixtures—or are we left feeling more "unmoored"? Take, for example, this sentence from a *New Yorker* review of the movie *Trainspotting*: "Even though Begbie is fictional—even though he is fictional and Scottish—I still feel that if he caught me talking about him in public he would crack the rim off a beer glass and rewrite my face."[2] Movies—Scotland—fiction—writing—violence. As I read this while revising this book, its features stood out in remarkably ordered fashion. With the current change in technologies, Scotland has reemerged from the United Kingdom as a subject of—and center for making—movies: an electronic genre in which the feature of "fiction" is being deployed experimentally to produce pleasure through altering disciplinary narratives. Like an aliterate in regard to literacy, the main character, we are told, has "chosen not to choose" the standard developmental routes regarding self-knowledge and work. Amid these disruptions of discipline, profession, and nation, writing—decentered but not disempowered (as in a screenplay)—reappears. It speaks, however, not with the firm calm of the Leech-gatherer wielding his staff and explaining himself, but in an image of the personal and public violence of change.

Writing Violence

I began this book by recounting the physical violence of a burning token booth in the late twentieth century. The late eighteenth century in Britain certainly saw its share of violence of that kind, but it also experienced violence in writing. I am thinking of the writing we know as the Gothic, a label not tagged on afterward but defined from the start both in *Otranto* and its Prefaces (1764) and in Bishop Percy's *Reliques* (1765). Rather than interpreting, individually or collectively, pieces of Gothic fiction, I want here only to call attention to the fiction of the Gothic itself in Percy. I offer it as an initial example of the role of writing in the symbolic violence of forgetting which is the main concern of this chapter.

In "Appendix II On the Ancient Metrical Romances," Percy not only constructs the history of "poetry as history" we examined in Chapter 5, he also devotes considerable space to insisting upon a very particular lineage for his reliques. To claim the "idea of chivalry and its peculiar fictions" (346) as a valuable heritage for Britain, Percy must establish both an origin that valorizes it and a path to Britain which leaves it untainted by contact with European rivals and non-European "rude people[s]": "The opinion therefore seems very untenable which some learned and ingenious men have entertained, that the turn for chivalry, and the taste for that species of romantic fiction were caught by the Spaniards from the Arabians or Moors after their invasion of Spain" (342). Note that this issue is cast as a problem in "learn[ing]" and that Percy formally conducts it in that manner, providing an array of very long footnotes that repeat and elaborate the claims in the main text. The integrity of the nation, that is, was cast historically as the subject of newly specialized knowledge.

As part of that project, the "Mahometan nations" must be cast aside as an origin because they represented an ongoing religious and political threat to a Christian Britain. The only eligible non-Christians were those who remained firmly in the pre-Christian past: thus the fallen civilizations of Greece and Rome were secured as Britain's ancient heritage, lending it their accomplishments at no current risk. The turn from the Mahometans also allowed Percy to leave Catholic Spain—a religious and geopolitical rival in the present—out of the picture.

That left a link to be filled between the Greco-Roman and the British, and Percy's choice was "the Gothic nations of the North" (346). The turn to the Gothic in the late eighteenth century, in other words, was a crucial part of a disciplinary project to write up "nation" and "culture" and put them together. The Gothic and the North had the great advantage of being as obscure as necessary. The legacy of that obscurity includes the historical notion of the *Dark Ages* as a mysteriously romantic time that gave way to an enlightened present; it also includes our ongoing fascination with what

Gothicism—with its strange mix of chivalry haunted by trips to Catholic countries and hints of the forbidden East—was and, to a large extent, still is. In the late eighteenth century, I am suggesting, it was a site for the symbolic violence of selective forgetting and remembering—a reason, perhaps, for its resurgent popularity, in writing and in film, today.

Women have been, of course, the primary victims in Gothic fiction, but there is another compelling historical link between Gothicism and women writers: Percy used the Mahometans' treatment of women to dismiss them from his history. "From the local customs and situation," he claimed,

> from the known manners and opinions of the Gothic nations in the north, we can easily account for all the ideas of chivalry and its peculiar fiction(s). For, not to mention their distinguished respect for the fair sex, so different from the manners of the Mahometan nations, their national and domestic history so naturally assumes all the wonders of this species of fabling, that almost all their historical narratives appear regular romances. (346)

As we saw, however, in Eliza Haywood's comment on the Mahometans (epigraph to Chapter 2), that "respect" has been double-edged, particularly in regard to women and writing, since Percy's time.

In describing the functions of Authorship in Chapter 6, for example, I foregrounded its economic role, using the examples of the Stephen King Book Club and the attributing of a poem to Shakespeare. Authorship also, however, facilitates other forms of valorization and hierarchy; Shakespeare, whatever the work, for example, over King. In serving our economy in this manner, that is, Authorship also serves us up—arranges us, pigeonholes us—in historically and politically specific ways; the classification of Author is part of a classificatory *system* in which differences of various kinds take on a variety of different functions. Gender, for example, is centered in *The Female Spectator* not only by the title, but also by the now habitual opening of the genre. In *having* to turn to an "Account" of the Author, the writing makes known the identity of the writer *and therefore* its gender: Haywood turns immediately to the issue of her own "Beauty" and "my Sex." The gender of the writer had, of course, been an issue in some earlier writing, but, as long as few people could write and read and little was printed, that category was a *relatively* uncontested site. But once Anne Finch became, in her words, "an intruder on the rights of men,"[3] and Mary Astell proposed to parcel out the "Prerogatives" of literacy,[4] power over the now rapidly proliferating work of writing began to become an issue, and the gender of the Author became, potentially, a powerful *un*known.

What I am suggesting, quite simply, is that one consequence of this crucial feature of modern Authorship—Author-*before*-work—a consequence so obvious that we easily overlook it—is that we *want* to find out whether the writer is male or female, and we *do*. The Author function enacts an institutionalized form of "outing." As the Author becomes the primary means of classifying texts, gender becomes a newly potent means of classifying Authors. The results were more texts *and* a possible means of categorizing them. The advent of *Authorial* professionalism at mid century, in other words, both facilitated the flow of print and foregrounded a means of regulating that flow.

In regard to the flow of conversation in and out of periodicals, for example, Stephen Copley notes a "paradoxical mixture" for women "of enfranchisement and disablement."[5] They are included, often centered, in conversation as judges of "learning," but "precisely because they are not professionally engaged" in making it: the "area of their sovereignty . . . remains the specialized one of consumption" (75). That situation was dramatized in *The Female Spectator* by Eliza Haywood's sarcastic comparison of the situation of women in France and England. After asserting that "Women are capable of attaining a thorough Knowledge in the most abstruse Sciences," she notes that "we cannot," however, "all have Patience to go through the Drudgery of School-Learning" (104). The French solution is "their most agreeable Manner of conversation" with *men*. When visiting there, she writes,

> I have been sometimes more edified by a single Sentence laugh'd out, than by a formal, stiff, pedantick Harangue of an Hour long.

But this is the least Advantage a French Lady reaps from her
Regard for Men of Learning.—Has she an Inclination to Philosophy, Theology, History, Astronomy, or in fine, any particular Study,
she has only to make Mention of it, and is certain of receiving a
Letter the next Day, in which is contained the whole Pith and Mar-
row of the Science, and at one View takes in the Substance of I
know not how many Volumes. (106–7)

"The Men," she concludes, "are the industrious Bees."

Haywood was of course, mocking France and men, as well as
many women. And, certainly her own productivity confirms that
the woman-and-consumption scenario—despite its very real power
over men and women—did not preclude extraordinary productivity by the latter. The problem for women who did produce became,
with the advent of Literature as a *regulated* flow, a matter of consumption and ongoing circulation. Let me try to frame the difficulties by invoking, one last time, Wordsworth's "experiment." As
I suggested earlier, in using that term to describe *Lyrical Ballads*,
Wordsworth was participating in a crucial shift in its meaning. It
continued to be a synonym—as it had throughout the eighteenth
century—for *experience* and for *trial*, but it was also increasingly deployed—as suggested by Wordsworth's quantitative and mecha-
nistic sense of "pleasure"—in its modern disciplinary sense of a
methodological procedure for producing knowledge. To recover
this idea of Literature as an experiment *today* thus carries two important consequences that point to the concluding part of my argument: how do we explain the actual fate of women writers in an
Author-centered, gender-conscious economy of print?

First, if Literature is an experiment not only in terms of experience—as in the titles of many anthologies of Literature—but also
in the now more scientific sense, we have an alternative, as I hinted
in the Argument, to the organic metaphors of birth and death
which now trouble discussions of the historicity of Literature.
Experiments do not "die," but they lead—if the funding is still
there—to other experiments after results are assessed. However,
one cannot use *experiment* in this way without facing the second
consequence: engendering. The modern binary of Arts versus Sci-

ences forming at the end of the eighteenth century, in which the new emphasis on experiment played a role, entailed, as we saw in Chapter 2, an engendering of knowledge which functioned to exclude women from certain areas. Wordsworth's casting of the lyric as an experiment could well, in that sense, have functioned to further the remasculinization of British Literature at the turn into the nineteenth century. At that point, both male and female Authorship had helped to turn deceleration into a substantial "rise," but we are only now beginning to cope with the shape that rise assumed. What happened to women writers in what I call The Great Forgetting is, I shall show, a crucial link between the period we call Romantic and the category we call Literature. To emphasize its ongoing power, I will begin with a recent attempt by a modern-day Romantic to conserve that category.

Keeping Up

"The great irony" of Harold Bloom's *The Western Canon*, writes Charles McGrath in the *New Yorker*, is that it

> may contribute to the very state of affairs Bloom so fiercely deplores. By tacking on that handy, media-friendly list—by resorting to the quintessential soundbite genre—Bloom has probably condemned his own book to the sad and inexorable canonical fate. You can talk about it endlessly without reading a single word.[6]

That may be a "great" irony, but it misses a much greater one: endless discourse over objects left unread is not simply the "fate" of the canon; it makes modern canonicity possible. In fact, thanks to David Kaufer and Kathleen Carley's extraordinary exploration of print culture, *Communication at a Distance*, we even have a term for this phenomenon: *reverse vicariousness* (66).

Calling into question theories of communication which "start with the supposition that individuals are *already* engaged in transactions with texts" (emphasis mine), Kaufer and Carley—as we saw in Chapter 6—focus on the ways in which contact—over the spatial, temporal, and social distances opened by print—is *initially* established (12–13). "Having the opportunity to read," they argue, is only part of the story. . . . the potential reader needs to know that the text exists. This knowledge can come through the text itself, through reviews, and through word of mouth. . . . Even nonreaders can positively register at social gatherings that they "know of" the book without actually having seen or read it first hand. We might call this phenomenon *reverse vicariousness,* because we normally think of immediate viewing or reading as vicarious experiences for face-to-face interaction. But, in this case, a viewer or reader uses face-to-face interaction to experience the viewer or reader role vicariously. (66)

If we want to teach ourselves and our students more than what texts might *mean*—if we want to understand their persistence and their power—then reverse vicariousness points to a deep irony in our standard pedagogical practice: we insist upon engaging texts in precisely the manner—individual close reading—that much of their public does not. To grasp these *other* kinds of interaction, perhaps some syllabi and tutorial lists should feature not just "reading" lists but "do-not-read" lists. "For next week, please do not read Canto I of *Don Juan*."

Again, bear with me here—I recognize the problems (and additional ironies) such a gesture poses, but I take it, and offer it here, as a tonic that can help restore to literary study a sense of the social life of texts. "The phenomenon of reverse vicariousness" in the words of Kaufer and Carley, "is fundamental, widespread, and too often misidentified with the stigma of 'low culture'"—a stigma that

rears its head every time an educator complains that students receive most of their information from a less rather than a more demanding medium: from television and radio rather than quality newspapers; from movies rather than books; from word of mouth rather than reading.

Whatever their other value, what these high/low judgments mask is that reverse vicariousness "is not so much an issue of reading skills and literacy as an issue of belonging, usually with peers." It is a *social* issue: "to *keep up* with the vogue information of culture is to maintain one's ties to it and to the others who are doing their part to keep up as well" (66–67; emphasis mine).

"Keeping up" became a very particular problem for a particular group at the particular historical moment that Authorial momentum began to turn Britain into an information culture. By casting the fate of women authors—in the terms of reverse vicariousness—as a struggle to keep up, I am not positing a Golden Age for women and their writing prior to Romanticism.[7] I *am* arguing, however, that the situation for women writing changed substantially and rather abruptly at the turn into the nineteenth century: earlier forms of subordination were reproduced with a difference—a difference in both kind and degree. In fact, my specific argument is that it was changes in the modes of reproduction themselves which effected this shift into The Great Forgetting—a Great Forgetting that became, as I have suggested, The Great Tradition. Forgetting, in this case, was neither causal nor natural; it was, rather, the result of what was reproduced, for whom, and how. In terms of the reverse vicariousness by which texts circulate in a print culture, it was a matter of whose texts, read or *even unread*, did get talked about and reproduced and whose texts, unread or *even read*, slipped into silence and out of production.

Acts of reproduction require labor and knowledge; what is reproduced, how frequently, and to what ends depend upon the ways that labor and knowledge are organized. And those ways, as we have seen, reproduce and constitute each other. The reproduction of the social and literary orders in Britain during the period we call Romanticism—and thus the fate of women writing—was configured by new divisions. The changes that can help us remember the Forgetting were as follows: in regard to the division of labor, shifts in the labor of reproduction, on the one hand, and in the reproduction of labor, on the other; in regard to the division of knowledge, shifts in the forms of reproducing knowledge and in the forms of knowledge reproduced.

I will begin with the labor of reproduction, in biological terms, since, despite some recent cinematic fantasies, it is work that uniquely impacts women; while certainly not precluding other kinds of work, it can conflict with them. Britain, unlike some other

European countries, such as France, experienced, as we have seen, a steep rise in population during the latter half of the eighteenth century. Although some countries did experience comparable growth, the primary reasons differed. The increase in Sweden, for example, was due primarily to declining mortality rates.[8] The rise in Britain, however, was largely the work of women; the acceleration of growth rates during the long eighteenth century, according to Roger Schofield, "owed far more to a rise in fertility than to a fall in mortality" (70). The gross reproductive rate—remember Abelove—a measure of the average number of daughters that would be born to a woman during her lifetime, rose from roughly two to three between 1681 and 1816; this means that the average woman had one-and-a-half as many children as she had before. More than half of that increase occurred during the initial decades we call Romantic, in only thirty-five years from 1781 to 1816.

These figures give new meaning to contemporary scholarly debates over the rise of the Domestic Woman and the ideology of male and female separate spheres. The issue of whether that literature was, in Linda Colley's words, "descriptive" or "didactic" needs to be addressed in terms of data confirming this startling increase in the labor of reproduction—both pre- and postnatal—and thus the amount of time and energy spent by women in the home and on the family.[9] I say *by women* in regard to *postnatal* because, despite arguments as to whether women were better or worse off under the preindustrial household economy, social historians agree that child care remained women's work under both regimes.

They also agree that the range of occupational alternatives for women constricted during the late eighteenth century. In agriculture, for example, a shift in crops toward wheat and rye led to increasing use of the heavier hand scythe employed by men, supplanting the light sickle used by women,[10] and enclosure increasingly closed off the option, popular among women, of tending small herds of dairy cows. Through most of the eighteenth century, 60 percent of the entire population of many rural communities—almost half of them women—were "servants in husbandry": young unmarrieds on annual contract to work as resident servants in farmers' households. But the number of those positions decreased drastically at the turn into the nineteenth century, as the population boom increased the alternative—and cheaper—supply of poor, landless adult *male* laborers.[11] Since that boom was fueled by the rise in the gross reproductive rate, many women went effectively from husbandry to husbands—and the increasing labor of reproduction.

The timing and intensity of that rise—one might say its Romantic nature—were tied to a central feature of agrarian and early industrial capitalism in Britain: the boom/slump cycles that began in earnest in the 1780s and 1790s. Landowners and industrialists, hoping to hold onto their workforces between harvests, on the one hand, and high demand, on the other, financed substantial increases in poor relief, payments reaching an unprecedented 2 percent of the gross national product during the Romantic period. If Schofield's latest take on the Cambridge population data is correct, then those payments are a key to the historicity of the population change. After demonstrating that "the great acceleration in population growth during the long eighteenth century . . . was principally due to earlier marriage" by women (95)—between 1716 and 1816, the average age fell about four years from 26.4 to 22.6—Schofield focuses on an extraordinary turn in the second quarter of the nineteenth century, just as the Romantic period, as conventionally dated, drew to a close. The nuptial age rose rapidly, reaching, by 1841, "a point very close to where it had been in 1741"; the gross reproductive rate fell accordingly.

In a provocative turn upon the Malthusian notion of the preventive check, Schofield points out that this seemingly strange reversal coincided precisely with the agitation for, and passage of, the new Poor Law in 1834. The correlation suggests, he argues, that early marriage with more children was a more viable option for women in a time of fewer economic alternatives and welfare payments keyed to prices and family size. The politics of this hypothesis clearly require more discussion, but the statistical picture of the 1780s through 1830s Schofield presents should alert us, particularly those of us interested in Romanticism, in particular, and in literature and history, in general, to new ways of linking productivity and periodization, literary and otherwise.

The women highlighted in this picture so far, were, of course, wage-earning members of the lower orders, and thus the most *direct* effect on literary activity of these changes was on the small but significant population of, and vogue for, "primitive" women poets: Barber, Leapor, Lewis, West, Collier, Hands, Candler, Years- ley.[12] First, and most obviously, the work of writing had to com- pete with these shifts in the kind and quantity of other work, par- ticularly the reproductive, if these women were to write at all. But for that writing to assume the form and status of print, and cer- tainly for it not to be forgotten, reverse vicariousness had to be and remain at work. Its crucial workings were even thematized back then in Elizabeth Hands's extraordinary poem entitled "On the Supposition of the Book having been Published and Read," in which the second part of the supposition—being read—proves unfounded: the "gentlemen" and "ladies" in the poem discuss at length precisely those books—from the Bible to "*Poems*" by a "poor servant-maid"—which they have never read.[13]

The withdrawal of that means of circulation and remembering and the waning of this particular group of women writers were sig- naled at the end of the century by two events. First, with the pop- ulation rising and dispersing to the towns, the "natural" power of the "primitive" was displaced from rural work to a new geograph- ical and socioeconomic location: "I pay particular attention," wrote Mary Wollstonecraft in 1792, "to those in the middle class, because they appear to be in the most natural state."[14] Second, as the result of these consolidations of the lower and middle *orders* into larger, separate, and antagonistic *classes*, a gap opened between writers from each group which the links of patronage and subscription, as well as gender, could no longer close—a gap dramatically evidenced by Ann Yearsley's battles with Hannah More and Elizabeth Mon- tagu.[15]

Since Schofield does not break down the gross reproductive rate increase by socioeconomic rank, we cannot, as of yet, know the immediate effects of the increasing labor of reproduction on the women writers of the newly forming middle class. There is, however, a less direct, but equally compelling, connection. It goes, roughly, like this: more births, more workers, more competition for jobs, more changes in the competitive structure of the job market. In terms of the shifts in the division of labor I mentioned earlier, an increase in the labor of reproduction—and thus of population—led to a new form of the reproduction of labor. That form was modern professionalism, and we now need to place the authorial version into this larger context. To perpetuate their prerogatives and police their membership in the face of new kinds of work and new kinds of competition for that work, an increasing number of occupational groups professionalized. Professionalism thus superseded on a national scale earlier and local forms of occupational monopoly such as craft guilds and trading companies.[16] Its appearance in the latter half of the eighteenth century, as we have seen, was marked lexically by the debuts of both the word *professional*, as an adjective describing a kind of behavior, and of terms of difference such as *amateur.*

The professional/amateur binary is particularly telling historically because it marks the need for new forms of exclusivity in the job market. The boundary behavior of the standard eighteenth-century professions—the church, the law, and medicine—had simply been, as we have seen, the behavior of gentlemen. Now women, linked by love to amateur status—the status of one who loves, could, along with excess men, be excluded from particularly profitable kinds of work—excluded not by the increasingly porous distinction of gentility, but by the newly valorized professional criterion of earned expertise—a criterion that, for the work of writing, was increasingly regulated—as I argued earlier—by the burgeoning institutions of criticism.

Burdened, at least indirectly, by the increasing labor of reproduction and threatened directly with exclusion by the new professional reproduction of labor, middle-class women writers still could, and did, write. The form of exclusion for authors, as I have been emphasizing, was not of the more absolute kind—formal association and certification that explicitly exclude undesirables. Of the two components of work whose ratio—as we saw in Chapter 4—sociologists use to describe professional status, women could, with difficulty, access *technicality*—the systematic body of knowledge justifying competence in a field—but not *indetermination*—

"the bases of [an occupation's] mystique, the sources of its legitimations." The combination of technicality *and* indetermination underpins the professional's status in capitalism as the source, as I argued earlier, of *both* productive labor *and* surplus value. In regard to the production and circulation of *texts*, that surplus derives largely from the amplifying power of reverse vicariousness.

To recognize the connection of that power to professional exclusion is to see why the moment of great amplification we call Romanticism was also the moment of The Great Forgetting. Occasioned by the shifts in the division of labor which I have just detailed, that Forgetting transpired through complementary shifts in the division of knowledge. At precisely the same time that the population boom and economic cycles reworked work, the forms of reproducing literary knowledge changed, as that knowledge itself changed form. The two primary venues cited by Roger Lonsdale for poetic publication by eighteenth-century women, for example, subscription and periodicals, saw substantial change in the 1790s.

At its most effective, subscription enacted a pre–information culture version of reverse vicariousness, the amplified text not only unread but initially even unwritten. By the end of the century, however, its viability was being undermined by the aforementioned problem of class and by the changing dimensions of the textual marketplace. The Author-centered boom in publication, now documented by the *ESTC* totals, matched the intensity of the contemporaneous population boom, magnifying the competition for readerly attention, and thus profit, beyond the personally delimited range of subscription—just as, I might add, the increase in workers overwhelmed the geographically delimited power of the guilds. Alternative forms of textual access, such as the circulating library, also established themselves at that time, as did new opportunities for authorial control and profit from publication, thanks to the 1774 changes in copyright discussed earlier. By the first decade of the nineteenth century, subscription was no longer a very desirable publication alternative.

Periodicals, on the other hand, did not fade from view but multiplied. However, that very multiplicity posed new problems for women writers, for the multiplication was also a fragmentation, as Klancher and others have detailed, of the eighteenth-century public voice. That anonymous voice of the representative observer, although fundamentally patriarchal, allowed for the literary cross-dressing that enlivened periodicals and other genres throughout the century, from Addison and Steele's decision to "fair-sex" it to Haywood's playful assumption of their spectatorial stance in the 1740s to the mass masquerade of readers-turned-writers which literally fueled the proliferation of periodicals, and periodical forms, in the 1760s and 1770s.

No single event illustrates so clearly the demise of these vicarious reversals—and the cost in reverse vicariousness for women writers—than the founding in 1802 of the *Edinburgh Review*. To quote John Hayden, "all of the old ways began to change."[17] This was, I would argue, the first fully *professional* review, in the modern sense of professionalism I described earlier. Its editorial policy, that is, was doubly exclusive. Although a few women eventually became contributors, it initially employed, as Hayden puts it, *only* "gentlemen writers" who were at first unpaid but were soon recompensed at newly professional levels. Its content was also newly exclusive, dropping the inclusive coverage of earlier reviews in favor of eight or nine articles that were themselves more judgmental than the heavily descriptive reviews of the past. They were usually published anonymously, but because they were longer and the writers were, in Hayden's words, "encourage[d] . . . to develop their personal views and style,"[18] the anonymity now functioned to channel the reverse vicariousness of literary discourse into what became, in telling ways, an old-boys network—our continued fascination with Francis Jeffrey's "This will never do" tiff with Wordsworth being only one example—dare I ask, by the way, how many of us have read the entire review and the entire *Excursion*?

The *Edinburgh Review* also helped to masculinize the literary further by juxtaposing its reviews with a wide range of newly specialized treatments of traditionally masculine subjects, particularly economics and politics. Through such juxtaposition, the literary "conversation" of the eighteenth century, which subordinated but did not systematically exclude writing by women, became a professionalized and more exclusive field, among other fields, to *study*. I will end, then, by locating this new disciplinary division of knowledge in the schools, where, once again, the same Romantic dates surface: "the strengthening of the subject [of English] and its extension to schools generally," reports Ian Michael, occurred "about 1790"; "by 1813 at least a section of school could be known as 'the English Department.'"[19]

The rise of schools as the new hotbed of reverse vicariousness and the rise of English education within those schools greatly accelerated The Great Forgetting in at least two important ways. First, the schools were, of course, and remained for quite some time, the province of males. Second, a primary tool for teaching English from the eighteenth century forward was the anthology, and, as Michael has shown in his stunning statistical analyses of books used in schools, the school anthology was, and largely remains, one of the most masculinized genres.[20] This was, at least through the eighteenth century, a matter not of appreciation but imitation, since the selections were supposed to function primarily as models for proper—that is, manly—behavior, literary and otherwise. Only one female poet—Elizabeth Carter—made Michael's ranking of the top eleven writers, by frequency of representation, in anthologies from the last thirty years of the eighteenth century (198). In the anthologies he studied from the first seven decades of the nineteenth century, only Felicia Hemans makes the top thirteen (236).

Clearly, then, there is much remembering to be done, and admirable progress has recently been made. But my premise for this chapter is that we also need to find out how we forgot. Our present struggle with yet another new technology highlights the importance of that scholarly responsibility. It is especially pressing given the additional parallels to a present in which professionals are being proletarianized, disciplinarity is under siege, Newt Gingrich is echoing Malthus, and Bloom—no, I haven't read the book—is anthologizing literature.

CODA: Finding Our Own Business

Anthologizing at the turn into the twenty-first century is risky business for everyone. Under the traditional canonical imperative of remembering what is "greatest," it risks reinscribing The Great Forgetting—a matter, as I have just tried to argue, not only of leaving out writers but of missing out on the social life of texts. To remedy that Forgetting by recirculating what was forgotten, however, risks what David Simpson has described as the anthological sublime: what do we do with all of this newly available material?[21] In both cases, we are left trying not to miss out on what we should be busy doing. What is—or should be—our business?

To ask that question is not to mark ourselves off as obsessively self-reflexive humanists or, less charitably, muddle-headed intellectuals who—unlike workers in the "real" world—never quite know what we are really doing. It is, rather, to link us historically to that world of work, where, in the latter half of the twentieth century, reclassifications of knowledge and of labor have put *What is our business?* on everyone's lips. Listen to Ken Auletta's description of the fate of the company that owns the *New York Times*:

> Like the railroads, which earlier in this century thought that they were in the railroad rather than the transportation business, or like the networks, which thought they were in the single-channel rather than the program business and ignored or fought cable, the Times Company was late to realize that it is in the information rather than the newspaper business.[22]

Such realizations—what is the *ongoing* nature of one's business?—are not easy tasks, for the cognitive terrain is often obscured by what I called in Chapter 7 *metonymic displacement,* in which the part or individual instance stands for the whole category.

To place Literature in the history of writing—the job of this book—is the equivalent strategically of placing trains within the rubric of transportation. It allows the overall enterprise a future by clarifying the temporality of the vehicles that have sustained it. Clearly there are now alternatives to trains and to the traditional forms of Literature. And—forgive me for stretching the comparison—there are just as clearly ways not only to continue to value and use trains and Literature but also to adapt them to new environments and technologies: thus airport-terminal shuttles, monorails, metros, and bullet trains, as well as course-specific anthologies, electronic editions, Austen on video, and hypertext/close readings.

By telling this history of writing as a tale about the advent of new technologies—framed by Pope's complaint against writing in the eighteenth century and Harry Kaufman's cinematic fate in the twentieth—I am not only making Literature part of the work of writing; I am also suggesting that it may behoove us to think of that work as itself an instance of a more encompassing, longer-term enterprise: mediating society's encounters with such change. Mediation may entail varying degrees of resistance, accommodation, and transformation. Britain's long eighteenth-century encounter with writing was mediated under the sign of profitable pleasure, whether articulated as a disciplinary imperative to "entertain and instruct," a professional rationale of the joy of intellectual work, or a literary claim to the most pleasurable kind of knowledge. Current anthologizers of "great" writing thus risk mistaking the means (canonical lists) for a historically specific end (experiencing the technology itself as pleasurable).

As new technologies mix with the old, means and ends alter for all, straining established agendas. To relieve the strain, we need to realign the past and present within new kinds of histories. In the one you have just read, issues of pleasure and comfort arise from lining up the ways we know and work with the technologies we deploy. Reverse vicariousness is a particularly useful cognitive tool for that task, since *vicariousness* not only links pleasure to mediation, but etymologically centers "change" (Latin *vicis*) in surprising (reverse) ways. This book is about the changes wrought by the work of writing, and, of course, it also is one: a written work that conducts its business by reversing the standard displacement of writing by Literature—opening both, perhaps, to new ways of knowing. I wrote it to recover the past, but I hope that—in the reading—it also helps us to negotiate change in the present.

NOTES

The Argument: Writing as a New Technology

Epigraph: Robert Potts, "Why Censors Can't Save Us," *The Guardian,* 22 March 1996: 3.

1. Richard Perez-Pena, "Attackers Set Fire to Token Clerk in Brooklyn Subway Station," *New York Times,* 27 November 1995: B1, B3.

2. See my use of Dryden as an example of this astonishment in Chapter 1.

3. In using this shorthand, I am following the example of Raymond Williams, *Writing in Society* (London: Verso, 1983) 1–7.

4. J. Paul Hunter, *Before Novels: The Cultural Contexts of Eighteenth-Century English Fiction* (New York: Norton, 1990) 67. Hunter's argument broadly conforms to Lawrence Stone's hypothesis of an educational and literary slump from the Restoration until the last quarter of the eighteenth century. Geoffrey Holmes and Daniel Szechi have marshaled the evidence for the opposing point of view, turning to figures and analysis from David Cressy and Roger Schofield to argue that "the improvement in literacy was strongly sustained well into the eighteenth century." Both arguments are complicated by such thorny issues as choosing the criterion for literacy as well as apparent variations in literacy rates among England, Scotland, and Wales, between urban and rural, and across social and economic ranks. My point in raising this controversy is to highlight what we do know with more certainty: 1) the amount of printed material increased substantially during the eighteenth century, particularly in its last two decades; and 2) more and more people contributed to that increase, particularly after mid century (see Chapter 6). See Lawrence Stone, "The Educational Revolution in England, 1560–1640," *Past and Present* 28 (1964): 41–80 and "Literacy and Education in England, 1640–1900," *Past and Present* 42 (1969): 69–139; Geoffrey Holmes and Daniel Szechi, *The Age of Oligarchy: Pre-Industrial Britain, 1722–1783,* ed. Geoffrey Holmes, Foundations of Modern Britain (London: Longmans, 1993); David Cressy, *Literacy and the Social Order: Reading and Writing in Tudor and Stuart England* (Cambridge: Cambridge Uni-

versity Press, 1980); R. S. Schofield, "The Measurement of Literacy in Pre-Industrial England," in *Literacy in Traditional Societies,* ed. Jack Goody (Cambridge: Cambridge University Press, 1968) 311–25 and "Dimensions of Illiteracy, 1750–1850," *Explorations in Economic History* 10 (1973): 437–54. Also useful in sorting out the debate are Michael Sanderson, "Literacy and Social Mobility in the Industrial Revolution in England," *Past and Present* 56 (August 1972): 77–92 and W. B. Stephens, "Literacy in England, Scotland, and Wales, 1500–1900," *History of Education Quarterly* 30, no. 4 (Winter 1990): 545–72.

    5. For an overview of the growth of the newspaper, see Henri-Jean Martin, *The History and Power of Writing,* trans. Lydia G. Cochrane (Chicago: University of Chicago Press, 1988, trans. 1994) 414–16.

    6. Samuel Johnson, *"The Adventurer* 115, 11 December 1753," in *The Yale Edition of the Works of Samuel Johnson,* ed. W. J. Bate, John M. Bullitt, and C. F. Powell, vol. II (New Haven: Yale University Press, 1963) 457.

    7. Martin, *History and Power of Writing* 355. See, as well, Raymond Williams, *The Long Revolution: An Analysis of the Democratic, Industrial, and Cultural Changes Transforming Our Society* (New York: Columbia University Press, 1961) 156–213; for a particularly comprehensive effort to argue for the eighteenth century as the age that saw the transformation of Britain into a print culture, see Alvin Kernan, *Samuel Johnson and the Impact of Print* (Princeton, Princeton University Press, 1987). Marcus Walsh cannily observes that Kernan tends to privilege "a Romantic conception of literature over an earlier conception of letters" (160), but his concern over whether Kernan "very much overstates the extent and suddenness of the changes in libraries in the eighteenth century, and very much overdramatizes the sense of *angst* this produced among eighteenth-century writers" (155) is less convincing. His examples of college library growth in the previous century and of some earlier expressions of concern about the spread of print do not address the new range of occasions for and kinds of print, the increasing number of users, and the heightened self-reflexivity of the proliferation they produced. See Marcus Walsh, "The Superfoetation of Literature: Attitudes to the Printed Book in the Eighteenth Century," *British Journal for Eighteenth-Century Studies* 15, no. 2 (1992): 151–61.

    8. In contributing to a "history of writing," I join Nancy Armstrong and Leonard Tennenhouse in both, as they put it, "privileg[ing] writing among the various changes that are said to have inaugurated our age" and showing how our standard histories have worked by "simultaneously empowering writing and rendering it transparent." I share with them the sense "that poststructuralism inadvertently collaborates with traditional historiography in refusing to grant writing much causality, if any at all," as well as a debt to Foucault in working out an alternative. Our concerns thus frequently overlap—for example, the Author, Literature, intellectual labor, the novel—but those overlaps are also sites for what I hope our readers experience as productive disagreement. See

Nancy Armstrong and Leonard Tennenhouse, *The Imaginary Puritan: Literature, Intellectual Labor, and the Origins of Personal Life,* ed. Stephen Greenblatt, The New Historicism: Studies in Cultural Poetics 21 (Berkeley: University of California Press, 1992) 5–7.

The concern with writing I share with Foucault can be grasped in terms of the concept of visibility. For him, modern power is "invisibl[y]" productive of "compulsory visibility." That is why the importance of the panopticon in marking the onset of that power was not whether it was, or could be, built, but that it wasn't and didn't have to be: it was written. Forms of writing became forms of visibility, but what they made visible was not themselves but the modern subject—a self whose subjectivity is constituted by all of the ways it knows itself to be visible. This book shifts the pattern of visibility, complementing Foucault's emphasis on the role of writing in forming subjects with an analysis of writing's own history forms. To describe that role, Foucault uses the phrase I have chosen for my title, the "work of writing" ("un travail ininterrompu d'ecriture")—a usage of which I was unaware or had let slip from memory when I first made that choice, but which certainly confirms the utility of the phrase. See Michel Foucault, *Discipline and Punish: The Birth of the Prison,* trans. Alan Sheridan (New York: Vintage Books, 1979) 187–92, 197.

9. David McNally, *Political Economy and the Rise of Capitalism: A Reinterpretation* (Berkeley: University of California Press, 1988) 1. Here and in Chapter 1, I stress McNally's take on political economy because it allows for the work of writing. Whereas the traditional view sees political economy "as an intellectual *reflection* of the ascendence of merchants and manufacturers" (emphasis mine), McNally reconceives the "rise of capitalism" as "the product of an immense transformation in the social relationships of landed society"—a transformation in which political economy was an "active element." That activity is made visible by McNally's centering of the "agrarian economy" as the location where reformers of husbandry produced knowledge—in writing—in order to induce change in the use of the land and in the politics of the commonwealth (xi, 1, 40).

10. Charles Bazerman, "How Natural Philosophers Can Cooperate: The Literary Technology of Coordinated Investigation in Joseph Priestley's *History and Present State of Electricity* (1967)," in *Textual Dynamics of the Professions: Historical and Contemporary Studies of Writing in Professional Communities,* ed. Charles Bazerman and James Paradis (Madison: University of Wisconsin Press, 1991).

11. Hume's argument regarding "havoc" concludes *An Enquiry Concerning Human Understanding*.

12. For the eighteenth-century origins of the subject of English, for example, see my Chapter 3 and Robert Crawford, *Devolving English Literature* (Oxford: Clarendon Press, 1992) 16–110.

13. On the Sunday schools, see Richard D. Altick, *The English Common Reader: A Social History of the Mass Reading Public, 1800–1900* (Chicago: University of Chicago Press, 1967) 68. On the issue of oral and written examinations, see Geoffrey S. Holmes, *Augustan England: Professions, State and Society, 1680–1730* (London: Allen and Unwin, 1982) 274.

14. In his Foreword to Martin, Pierre Chaunu refers to "the short reign of the Gutenberg Galaxy" (xiv).

15. See Robert Pattison, *On Literacy: The Politics of the Word from Homer to the Age of Rock* (New York: Oxford University Press, 1982, rpt. 1984) vii.

16. See Kernan, *Samuel Johnson and the Impact of Print;* Raymond Williams, *Keywords: A Vocabulary of Culture and Society*, 2nd ed. (New York: Oxford University Press, 1976, 1983) 184–85; Terry Eagleton, *Literary Theory* (Minneapolis: University of Minnesota Press, 1983) 18; Marilyn Butler, "Revising the Canon," *Times Literary Supplement,* 4–10 December 1987, 1349; Douglas Lane Patey, "The Eighteenth Century Invents the Canon," *Modern Language Studies* 18 (1988): 17–37; James Engell, *Forming the Critical Mind: Dryden to Coleridge* (Cambridge, Mass.: Harvard University Press, 1989) 127; Trevor Ross, "Copyright and the Invention of Tradition," *Eighteenth-Century Studies* 26 (Fall 1992): 1–28; Richard Bourke, *Romantic Discourse and Political Modernity: Wordsworth, the Intellectual and Cultural Critique* (New York: St. Martin's Press, 1993) 258; and Clifford Siskin, *The Historicity of Romantic Discourse* (New York: Oxford University Press, 1988), hereafter cited as *Historicity*. Also, see my discussion of Literature later in this Argument. Throughout this book, I refer to this narrowed range of writing with the capital letter: *L*iterature.

17. See the discussion of Defoe in Diana Laurenson and Alan Swingewood, *The Sociology of Literature* (London: MacGibbon and Kee, 1971) 131.

18. John Stuart Mill in his inaugural lecture at St. Andrews cited in Roy Lewis and Angus Maude, *Professional People* (London: Phoenix House, 1952) 210.

19. William Wordsworth, *The Prose Works of William Wordsworth,* ed. W. J. B. Owen and Jane Worthington Smyser, 3 vols., vol. I (Oxford: Clarendon Press, 1974) 116. For Williams's discussion of the historical ambiguities of *experiment,* see *Keywords* 126–29.

20. Bruce Robbins points out how critics as diverse as John Gross and Terry Eagleton "both subscribe, with differences that are surprisingly slight, given the magnitude of the political gulf between them, to the professional myth: we have fallen into lamentable specialization from a formerly higher, more public, and more adversarial estate." See Bruce Robbins, "Oppositional Professionals: Theory and the Narratives of Professionalization," in *Consequences of Theory: Selected Papers from the English Institute,* ed. Jonathan Arac and Barbara Johnson (Baltimore: Johns Hopkins University Press, 1990) 5; John Gross, *The Rise and Fall of the Man of Letters* (New York: Macmillan, 1969); and Terry Eagle-

ton, *The Function of Criticism: From "The Spectator" to Poststructuralism* (London: Verso, 1984). For a particularly entertaining version of the "Decline-of-Literature" tale, see Brian McCrea, *Addison and Steele Are Dead: The English Department, Its Canon, and the Professionalization of Literary Criticism* (Newark: University of Delaware Press, 1990). For a telling critique of McCrae's assumptions, see Anthony Vaver, "Professionalizing English Studies: From the Eighteenth-Century Social Critic to the Postmodern Literary Theorist," *Minnesota Review* 43/44 (1995): 228–35.

21. We suggested this term in a joint presentation at the North American Society for the Study of Romanticism Conference held at Duke University, November 1994. For a very different take on this problem of periodization, see Marshall Brown, *Preromanticism* (Stanford: Stanford University Press, 1991).

22. For a discussion of the 1662 Print Act and its lapse thirty-two years later, see John Feather, *A History of British Publishing* (London: Routledge, 1988) 50–83.

23. Roger Lonsdale, ed., *Eighteenth-Century Women Poets* (Oxford: Oxford University Press, 1989) 43.

24. See Martin, *History and Power of Writing* 404–11 and Feather, *History of British Publishing* 135–36.

25. See Martin, *History and Power of Writing* 434–37.

26. See Lee Erickson, *The Economy of Literary Form: English Literature and the Industrialization of Publishing* (Baltimore: Johns Hopkins University Press, 1996) 19–39. For the libraries, see Feather, *History of British Publishing* 142–44.

27. The publishers themselves joined with booksellers in 1829 in a short-lived attempt to set bookselling regulations; the Booksellers' Association evolved from that effort, but it also failed, disbanding itself in 1852. See Feather, *History of British Publishing* 145–46.

28. See Franklin E. Court, "The Social and Historical Significance of the First English Literature Professorship in England," *PMLA* 103, no. 5 (1988): 796–807.

29. Ian Michael, *The Teaching of English from the Sixteenth Century to 1870* (Cambridge: Cambridge University Press, 1987) 377.

30. Philip Elliott, *The Sociology of the Professions* (New York: Herder and Herder, 1972) 42.

31. See Elliott 32–40 and W. J. Reader, *Professional Men: The Rise of the Professional Classes in Nineteenth-Century England* (London: Weidenfeld and Nicolson, 1966) 16, 19, 54.

32. My argument here about professionalization highlights the need for further inquiries into the role of writing in the construction of modern jurisprudence and the codification of the law. Richard Helgerson focuses on the earlier work of writing in the Renaissance in *Forms of Nationhood: The Elizabethan Writing of England* (Chicago: University of Chicago Press, 1992). As

this book went to press, Mark Schoenfield published *The Professional Words-worth: Law, Labor, and the Poet's Contract* (Athens: University of Georgia Press, 1996). Both John Barrell and Peter de Bolla are currently at work on studies interrelating writing and the law during the long eighteenth century.

33. A. M. Carr-Saunders and P. A. Wilson, *The Professions* (Oxford: Clarendon Press, 1933) 310–11.

34. Doron Swade, "The Difference Engine," in *Cultural Babbage: Technology and the History of Culture,* ed. Francis Spufford and Jenny Uglow (London: Faber and Faber, forthcoming 1997).

35. Until the sixth edition, 1832 was the date cited by the *Norton Anthology of English Literature* as the end of Romanticism; it has now been rounded off to 1830. See M. H. Abrams, ed., *The Norton Anthology of English Literature,* 6th ed., vol. 2 (New York: Norton, 1993) vii.

36. My point here is the persistence—from a history of Literature into a history of writing—of the dates, not whether the period they enclose should be labeled "Romantic."

37. See Jerome McGann, *The Romantic Ideology: A Critical Investigation* (Chicago: University of Chicago Press, 1983) and Siskin, *Historicity.*

38. For an explanation of "spontaneity," "intensity," and "depth" as textual "effects," see *Historicity* 27–28.

39. I am not arguing about whether there were "mad" authors prior to the late eighteenth century, nor am I arguing about whether particular authors from that time were "really" mad—nor even whether some of those authors came to believe that to be authors, they *should* be. My points are, first, that in literary historical accounts from that time, and of that time, "madness"—and the other attributes I have named—are frequently linked to "authorship," and that, second, within standard, psychologized conceptions of Literature as the product of "imagination," those links are invested with considerable explanatory power.

40. Steven Johnson, "Strange Attraction," *Lingua Franca* 6 (March/April 1996): 50.

41. Ralph Cohen, "History and Genre," *New Literary History* 17, no. 2 (1986): 207. See also *Historicity* 21–25.

42. Charles Bazerman, *Shaping Written Knowledge: The Genre and Activity of the Experimental Article in Science* (Madison: University of Wisconsin Press, 1988) 62.

43. See, for example, Leslie Santee Siskin, *Realms of Knowledge: Academic Departments in Secondary Schools,* Education Policy Perspective Series (London: Falmer Press, 1994); Tony Becher, *Academic Tribes and Territories: Intellectual Enquiry and the Cultures of Disciplines* (Milton Keynes: The Society for Research into Higher Education, and Open University Press, 1989) 139–45; and Burton R. Clark, "The Organizational Conception," in *Perspectives on Higher Education:*

Eight Disciplinary and Comparative Views, ed. Burton R. Clark (Berkeley: University of California Press, 1984) 106–31.

44. See my argument in *Historicity* 10–11, 20–23.

45. J. G. A. Pocock, "Texts as Events: Reflections on the History of Political Thought," in *Politics of Discourse: The Literature and History of Seventeenth-Century England,* ed. Kevin Sharpe and Steven N. Zwicker (Berkeley: University of California Press, 1987) 29.

46. Kevin Sharpe and Steven N. Zwicker, "Introduction," in *Politics of Discourse* 10–15.

47. Cohen, "History and Genre" 213.

48. By linking modernity to control, I risk inducing in response a humanities version of what social scientists call *metaphysical pathos*—the "underlying mood of pessimism" enveloping arguments, such as that of Max Weber on rationalization, that "all large-scale social activity necessarily results in bureaucracy and the loss of democratic freedom." This version of *mp* reads recent efforts within the humanities to theorize and historicize "large-scale social activity" as cynical variations of the rationalization thesis and thus as politicized pessimism that denies, or cannot account for, the positive values associated with Literature.

For a classic example of humanistic *mp*, see Don Bialostosky's review of *The Historicity of Romantic Discourse.* Not only does he worry over a threatened democracy and the fate of Literature, but he also formalizes those concerns into a pessimism/optimism binary using my book and Jonathan Arac's supposedly more "affirm[ing]" *Critical Genealogies.* Foucault is the fall guy—actually guys, since he is developmentally disciplined into an "earlier" version and a "later" one. The second is, of course, wiser and thus a candidate for the resurrection sequence of the review: its strategy for dispelling the gloom of large-scale historical change by changing the scale—by making change personal. The difference between the improved Foucault, properly read, and William Wordsworth "may be less consequential," Bialostosky ventures, "than it at first appears." The passing—and any pathos in the passing—of two centuries is thus of less and less consequence as Wordsworth's "vision of a democracy of active and disciplined sensibilities" is made to seem more and more like the mature Foucault's "vision of productive power." When past and present collapse into one another, it would not only, in Bialostosky's words, "be premature and unwise to put [Wordsworth's] regime in the past"; it would simply be futile. Let me add that what I tried to affirm in *Historicity*—and what I am trying to reaffirm innovatively in *Work*—is neither this review's attempt to assert a comforting sense of continuity nor the tempting titillations of absolute discontinuity, but the value of a history that can manage both desires—and thus articulate our mixed relationship to the past. In doing so, such a history can engage the issue of control *and* the values associated with Literature, thus putting the latter into a new—

and not necessarily pessimistic—dialogue with the present. Control enters the discussion not to assert the inevitable workings of an abstract process such as rationalization, but to point to historically and geographically contingent strategies used to work with a specific technology. Any metaphysical threat posed by those strategies is lessened by the likelihood that they will themselves be disrupted by technological change. See Don Bialostosky, "Review of Jonathan Arac, *Critical Genealogies: Historical Situations for Postmodern Literary Studies* and Clifford Siskin, "The Historicity of Romantic Discourse," *The Wordsworth Circle* 19 (Summer 1988): 194–99. This review, which mixes many valuable insights with the *mp*, was revised to form part of Don H. Bialostosky, *Wordsworth, Dialogics, and the Practice of Criticism* (New York: Cambridge University Press, 1992). For the definition of *mp* which I am using, see Nicholas Abercrombie, Stephen Hill, and Bryan S. Turner, *The Penguin Dictionary of Sociology* (Harmondsworth, U.K.: Penguin, 1984) 133. See also A. W. Gouldner, "Metaphysical Pathos and the Theory of Bureaucracy," *American Political Science Review* 49 (1955): 496–507.

49. David Shumway and Ellen Messer-Davidow, "Disciplinarity: An Introduction," *Poetics Today* 12, no. 2 (Summer 1991): 202.

50. Quoted in A. J. Youngson, *The Scientific Revolution in Victorian Medicine Philosophy and Fiction: Essay in Literary Aesthetics* (New York: Homes and Meier, 1979) 9.

51. Robert Dingwall, "Introduction," in *The Sociology of the Professions: Lawyers, Doctors and Others,* ed. Robert Dingwall and Philip Lewis (London: Macmillan, 1983) 12.

52. Felix Schelling, *The English Lyric* (Port Washington, N.Y.: Kennikat Press, 1913, rpt. 1967) 148.

53. See Lionel Gossman, "Literature and Education," *New Literary History* XIII, no. 2 (Winter 1982): 341–71; Gerald Graff, *Professing Literature: An Institutional History* (Chicago: University of Chicago Press, 1987); and Ian Small and Josephine Guy, "The 'Literary,' Aestheticism and the Founding of English as a Discipline," *English Literature in Transition, 1880–1920* 33, no. 4 (1990): 443–53. In *Literary Theory,* Eagleton's account of "Literature" and "English" pauses briefly in the eighteenth century before focusing on the nineteenth and twentieth.

54. Raymond Williams, *Problems in Materialism and Culture* (London: Verso, 1980) 50.

55. Peter Hohendahl, *The Institution of Criticism* (Ithaca: Cornell University Press, 1982) 226.

56. Both Martin and Anderson do point to the need to emphasize difference. Martin argues that "printed matter . . . created new cultural solidarities" that were "national in character" (449). Anderson was particularly careful in his 1991 revision to attend to variations among nationalisms in terms of timing and

of the differing roles of the "local" and the "metropole." See Benedict Anderson, *Imagined Communities: Reflections on the Origin and Spread of Nationalism,* rev. (London: Verso, 1983, rev. 1991) xiii.

57. See the discussion of exclusion in Shumway and Messer-Davidow, "Disciplinarity" 205–6. In foregrounding gender differentiation throughout this book, I am indebted to the pioneering work—both archival and conceptual—of Anne Mellor. See, in particular, *Romanticism and Gender* (New York: Routledge, 1992).

58. Ellen Messer-Davidow, "Know-How," in *(En)Gendering Knowledge: Feminists in Academe,* ed. Joan E. Hartman and Ellen Messer-Davidow (Knoxville: University of Tennessee Press, 1991) 289.

59. Compare my argument, for example, with that of Nicholas Hudson in *Writing and European Thought, 1600–1830* (Cambridge: Cambridge University Press, 1974). Hudson traces a "'demystification' of writing from the seventeenth to the late eighteenth century" in which concerns about its "destructive influence" were "reconcile[d]," during "the Romantic age," with a sense of its "advantages." Although clearly sharing the trajectory of what I have termed *naturalization,* Hudson's argument differs in his determination to "stay close to what scholars from the Renaissance to the Romantic era were themselves saying about writing," particularly in terms of an oral/written binary (7, 2, xii). This form of "close[ness]" is very useful, but I seek here to engage writing not only as an idea to be debated but as an interactive technology—one whose power can be gauged more precisely within a material history of the ways its various kinds are produced, mixed, circulated, reviewed, and reproduced.

Those practices are also largely absent from Timothy J. Reiss, *The Meaning of Literature* (Ithaca: Cornell University Press, 1992) but he does combine close attention to what was said about Literature with a startling capacity to—geographically and temporally—"zoom out." Using examples from across Western Europe, Reiss plots a large-scale scenario that subordinates, conceptually and chronologically, what he calls the late seventeenth- and early eighteenth-century "invention" (70) of Literature within a "discursive transformation" (3) which occurred a century earlier; Literature's acquisition of a "wholly new dimension of meaning" (229) "consolidated" changes dating from a Europe-wide social crisis spanning the century from 1550 to 1650. With the consolidation complete by the "first two decades of the eighteenth" (3, 42) the rest of that century and the turn into the next are subordinated even further as a "later development and sealing" (262). Reiss puts Literature, in other words, into a history of "discursive class" (3) rather than a history of writing and thus addresses not the proliferation of a technology but changes in "meaning." This produces very useful insights into the politics of literary activity, including issues of gender and the function of the novel (see his Chapters 3 and 7); however, in not attending to how, where, and when writing spread, this approach does not engage the classificatory role of Literature in domesticating that tech-nology—in Britain, in the (long) eighteenth century, and in conjunction with new ways of knowing and working.

Chapter 1. Writing Havoc

Epigraphs: The first quotation is from Alexander Pope, *The Poems of Alexander Pope,* ed. John Butt, 2nd ed., The Twickenham Edition of the Poems of Alexan-der Pope, vol. IV (London: Methuen, 1939, 1953) 96. The first folio was pub-lished January 2, 1735, with a title-page date of 1734. All quotations from Pope are taken from this edition, hereafter cited as *Pope.* The second quotation is from William Wordsworth, *The Poetical Works of William Wordsworth,* ed. E. De Selincourt and Helen Darbishire, vol. II (Oxford: Clarendon Press, 1940–49) 235–40. All quotations from Wordsworth's verse are taken from this edition, hereafter cited as *Wordsworth.*

1. Negative references to "blood-suck," "blood-suckers," and "blood-suck-ing" appear in the sixteenth century. Dryden provided an early link between that usage and "leech" in *The Medal* (1682) where he described witnesses before the grand jury who refused to indict the Earl of Shaftesbury as those "that leech-like, liv'd on blood, / Sucking for them were med'cinally good; / But when they fasten'd on *their* fester'd sore, / Then justice and religion they for-swore" (149–52). John Dryden, *The Poetical Works of Dryden,* ed. George R. Noyes, The Cambridge Poets (Cambridge, Mass.: Riverside Press, 1909, rev. 1950). All quotations from Dryden are taken from this edition, hereafter cited as *Dryden.*

2. The leech is, in fact, regaining medical attention in the late twentieth cen-tury with the rising interest in "natural" and "home" remedies and the efforts by biotech companies to find new kinds of drugs. The Genentech Corporation, for example, maintains a Web page on research into the leech's clotting agents, http://www.gene.com/ae/TSN/SS/leeches_background.html. For an analysis of how the figure of the leech connects Romanticism to the present, see Ira Liv-ingston, *Arrow of Chaos: Romanticism and Postmodernity,* ed. Sandra Buckley, Michael Hardt, and Brian Massumi, Theory Out of Bounds 9 (Minneapolis: University of Minnesota Press, 1996) 180–83, 198–212.

3. Advances in surgery provided some of the alternatives as that field was professionalized between "Arbuthnot" and "Resolution": "Few episodes in medical history are more remarkable," observe Carr-Saunders and Wilson in *The Professions* "than the rapid rise of the surgeons in the latter half of the eight-eenth century" (75). It should be noted, however, that some of the new uses for leeches today are in surgery, particularly to maintain blood flow during new microsurgical procedures.

4. Steven Knapp, *Personification and the Sublime: Milton to Coleridge* (Cam-bridge, Mass.: Harvard University Press, 1985) 119.

5. The naming of "it" becomes an increasingly important task during the eighteenth century as the size, number, and variety of crowds increase and as the role of writing in their formation is naturalized. This naming is what scholars of the crowd and mob study; in fact, their scholarship continues the undertaking into the present day. Witness the widespread influence of Habermas's effort on eighteenth-century studies: for many historians and critics, the label *public sphere* gives an empowering coherence to the past. That coherence also carries a nostalgic appeal in the present, as new forms of multiplicity—webs that are worldwide—arise from the current technological shift from writing/reading/print to electronic media. For the crowd in the eighteenth century, see Michael Hill, "Reading, Writing, and 'Rioting': A Genealogy of the Crowd in the Age of Print" (Ph.D. dissertation, State University of New York at Stony Brook, N.Y., 1994).

6. For shifting fortunes, see "there may come another day to me" ("Resolution and Independence" 34) and "of fortunes sharpe adversitee" (*Troilus and Criseide* III.1625) and for communication see "But now his voice to me was like a stream / Scare heard" ("Resolution and Independence" 106–7) and "Oon ere it herde, at tothir out it wente" (*Troilus and Criseide* IV.434).

7. See *Historicity* 193.

8. See, for example, Harold Bloom, *The Visionary Company: A Reading of English Romanticism* (Ithaca: Cornell University Press, 1961) and the end-of-decade collection *Romanticism and Consciousness: Essays in Criticism,* ed. Harold Bloom (New York: Norton, 1970).

9. See, in particular, *Historicity* 7–8, 56.

10. This argument is a primary connection between my previous book, *Historicity,* and this one. See, in particular, 176–77.

11. Identity and work interrelate in different ways at different historical moments. My point here is that during the eighteenth century that link becomes particularly intimate and important as both the self and work are reconfigured in developmental terms: the former as "something evermore about to be" and the latter as professions requiring an ongoing education.

12. I am not claiming, of course, that the madness is "caused" by the professionalization of identity—we now know that hatters suffered from the materials they worked with and that problems once thought to be psychological are now being explained as chemical—but that these cases of madness have been classified and experienced in occupational terms.

13. Alan Bewell, *Wordsworth and the Enlightenment: Nature, Man, and Society in the Experimental Poetry* (New Haven: Yale University Press, 1989) 176.

14. Sarah Egerton, "The Female Advocate, or, An Answere to a Late Satyr Against the Pride, Lust and Inconstancy, etc. of Woman," in *First Feminists: British Women Writers, 1578–1799,* ed. Moira Ferguson (Bloomington: Indiana University Press, 1985) 154.

15. Anonymous, "Preface to *Constantia*," reprinted in *Eighteenth-Century British Novelists on the Novel*, ed. George L. Barnett (New York: Appleton-Century-Crofts, 1751, 1968) 91, 94.

16. See Oliver Goldsmith on a "just balance between patronage and the press" in Oliver Goldsmith, *The Collected Works of Oliver Goldsmith*, ed. Arthur Friedman, vol. I (Oxford: Clarendon Press, 1966) 310–11, 498–504.

17. E. S. Dallas, *The Gay Science*, 2 vols., vol. 2 (London, 1866, rpt. New York: Johnson Reprint Corp., 1969) 299.

18. Anne Finch, *The Poems of Anne Countess of Winchilsea*, ed. Myra Reynolds (Chicago: University of Chicago Press, 1903) 9.

19. The concluding couplets of "Cooper's Hill" were widely admired and imitated by Finch's contemporaries:

O could I flow like thee, and make thy stream
My great example, as it is my theme!
Though deep, yet clear, though gentle, yet not dull,
Strong without rage, without o'erflowing full.

20. See Lonsdale, ed., *Eighteenth-Century Women Poets* 497.

21. For an even more bizarre twist on gender and high romantic description, see Coleridge's "Ode to Georgiana, Duchess of Devonshire," written in response to her poem "Passage over Mount Gothard." Structured around the refrain "O Lady, nursed in pomp and pleasure! / Whence learn'd you that heroic measure," the ode's focus, announced in a subtitle, is not the Duchess's heroic quatrains but her twenty-fourth stanza, a tribute to William Tell's assassination of the Austrian "tyrant." Having elevated her politics over her poetry, but through a question that disparages her background, Coleridge manages to condescend to both. She is then in a position to receive his praise, which turns out to be neither poetical, nor political, but biological: her instinct for "Liberty" derives from being a "Mother!" Thus, after attempting the kind of poetry which Eliza forgoes, the Duchess is put back in her proper place.

22. See the note itself and David Perkins's brief discussion of the controversy in *English Romantic Writers*, ed. David Perkins (New York: Harcourt Brace Jovanovich, 1967) 434.

23. Eliza's anonymity—like the widespread anonymity of electronic communication today—raises the possibility of yet another ironic twist: was she a woman?

24. Critical fascination with Coleridge's infirmities demonstrates the ongoing power of the "psychologizing" I discussed in the previous section. See my argument regarding our own addiction to portrayals of Coleridge as an addict in *Historicity* 180–90.

25. *The German Ideology*, in Karl Marx and Frederick Engels, *Marx and*

Engels: 1845–47, Karl Marx, Frederick Engels: Collected Works, vol. V (Moscow: Progress Publishers, 1976) 236.

26. Henry Abelove, "Some Speculations on the History of Sexual Intercourse during the Long Eighteenth Century in England," *Genders* 6 (Fall 1989): 128.

27. Thomas Laqueur agrees that the incidence of "intercourse, so called" increased, but he argues that this was not an issue of the "popularity" of the act: "Within marriage, the evidence suggests, there was little change [in the frequency of intercourse]. But as the barriers to nuptiality eased, access to sexual intercourse did become greater; the franchise, so to speak, for indulging in it was lowered" (200).

Abelove, however, does not claim that individuals engaged in *more* sexual activity than in the past, but that more of them devoted that activity to reproductive intercourse. If Laqueur is right, the reason was greater access to marriage as the situation in which intercourse was "indulg[ed]," but the result would still be that intercourse claimed a higher percentage of the total number of sexual acts performed in England: it became, that is, more popular—not necessarily more desired—compared with the other acts. Laqueur agrees, I should add, with Abelove regarding the fate of the other acts: "compared to earlier periods, there was certainly open hostility to nonreproductive sexuality" (198). See Thomas Laqueur, "Sexual Desire and the Market Economy During the Industrial Revolution," in *Discourses of Sexuality from Aristotle to AIDS,* ed. Domna C. Stanton (Ann Arbor: University of Michigan Press, 1992) 185–215.

28. "Outlines of a Critique of Political Economy" in *Marx and Engels* III.419.

29. Eugene Rotwein, *David Hume: Writings on Economics* (Madison: University of Wisconsin Press, 1955, 1970) x.

30. Edwin Greenlaw, *The Province of Literary History* (Port Washington, N.Y.: Kennikat Press, 1931, rpt. 1968) 72.

31. "Of the Study of History," in David Hume, *Philosophical Works of David Hume,* ed. T. H. Green and T. H. Grose, 4 vols., vol IV (London: Scientia Verlag Aalen, 1882, 1964) 390. See Rotwein's discussion, xxvii–xxviii.

32. Bazerman, "How Natural Philosophers Can Cooperate" 16.

33. David Hume, *Enquiries Concerning the Human Understanding and Concerning the Principles of Morals,* ed. L. A. Selby-Bigge and P. H. Nidditch, 3rd ed. (Oxford: Clarendon Press, 1902, 1975) 5, 17. See also David Hume, *A Treatise of Human Nature,* ed. L. A. Selby-Bigge, 2nd ed. (Oxford: Clarendon Press, 1978).

34. This assessment, made between "Arbuthnot" and "Resolution," appears to share explanatory strategies with both texts: Pope's sense of a proliferating "press" that threatens the unwary and Wordsworth's developmental frame-

work which encourages—as I argue in *Historicity* (94–124)—ongoing revision of early work even into posthumous publication.

35. Peter Calvert, *The Concept of Class: An Historical Introduction* (New York: St. Martin's Press, 1982) 22, 12. For a powerful analysis of the connection between the advent of modern "classificatory thinking" and political economy, see Mary Poovey, "The Social Constitution of 'Class': Toward a History of Classificatory Thinking," in *Rethinking Class: Literary Studies and Social Formations,* ed. Wai Chee Dimock and Michael T. Gilmore, The Social Foundations of Aesthetic Forms (New York: Columbia University Press, 1994) 15–56.

Chapter 2. Engendering Disciplinarity

Epigraphs: The full title of the first quotation is "On Sir J— S— saying in a Sarcastic Manner, My Books would make me Mad. An Ode." See Lonsdale, ed., *Eighteenth-Century Women Poets* 41. The second quotation is from "A Letter from Cleora," from vol. II, book X, 230–37, reprinted in Eliza Haywood, *The Female Spectator: Being Selections From Mrs. Eliza Haywood's Periodical, First Published in Monthly Parts (1744–46),* ed. Gabrielle M. Firmager (London: Bristol Classical Press, 1993) 100–101.

1. "A Letter concerning French ladies, and how easily they improve themselves," from vol. II, book XII, 341–48, 1744–45, reprinted in Haywood, *Female Spectator* 107.

2. Keith Hoskin, "Education and the Genesis of Disciplinarity: The Unexpected Reversal," in *Knowledges: Historical and Critical Studies in Disciplinarity,* ed. Ellen Messer-Davidow, David R. Shumway, and David J. Sylvan (Charlottesville: University of Virginia Press, 1993) 276.

3. Nicholas Hans, *New Trends in Education in the Eighteenth Century* (London: Routledge, 1951) 15.

4. Mary Astell, *A Serious Proposal to the Ladies for the Advancement of Their True and Greatest Interest, Parts I and II* (New York: Source Book Press, 1701, 1970). Selections from both parts are available in *The Meridian Anthology of Early Women Writers: British Literary Women from Aphra Behn to Maria Edgeworth 1660–1800,* ed. Katherine M. Rogers and William McCarthy (New York: New American Library, 1987) 113–28.

5. The reference to "Nature" as part of what she "mean[s]" by "God" suggests that Astell may be considering a rather wide range of knowledges other than the theological.

6. *Women Critics, 1660–1820: An Anthology,* ed. Folger Collective (Bloomington: Indiana University Press, 1995) 9, hereafter cited as *Women Critics.*

7. "Preface to *Observations upon Experimental Philosophy,*" 1666, in *Women Critics* 13.

8. "Preface to *The Description of a New World, called the Blazing-World,*" 1668, in *Women Critics* 14.

9. Mary Lee, "The Ladies Retreat: or A Dialogue between Sir John Brute, Sir William Loveall, Melissa, and a Parson," in *First Feminists: British Women Writers 1578–1799*, ed. Moira Ferguson (Bloomington: Indiana University Press, 1701) 218–37.

10. Quoted in Londsdale, ed., *Eighteenth-Century Women Poets* 1.

11. Letter from Lady Mary Wortley Montagu to Lady Bute, 6 March 1753, in *Meridian Anthology* 207.

12. See Londsdale, ed., *Eighteenth-Century Women Poets* 54.

13. Letter from Lady Mary Wortley Montagu to Lady Bute, 28 January 1753, in *Meridian Anthology* 204–5.

14. *A Patchwork Screen for the Ladies* (London: E. Curll, 1723) in *Women Critics* 32, 30.

15. Cooper refers to three texts: Edward Philips, *Theatrum Poetarum* (1675); William Winstanley, *Lives of the Most Famous English Poets* (1687); and Giles Jacob, *Poetical Register, or Lives and Characters of the English Dramatic Poets* (1719–20). The Renaissance discourses included William Webbe's *A Discourse of English Poetrie* (1586) and Philip Sidney's *An Apology for Poetrie* (1595).

16. "Preface to *The Muses Library*," in *Women Critics* 73–79. The notion of all poems being parts of one ongoing Poem became a staple of Romantic theory and practice. See *Historicity* 112–13.

17. Women played a crucial role not only in the anthologizing of English Literature, but also in another crucial disciplinary area: the deification of Shakespeare. Samuel Johnson's Preface was preceded and followed by work by women, including that of Charlotte Lennox, *Shakespear Illustrated* (1753–54), which critiqued his plotting by turning to sources; Elizabeth Montagu, *An Essay on the Writings and Genius of Shakespear* (1769), which focused on his generic innovations; and Elizabeth Griffith, *The Morality of Shakespeare's Drama Illustrated* (1775), which pursued Johnson's focus on moral philosophy. See *Women Critics* xx.

18. Having taken great pains to define and historicize modern conceptions of *depth* and *development* in *Historicity,* I am trying to be particularly careful here not to identify any one familiar-sounding feature in Astell with a later concept: for example, *within = depth*. Instead, I am suggesting that certain features do appear to participate in ongoing reclassifications from which the later concepts emerge. See my argument regarding this kind of change in Clifford Siskin, "Working *The Prelude*: Foucault and the New History," in *The Prelude,* ed. Nigel Wood, Theory in Practice (Buckingham: Open University Press, 1993) 98–124:

> Aspects of what Foucault calls the "Author function," for example, certainly appear prior to the late eighteenth century, but . . . not until they are put into combination with narratives linking aesthetic depth and

individual development, as well as with rewritten copyright laws, is that most familiar form of the subject—the Creative Author—in place. (104–5)

19. Edmund Burke, *A Philosophical Enquiry into the Origin of Our Ideas of the Sublime and Beautiful*, ed. James T. Boulton (Notre Dame: University of Notre Dame Press, 1759, 1958).

20. Horace Walpole, *The Castle of Otranto: A Gothic Story*, ed. W. S. Lewis (Oxford: Oxford University Press, 1765, 1982) 108.

21. See *Oxford English Dictionary*.

22. Clara Reeve, "Preface to *The Old English Baron*," reprinted in Barnett, *Eighteenth-Century British Novelists on the Novel* 136–37.

23. Karen Swann, "The Sublime and the Vulgar," *College English* 52, no. 1 (January 1990): 9.

24. Jonathan Arac, "The Media of Sublimity: Johnson and Lamb on *King Lear*," *Studies in Romanticism* 26, no. 2 (1987): 209–20; Michael Hays, "Comedy as Being/Idea," *Studies in Romanticism* 26, no. 2 (1987): 221–30; Neil Hertz, *The End of the Line: Essays on Psychoanalysis and the Sublime* (New York: Columbia University Press, 1985).

25. R. S. Crane, *The Idea of the Humanities and Other Essays Critical and Historical*, vol. I (Chicago: University of Chicago Press, 1967) 106.

26. John Baillie, *An Essay on the Sublime* (1747) cited in Burke, *Philosophical Enquiry* xlv.

27. Longinus, "On the Sublime," in *Criticism: The Major Statements*, ed. Charles Kaplan (New York: St. Martin's Press, 1906, 1986) 93.

28. See my arguments regarding the valorization of work in the eighteenth century in Chapter 4 and in my essay, "Wordsworth's Prescriptions: Romanticism and Professional Power," in *The Romantics and Us: Essays on Literature and Culture*, ed. Gene W. Ruoff (New Brunswick, N.J.: Rutgers University Press, 1990) 303–21.

29. Boulton argues that "the link between sublimity and terror had been suggested before; it was used, consciously perhaps, in Thomson's *Seasons;* but Burke was the first to convert it into a system" (Burke, *Philosophical Enquiry* lvi).

30. Boulton notes that Baillie was the first to use the term "'sublime' . . . equally with beauty, [as] a general and accepted expression for use in aesthetics" (lii).

31. Boulton also points out that Addison uses the term "'sublime' . . . very infrequently" (xlix).

32. Eagleton is speaking of the Kantian sublime in Terry Eagleton, *The Ideology of the Aesthetic* (Cambridge: Basil Blackwell, 1990) 90.

33. Chaucer uses it in the Canon's Yeoman's Tale: "That we hadde in oure

matires sublymyng" (770). Larry D. Benson, ed., *The Riverside Chaucer,* 3rd ed. (Boston: Houghton Mifflin, 1987).

34. Samuel Johnson, *Lives of the English Poets,* ed. George Birbeck, vol. I (Oxford: Clarendon Press, 1905) 177.

35. Edmund Burke, *Reflections on the Revolution in France,* ed. Thomas H. D. Mahoney (New York: Liberal Arts Press, 1955) 216.

36. Boulton's examples are primarily within what we now think of as the arts, for he tends to place the *Enquiry* under the rubric of aesthetics (xc–cxxvii).

37. See Williams, *Keywords* 88–89.

38. Richard Münch and Neil J. Smelser, eds., *Theory of Culture* (Berkeley: University of California Press, 1992).

39. David Radcliffe, *Forms of Reflection: Genre and Culture in Meditational Writing* (Baltimore: Johns Hopkins University Press, 1993) x–xi.

40. Robert Mandrou, *From Humanism to Science, 1480–1700,* trans. Brian Pearce (New York: Penguin, 1978) 268.

41. David L. Wagner, "The Seven Liberal Arts and Classical Scholarship," in *The Seven Liberal Arts in the Middle Ages,* ed. David L. Wagner (Bloomington: Indiana University Press, 1986) 1–9.

42. Margaret Jacob, *The Cultural Meaning of the Scientific Revolution* (Philadelphia: Temple University Press, 1988) 136, 141.

43. John Barrell, *English Literature in History, 1730–1780* (New York: St. Martin's Press, 1983).

44. I want to thank the Stony Brook doctoral students in my Spring 1994 seminar "Engendering Disciplinarity" for their help in thinking through the issues engaged in this chapter. I would also like to thank Greg Laugero, whose use of the term *infrastructure* in his dissertation inspired my use of it here. See Greg Laugero, "Infrastructures of the Enlightenment: Road-Making, the Circulation of Print, and the Emergence of Literature" (Ph.D. dissertation, State University of New York at Stony Brook, 1994) and "Infrastructures of the Enlightenment: Road-making, the Public Sphere, and the Emergence of Literature," *Eighteenth-Century Studies* 29, no. 1 (Fall 1995): 45–68.

45. John Rajchman sees postanalytic philosophy as "more de-disciplinizing than interdisciplinary: less a collaboration between specialized fields than a questioning of basic assumptions in those fields and an attempt to create new ones." I use *dedisciplinarity* here in a different sense: as a move not to new disciplines, but a move from discipline to another unit of knowledge. See John Rajchman, "Philosophy in America," in *Post-Analytic Philosophy,* ed. John Rajchman and Cornell West (New York: Columbia University Press, 1985) xiii. Michael McKeon shares my wariness of "unhistorical thinking" in cultural studies. See "The Origins of Interdisciplinary Studies," *Eighteenth-Century Studies* 28, no. 1 (1994): 17–28.

46. Dietrich Rueschemeyer, *Power and the Division of Labour* (Stanford: Stanford University Press, 1986) 41.

47. Since this ironic connection is only visible from our historical perspective, I do not see any value in treating this as a political failure on Astell's part. Understanding the past, however, can help *us* make political sense of the present. For a harsher judgment of Astell, see Catherine Sharrock, "De-ciphering Women and De-scribing Authority: The Writings of Mary Astell," in *Women, Writing, History, 1640–1740,* ed. Isobel Grundy and Susan Wiseman (Athens: University of Georgia Press, 1992) 109–24: "Conditioned by her own internalized values, Astell's texts write themselves out of her conscious control and into the hands of patriarchy" (124). For a contemporary political problem that I think bears scrutiny with the fate of Astell in mind, see Messer-Davidow's *(En)Gendering Knowledge:*

> The disciplinary grid is like the domestic grid that, we discovered in the 1960s, disempowers women. Isolated in a compartment (a specialty or a home), each woman is prevented from knowing the structures of oppression and acting to change them. Paradoxically, we may have escaped from our domestic enclosures only to find ourselves two decades later ensconced in disciplinary ones. Twenty years ago, movement critique told us our separation would be our downfall; now professional ideology tells us specializations are the places to seek academic success. (289)

Chapter 3. Scottish Philosophy and English Literature

Epigraphs: The first quotation is from Thomas Blackwell, *An Inquiry into the Life and Writings of Homer,* in *Eighteenth-Century Critical Essays,* ed. Scott Elledge, vol. I (Ithaca: Cornell University Press, 1735) 433. The second quotation is from Lord John Russell to the Duke of Bedford, 27 April 1809, quoted in Spencer Walpole, *The Life of Lord John Russell,* 2nd ed., 2 vols., vol. I (London: Longmans, 1889) 43. I thank Anand C. Chitnis for this quotation. See Anand C. Chitnis, *The Scottish Enlightenment and Early Victorian English Society* (London: Croom Helm, 1986) 1.

1. Arthur R. King Jr. and John A. Brownell, *The Curriculum and the Disciplines of Knowledge: A Theory of Curriculum Practice* (New York: John Wiley and Sons, 1966) 39–40.

2. John Valdimir Price, "The Reading of Philosophical Literature," in *Books and Their Readers in Eighteenth-Century England,* ed. Isabel Rivers (New York: St. Martin's Press, 1982) 165.

3. Hume, *Enquiries* 162 and see Price, "Reading of Philosophical Literature" 166.

4. W. A. Speck, "The Eighteenth Century: England's Ancien Régime?," *British Journal for Eighteenth-Century Studies* 15, no. 2 (Fall 1992): 133. For the cen-

trality of Jacobitism in this debate, see J. C. D. Clark, "On Moving the Middle Ground: The Significance of Jacobitism in Historical Studies," in *The Jacobite Challenge,* ed. Eveline Cruickshanks and Jeremy Black (Edinburgh: John Donald Publishers, 1988) 177–88.

5. Gerald Newman, *The Rise of English Nationalism: A Cultural History, 1740–1830* (New York: St. Martin's Press, 1987).

6. Linda Colley, *Britons: Forging the Nation, 1707–1837* (New Haven: Yale University Press, 1992) 73, 131–32.

7. Paul Monod, *Jacobitism and the English People, 1688–1788* (Cambridge: Cambridge University Press, 1989) 350.

8. Otto Dann and John Dinwiddy, eds., *Nationalism in the Age of the French Revolution* (London: Hambledon Press, 1988) 3.

9. Robert Wuthnow, *Communities of Discourse: Ideology and Social Structure in the Reformation, the Enlightenment, and European Socialism* (Cambridge, Mass.: Harvard University Press, 1989) 256.

10. Murray G. H. Pittock, *Poetry and Jacobite Politics in Eighteenth-Century Britain and Ireland,* ed. Howard Erskine-Hill and John Richetti, Cambridge Studies in Eighteenth-Century English Literature and Thought (Cambridge: Cambridge University Press, 1994) 235.

11. Steve Bruce, "A Failure of the Imagination: Ethnicity and Nationalism in Scotland's History," *Scotia* XVII (1993): 8.

12. Howard Erskine-Hill, "Literature and the Jacobite Cause: Was There a Rhetoric of Jacobitism?" in *Ideology and Conspiracy: Aspects of Jacobitism, 1689–1759,* ed. Eveline Cruickshanks (Edinburgh: John Donald Publishers, 1982) 51–52.

13. For a particularly useful look at these controversies, especially in regard to the notion of distressed genres, see Susan Stewart, *Crimes of Writing: Problems in the Containment of Representation* (Durham, N.C.: Duke University Press, 1994).

14. Howard D. Weinbrot, *Britannia's Issue: The Rise of British Literature from Dryden to Ossian* (Cambridge: Cambridge University Press, 1993) 1–5.

15. Robert Crawford, *Devolving English Literature* (Oxford: Clarendon Press, 1992).

16. R. A. Houston, *Scottish Literacy and Scottish Identity: Illiteracy and Society in Scotland and Northern England 1600–1800,* ed. Peter Laslett, Roger Schofield, E. A. Wrigley, and Daniel Scott Smith, Cambridge Studies in Population, Economy and Society in Past Time, vol. 4 (Cambridge: Cambridge University Press, 1985) 266.

17. S. Leslie Hunter, *The Scottish Educational System* (Oxford: Pergamon Press, 1968) 2.

18. G. S. Osborne, *Change in Scottish Education* (London: Longmans, 1968) 10.

19. D. G. Palmer, *The Rise of English Studies: An Account of the Study of English Language and Literature from Its Origins to the Making of the Oxford English School* (Oxford: Oxford University Press, 1965) 5–9 and Gerald Wester Chapman, ed., *Literary Criticism in England, 1660–1800* (New York: Knopf, 1966) 266.

20. Harold Perkin, "The Historical Perspective," in *Perspectives on Higher Education: Eight Disciplinary and Comparative Views,* ed. Burton R. Clark (Berkeley: University of California Press, 1984) 32.

21. Richard B. Sher, *Church and University in the Scottish Enlightenment: The Moderate Literati of Edinburgh* (Princeton: Princeton University Press, 1985) 28 and Palmer, *Rise of English Studies* 72.

22. George Elder Davie, *The Democratic Intellect: Scotland and Her Universities in the Nineteenth Century* (Edinburgh: Edinburgh University Press, 1961) 4–5 and Chapman, ed., *Literary Criticism in England* 266–67.

23. For a study of specific innovations in curriculum and pedagogy, including class size, library use, and prizes, see David Hamilton, "Adam Smith and the Moral Economy of the Classroom," *Journal of Curriculum Studies* 12, no. 4 (1980): 281–98.

24. Cited in Chapman, ed., *Literary Criticism in England* 272.

25. Crane, *Idea of the Humanities* 103, 97.

26. George Campbell, *The Philosophy of Rhetoric,* ed. Lloyd F. Bitzer (Carbondale: Southern Illinois University Press, 1776, 1963) lxvii.

27. See R. S. Crane on the connection between the Scottish philosophers and Newtonian natural philosophy (*Idea of the Humanities* 106–10).

28. William S. McCormick, *Three Lectures on English Literature* (London: Alexander Gardner, 1889) 12.

29. Louis Kampf, "Gibbon and Hume," in *English Literature and British Philosophy: A Collection of Essays,* ed. S. P. Rosenbaum (Chicago: University of Chicago Press, 1971) 110.

30. John Stuart Mill, Inaugural Lecture at St. Andrews, 1867, cited in Roy Lewis and Angus Maude, *Professional People* (London: Phoenix House, 1952) 210.

31. John Stuart Mill, *The Autobiography of John Stuart Mill* (New York: Columbia University Press, 1924) 1070.

32. William Wordsworth, *The Prelude 1799, 1805, 1850,* ed. Jonathan Wordsworth, M. H. Abrams, and Stephen Gill (New York: Norton, 1979).

Chapter 4. The Georgic at Work

Epigraphs: The first quotation is from a poem published posthumously in 1806. See Lonsdale, ed., *Eighteenth-Century Women Poets* 474–75. The second quotation is from the version published in the 1800 edition of *Lyrical Ballads*. Wordsworth's later revisions are detailed in *Wordsworth* 4.65–67.

1. Robinson and the Prince entered into a preassignation contract for £20,000 after she attracted his attention while playing Perdita in a production of *The Winter's Tale*. He later refused to pay the bond, but Robinson, using letters he had sent her and the influence of another lover, Charles James Fox, eventually secured £5,000 and a £500 annuity. See Lonsdale, ed., *Eighteenth-Century Women Poets* 469. For the legal difficulties facing women during the long eighteenth century, see Susan Staves, *Married Women's Separate Property in England, 1660–1833* (Cambridge, Mass.: Harvard University Press, 1990).

2. See "Stanzas" in Lonsdale, ed., *Eighteenth-Century Women Poets* 475–76.

3. Eliot Freidson, "The Theory of Professions: State of the Art," in *The Sociology of the Professions: Lawyers, Doctors and Others,* ed. Robert Dingwall and Philip Lewis (London: Macmillan, 1983) 32–33.

4. Cohen, "History and Genre" 204.

5. The many efforts to articulate this issue include Gloria V. Engel and Richard H. Hall, "The Growing Industrialization of the Professions," in *The Professions and Their Prospects,* ed. Eliot Freidson (Beverly Hills, Calif.: Sage Publications, 1971) 75–88; Eliot Freidson, "Professionalization and the Organisation of Middle-Class Labour in Post-Industrial Society," *Sociological Review* Monograph 20 (1973): 47–59; Martin Oppenheimer, "The Proletarianization of the Professional," *Sociological Review* Monograph 20 (1973): 213–27; Terence Johnson, "The Professions in the Class Structure," in *Industrial Society: Class, Cleavage and Control,* ed. Richard Scase (New York: St. Martin's Press, 1977) 93–110; Magali Larson, "Proletarianization and Educated Labor," *Theory and Society* 9 (1980): 131–75; Charles Derber, "Toward a New Theory of Professionals as Workers: Advanced Capitalism and Postindustrial Labor," and John McKinlay, "Toward the Proletarianization of Physicians," both in *Professionals as Workers: Mental Labor in Advanced Capitalism,* ed. Charles Derber (Boston: C. K. Hall, 1982) 193–208, 37–62.

6. Robert Pear, "Doctors Fear They're Losing Status," *San Francisco Chronicle,* 31 December 1987, A16. This is reprinted from the *New York Times,* 26 December 1987, A1.

7. The apparent solution for many doctors in the 1990s has been to take on an additional professional identity as businessmen: to maintain professional control as doctors, they have banded together to form their own HMOs. I thank Leslie Siskin for this observation.

8. Jane Tompkins, "Me and My Shadow," *New Literary History* 19, no. 1 (Fall 1987): 169.

9. Dingwall, "Introduction," in *The Sociology of the Professions* 5. Dingwall is summarizing the views of Everett Hughes.

10. For the attitude of the eighteenth-century gentleman toward a "job," see W. J. Reader, *Professional Men: The Rise of the Professional Classes in Nineteenth-Century England* (London: Weidenfeld and Nicolson, 1966) 5.

11. The "term 'the myth of vocation,'" according to Ruth Danon, "derives from the studies of contemporary philosophers, sociologists, historians and laborers concerned with the problem of work in modern life. They make evident that we live in a work-centered culture and that this culture cannot be described simply in Weberian terms. The Protestant work ethic does not explain the expectation people have that they be made happy by their work." See Ruth Danon, *Work in the English Novel: The Myth of Vocation* (London: Croom Helm, 1985) 2.

12. See the references to Hippocrates in W. F. Bynum and Roy Porter, eds. *William Hunter and the Eighteenth-Century Medical World* (Cambridge: Cambridge University Press, 1985) 209, 212, 263, 327; Ivan Waddington, *The Medical Profession in the Industrial Revolution* (Dublin: Gill and Macmillan, 1984) 153; and Guy Williams, *The Age of Agony: The Art of Healing, 1700–1800* (Chicago: Academy Chicago, 1975, rpt. 1986) 7. The use of the Hippocratic oath to exclude surgeons from a "closed shop" is discussed in Frederick F. Cartwright, *A Social History of Medicine* (London: Longmans, 1977) 41–42. The public relations reduction of the classical past from a source of knowledge actively imitated and engaged into a self-justifying moral agenda for the professional present occurred later, becoming an ongoing—and, as humanists such as Allan Bloom have demonstrated—profitable project of modern professionals and professional groups.

13. Changes in the medical profession have received much of the attention in work focusing on the early and mid eighteenth century. See, for example, W. F. Bynum, "Physicians, Hospitals and Career Structures in Eighteenth-Century London," in *William Hunter,* ed. Bynum and Porter 105–28. Geoffrey S. Holmes, *Augustan England: Professions, State and Society, 1680–1730* (London: Allen and Unwin, 1982) addresses a full range of occupations in an attempt to combat the widespread notion that the professions became, as Wilfred Prest has put it, "a significant social presence only with the onset of the classical phase of industrialization." See Wilfred Prest, ed., *The Professions in Early Modern England* (London: Croom Helm, 1987) 5.

In his own work, Prest argues for a significant presence in the early modern period as well; his strategy is to try to undo empirically the assumption that the professions consisted primarily of gentlemen until the late eighteenth century. The issue of an ideal of gentlemanly behavior still remains, as does the question of the importance of self-classification in distinguishing professions from other occupations: as Prest himself admits,

> before the nineteenth century people do not seem to have debated the meaning of the term "profession," or what distinguished professions from other, less esteemed occupations; nor is there any evidence that particular prestige attached to occupations which claimed the status of professions. (13)

Prest also raises the important point that

> if what distinguishes a profession from any other occupation is the ability
> of its membership to determine directly or indirectly, who may pursue
> that particular vocation, then there were either very few or very many pro-
> fessions in early modern England. Few, if we are thinking of recognisable
> prototypes of modern professions, whether legal, medical or other; many,
> if we include all the craft guilds and trading companies whose members
> sought to maintain a monopoly on the practice of numerous callings and
> trades in particular localities. The historical puzzle is to explain, if pos-
> sible without embroiling ourselves in unprofitable debate about the attri-
> butes or definition of a true profession, why the national occupational
> monopoly form (represented by the professions) has expanded and flour-
> ished down to the present day, while the local occupational monopoly
> form (represented by the guilds) shrank and withered on the vine. (14)

The standard history of the professions which Prest is challenging—the one
that links professionalization to industrialization—is usually traced back to
work from the 1930s by A. M. Carr-Saunders and P. A. Wilson in Britain and
Talcott Parsons in the United States. See A. M. Carr-Saunders and P. A. Wilson, *The Professions* (Oxford: Clarendon Press, 1933) and Talcott Parsons, "The
Professions and Social Structure," *Social Forces* 17 (1939): 457–67. Explanations
have generally shifted from their descriptive and functionalist arguments to
historical and ideological ones, but that link has remained largely unopposed.
For a useful analytical survey of work on the professions up to the present
decade, see C. W. R. Gispen, "German Engineers and American Social Theory:
Historical Perspectives on Professionalization," *Comparative Studies in Society
and History* 30 (1988): 550–74. For important historical and ideological analyses, see Magali Sarfatti Larson, *The Rise of Professionalism: A Sociological Analysis* (Berkeley: University of California Press, 1977) and Rueschemeyer, *Power
and the Division of Labour*.

14. See the tables assembled in Reader, *Professional Men* 207–11, and the
observations of Philip Elliott regarding the sociology of Victorian professionalism in *The Sociology of the Professions* (New York: Herder and Herder) 54–57.

15. Those efforts that do attend to the late eighteenth and early nineteenth
centuries do not address literary activity. See Waddington, *The Medical Profession in the Industrial Revolution* and Larson, *The Rise of Professionalism*.

16. See W. F. Bynum's discussion of Johnson's definition in Bynum 111.

17. Both Reader 1–24 and Elliott 20–27 provide useful analyses of the gentlemanly nature of the professions in the eighteenth century. The restriction
to gentlemen functioned less as an absolute barrier—men of lesser status did
improve themselves by entering the professions in the seventeenth and eighteenth centuries—than as a means of valorizing certain kinds of work over other

kinds. I am describing how the work of writing helped to transform that hierarchy into its modern forms of professional versus amateur and intellectual versus manual labor.

18. Lyman Ray Patterson, *Copyright in Historical Perspective* (Nashville: Vanderbilt University Press, 1968) 143. In addition to Patterson, the following sources are also useful in tracking the history of copyright: Mark Rose, "The Author as Proprietor: *Donaldson v. Becket* and the Genealogy of Modern Authorship," *Representations* 23 (Summer 1988): 51–85 and *Authors and Owners: The Invention of Copyright* (Cambridge, Mass.: Harvard University Press, 1993); Deborah D. Rogers, "The Commercialization of Eighteenth-Century English Literature," *Clio* 18, no. 2 (1989): 171–78; Gwyn Walters, "The Booksellers in 1759 and 1774: The Battle for Literary Property," *Library* 5th series 29 (1974): 287–315; Terry Belanger, "From Bookseller to Publisher: Changes in the London Book Trade," in *Book Selling and Book Buying: Aspects of the Nineteenth-Century British and North American Book Trade,* ed. Richard G. Landon, ACRL Publications in Librarianship, vol. 40 (Chicago: American Library Association, 1978) 7–16 and "Publishers and Writers in Eighteenth-Century England," in *Books and Their Readers in Eighteenth-Century England,* ed. Isabel Rivers (New York: St. Martin's Press, 1982) 5–26; John Feather, *The Provincial Book Trade in Eighteenth-Century England* (Cambridge: Cambridge University Press, 1985) and *A History of British Publishing*; Martha Woodmansee, "The Genius and the Copyright: Economic and Legal Conditions of the Emergence of the 'Author'," *Eighteenth-Century Studies* 17, no. 4 (Summer 1984): 425–48; Robin Meyers and Michael Harris, eds., *Economics of the British Booktrade 1605–1939,* Publishing History Occasional Series, vol. 1 (Cambridge: Chadwyck-Healey, 1985); Marjorie Plant, *The English Book Trade: An Economic History of the Making and Sale of Books,* 2nd ed. (London: Allen and Unwin, 1965); R. M. Wiles, *Serial Publication in England Before 1750* (Cambridge: Cambridge University Press, 1957); and Trevor Ross, "Copyright and the Invention of Tradition," *Eighteenth-Century Studies* 26, no. 1 (Fall 1992): 1–28.

19. Belanger, "Publishers and Writers" 15.

20. The questions are reprinted in Patterson, *Copyright* 175.

21. Kernan, *Samuel Johnson and the Impact of Print* 283–87.

22. Trevor Ross, "How 'Poesy' Became Literature: Making and Reading the English Canon in the 18th Century," unpublished manuscript (1990) 8, 22–23. This essay was revised and published as "Copyright and the Invention of Tradition."

23. Hugh Amory, "*De facto* Copyright? Fielding's *Works* in Partnership 1769–1821," *Eighteenth-Century Studies* 17, no. 4 (Summer 1984): 453.

24. Letter to Beaumont, 3 June 1805, in William Wordsworth and Dorothy Wordsworth, *The Letters of William and Dorothy Wordsworth: The Early Years,*

1787–1805, ed. Ernest de Selincourt, rev. Chester L. Shaver, 2 vols., vol I (Oxford: Oxford University Press, 1967) 594–95.

25. Preface to *The Excursion* (1814) in *Prose* III.5.

26. Larson, *The Rise of Professionalism* xvi.

27. William MacDonald, *The Intellectual Worker and His Work* (London: Jonathan Cape, 1923) 65.

28. In *Historicity,* I inquire generically into the fourteen-book *Prelude* as a sonnet; Book VIII would then contain the turn from octet to sestet (122).

29. See William Wordsworth, *The Prelude 1799, 1805, 1850,* ed. Jonathan Wordsworth, M. H. Abrams, and Stephen Gill (New York: Norton, 1979) 468–69.

30. The first usage cited in the *Oxford English Dictionary* is from 1784.

31. Crane, *Idea of the Humanities* 104.

32. Stewart Clegg, Paul Boreham, and Geoff Dow, *Class, Politics and the Economy,* ed. John Rex, International Library of Sociology (London: Routledge, 1986) 6–13 and David Ricardo, *On the Principles of Political Economy and Taxation,* 2nd ed. (London: John Murray, 1819) iii.

33. Terence Johnson deploys these terms brilliantly in his analysis of the professions in the class structure in Scase, *Industrial Society* 99.

34. See Galperin's analysis of Wordsworth's reputation and career in *Revision and Authority in Wordsworth: The Interpretation of a Career* (Philadelphia: University of Pennsylvania Press, 1989).

35. M. H. Abrams, *Natural Supernaturalism: Tradition and Revolution in Romantic Literature* (New York: Norton, 1971) 183–87.

36. For an exploration of how "ironic spirals" map our "complex cultural plane," see Ira Livingston, "Wheel Within Wheel: A Cultural Physics of Irony" (Ph.D. dissertation, Stanford University, 1990).

37. See *Historicity* 116–23.

38. Michel Foucault, *The Archaeology of Knowledge and The Discourse on Language,* trans. A. M. Sheridan Smith (New York: Pantheon Books, 1972) 222.

39. Anthony Low, *The Georgic Revolution* (Princeton: Princeton University Press, 1985) 4.

40. In addition to Low 14, see Raymond Williams, *The Country and the City* (New York: Oxford University Press, 1973) 13–34; Stephen Orgel, *The Illusion of Power* (Berkeley: University of California Press, 1975) 37–58; and James Turner, *The Politics of Landscape: Rural Scenery and Society in English Poetry 1630–1660* (Cambridge, Mass.: Harvard University Press, 1979) 116–85.

41. See *Historicity* 87–88.

42. See L. P. Wilkinson's discussion of Addison's essay in his translation of *The Georgics.* Virgil, *The Georgics,* trans. L. P. Wilkinson (Harmondsworth, U.K.: Penguin, 1982) 34.

43. For an analysis of the history of the "artist as hero," see Robert Folkenflik, "Patronage and the Poet Hero," *Huntington Library Quarterly* 48 (1985): 363–79 and Robert Folkenflik, *The English Hero, 1660–1800* (Newark: University of Delaware Press, 1982).

44. See Alexandre Beljame, *Men of Letters and the English Public in the Eighteenth Century 1660–1744, Dryden, Addison, Pope,* ed. Bonamy Dobree, trans. E. O. Lorimer (London: Kegan Paul, Trench, Trubner and Co., Ltd., 1948) 363.

45. Folkenflik, "Patronage and the Poet Hero" 363.

46. Walter Raleigh, *Some Authors* (Oxford: Oxford University Press, 1923) 159; cited in *Dryden* lvii.

47. M. H. Abrams, ed., *The Norton Anthology of English Literature*, 5th ed., 2 vols., vol I (New York: Norton, 1986) 1788–89.

48. From Dryden's Dedication to *The Georgics* in *Dryden* 443.

49. Quotations from *The Castle of Indolence* are taken from James Thomson, *Liberty, The Castle of Indolence and Other Poems,* ed. James Sambrook (Oxford: Clarendon Press, 1986). See the note in this edition (391) regarding possible sources for these mechanical images.

50. Barrell, *English Literature in History* 87.

51. Adam Smith, *An Inquiry into the Nature and Causes of The Wealth of Nations,* ed. Edwin Cannan (New York: Modern Library, 1776, 1937) 5.

52. See Barrell's analysis of Smith's *examinations* as a solution to a "political problem" (29). I am suggesting that what Smith calls "contemplation" becomes an essential feature of professional work.

53. See Williams, *Keywords* 41.

54. Sir Joshua Reynolds, *Discourses on Art With Selections from The Idler,* ed. Stephen O. Mitchell (New York: Bobbs-Merrill, 1965) 142.

55. Michel Foucault, "The Father's 'No,'" in *Language, Counter-Memory, Practice: Selected Essays and Interviews by Michel Foucault,* ed. Donald F. Bouchard (Ithaca: Cornell University Press, 1977) 73.

56. "The psychological dimension in our culture," observes Foucault, "is the negation of epic perceptions" (75).

57. See *Historicity* 73 on the sense of occupational inadequacy in the late eighteenth century.

58. Among the earliest full-length treatments was Kurt Heinzelman, *The Economics of Imagination* (Amherst: University of Massachusetts Press, 1980). Heinzelman has also edited a special issue of *Texas Studies in Language and Literature* 33, no. 2 (1991) on the georgic and Romanticism; in that issue, see Kurt Heinzelman, "Roman Georgic in a Georgian Age: A Theory of Romantic Genre," 182–214 and Bruce Graver, "Wordsworth's Georgic Beginnings" 137–59. Also of interest is Bruce Graver, "Wordsworth's Georgic Pastoral: *Otium* and *Labor* in *Michael,*" *European Romantic Review* 1, no. 2 (1991): 119–34. Of particular relevance to my argument is Annabel Patterson's analysis of

Wordsworth's "hard pastoral whose entire rationale is georgic" in Annabel Patterson, *Pastoral and Ideology: Virgil to Valéry* (Berkeley: University of California Press, 1987) 263–84. This remarkable book supplements my argument in two important ways. First, she shows how "the arbiters of European culture since Virgil" have turned to the *Eclogues* "as a paradigm of the intellectual's dilemma" (10). That turn necessarily involves the georgic because "Virgilian pastoral would have indicated its liminal status on the borders of georgic even if the *Georgics* had never been written" (134). Thus my analysis of the Wordsworthian use of the pastoral/georgic distinction to portray "intellectual" behavior in *professional* terms can be placed within a history of earlier portrayals in different terms.

Second, Patterson, expanding on an earlier effort (Annabel Patterson, "Wordsworth's Georgic: Genre and Structure in *The Excursion*," *The Wordsworth Circle* 9, no. 2 [Spring 1978]: 145–54) also sees a mix of pastoral and georgic in Wordsworth. Her concern, however, is with the "ethical dilemma posed by rural labor" and Wordsworth's "solution" to it: an endorsement, both of its "necessity" and its "dignity," which makes the "hardship . . . *natural*" and therefore capable of "ennobl[ing] the spectator" (281–82). This analysis of "the socioeconomic conflicts that underwrite the literary ones" (280) is thus very useful, but the issue requires further attention, for her inquiry into Wordsworth's descriptions of his own work is subordinated to judging his depictions of, and reactions to, the labor of others. Having ignored the professional aspect of Wordsworth's mix, Patterson sees *The Excursion* as "an (aberrant) phase" between the early and late *Preludes*. But the call for "education" which she cites as indicative of *The Excursion*'s aberration is also, as I show here, the professional impetus behind all of the autobiographical efforts.

59. Among the most insightful discussions of Romantic pastoral are Herbert Lindenberger, "The Idyllic Moment: On Pastoral and Romanticism," *College English* 34, no. 3 (1972): 335–51 and Lore Metzger, *One Foot in Eden: Modes of Pastoral in Romantic Poetry* (Chapel Hill: University of North Carolina Press, 1986). Lindenberger stresses "The precariousness, the tensions, the historical dislocations which give idyllic moments their intensity—and also their momentariness" (351) in order to raise theoretical questions regarding literary periodization. Metzger asserts that "pastoral most frequently functions in English Romantic poetry to articulate radical ends of social reform attenuated by an insistence on conservative means" (xiv).

60. All quotations from *The Prelude* in this chapter, unless otherwise noted, are from the edition edited by Jonathan Wordsworth, M. H. Abrams, and Stephen Gill.

61. Patterson quotes approvingly (*Pastoral and Ideology*, 278) from Fredric Jameson, *The Political Unconscious: Narrative as a Socially Symbolic Act* (Ithaca: Cornell University Press, 1981) that

> one cannot without intellectual dishonesty assimilate the "production" of
> texts . . . to the production of goods by factory workers: writing and
> thinking are not alienated labor in that sense, and it is surely fatuous for
> intellectuals to seek to glamorize their tasks . . . by assimilating them
> to real work on the assembly line and to the experience of the resistance
> of matter in genuine manual labor. (45)

She uses the argument to caution against the "attractions" of Wordsworth's
"claim" of "the hard pastoral of the mind at serious work," citing Kurt Heinzelman's use of the phrase "'a labor theory of poetic value'" (in *The Economics of
the Imagination* 221). To point out that "such appropriations of Marxist terminology" are problematic, however, is only the first step in coming to terms
with the issue of Wordsworth, Romanticism, and the professionalization of
work. Historicizing the terminology itself is the next step: the relationship, for
example, between Romantic discourse and Jameson's key (and ultimately *self-*
glamorizing) adjectives—"real" and "genuine." For some angles on the Roman-
tic/Marxist connection, see my review of David Aers, Jonathan Cook, and
David Punter, *Romanticism and Ideology: Studies in English Writing, 1765–1830*
(London: Routledge, 1981) in *Comparative Literature Studies* 21, no. 2 (Summer
1984): 228–32 and also *Historicity* 142–43.

62. Other writers also brought the pastoral and georgic together in different ways, producing, as Patterson asserts in speaking of Sir Francis Bacon, a
"relationship between the two genres [which] became, in effect, a sign-system
for other sets of relationships and arguments" (134). Wordsworth's combination, for example, shows both continuity and discontinuity with Bacon's
"Georgics of the Mind." It does link intellectual labor with images from nature,
but both the nature of that kind of labor—from the inductive method of
Baconian science to Wordsworth's deep knowledge of the developing self—
and the nature of nature—from a source of "sweeten[ing]" (Patterson, *Pastoral
and Ideology* 137) images of order to a conceptual category that redefines "real"
feelings, language, and behavior—underwent significant change. In addition,
Wordsworth's mixture entails not the mutual modification described by Patterson (Bacon's "pastoralized georgic" 138), but the assertion of their simul-
taneity in the activity of the professional.

Chapter 5. The Lyricization of Labor

Epigraphs: For the first quotation, see Lonsdale, *Eighteenth-Century Women
Poets* 384. These lines are spoken by a "man of rank." I thank Maxine Berg for
the second quotation which she found in J. L. Hammond and B. Hammond,
The Skilled Labourer 1760–1832 (New York: Longmans, 1919, 1970) 149. See
Maxine Berg, "Women's Work, Mechanisation and the Early Phases of Indus-

trialisation in England," in *The Historical Meanings of Work*, ed. Patrick Joyce (Cambridge: Cambridge University Press, 1987) 78.

1. Daniel Albright, *Lyricality in English Literature* (Lincoln: University of Nebraska Press, 1985) 3.

2. Felix Schelling, *The English Lyric* (Port Washington, N.Y.: Kennikat Press, 1913, 1967).

3. Joseph Trapp, *Lectures on Poetry* (London, 1742) 203.

4. Anna Laetitia Aikin, "Preface," in *The Poetical Works of Mr. William Collins*, ed. Anna Laetitia Aikin (London, 1797) iii.

5. John Stuart Mill, "Thoughts on Poetry and Its Varieties," in *Collected Works of John Stuart Mill*, ed. John M. Robson and Jack Stillinger, vol. I (London: Routledge, 1981) 359. See Richard Feingold's discussion of this passage in Richard Feingold, *Moralized Song: The Character of Augustan Lyricism* (New Brunswick, N.J.: Rutgers University Press, 1989) 2–3.

6. Dale Spender and Janet Todd, eds., *British Women Writers: An Anthology from the Fourteenth Century to the Present* (New York: Peter Bedrick Books, 1989).

7. See Ian Watt, *The Rise of the Novel* (Berkeley: University of California Press, 1957); Nancy Armstrong, *Desire and Domestic Fiction: A Political History of the Novel* (New York: Oxford University Press, 1987); John Bender, *Imagining the Penitentiary: Fiction and the Architecture of the Mind in Eighteenth-Century England* (Chicago: University of Chicago Press, 1987); and Michael McKeon, *The Origins of the English Novel 1600–1740* (Baltimore: Johns Hopkins University Press, 1987).

8. See *Historicity* 15–36.

9. Paul de Man, "Lyric and Modernity," in *Forms of Lyric: Selected Papers from the English Institute*, ed. Reuben A. Brower (New York: Columbia University Press, 1970) 151.

10. Chaviva Hošek and Patricia Parker, eds., *Lyric Poetry: Beyond New Criticism* (Ithaca: Cornell University Press, 1985) 17.

11. Cohen, "History and Genre" 210.

12. Eric Partridge, *Eighteenth Century English Romantic Poetry (Up till the Publication of the "Lyrical Ballads," 1798)* (Paris, 1924; rpt. London: Norwood Editions, 1979).

13. Joel Fineman, *Shakespeare's Perjured Eye: The Invention of Poetic Subjectivity in the Sonnets* (Berkeley: University of California Press, 1986).

14. Thomas Percy, *Reliques of Ancient English Poetry Consisting of Old Heroic Ballads, Songs, and Other Pieces of Our Earlier Poets, Together with Some Few of Later Date*, ed. Henry B. Wheatley (New York: Dover Publications, 1765, 1886, 1966) 339.

15. McNally, *Political Economy* 37.

16. G. K. Hunter, "Drab and Golden Lyrics of the Renaissance," in *Forms of*

Lyric: Selected Papers from the English Institute, ed. Reuben A. Brower (New York: Columbia University Press, 1970) 13.

17. Stuart Curran, *Poetic Form and British Romanticism* (New York: Oxford University Press, 1986) 67. David Radcliffe makes an important argument linking the "lyric ode as a critical genre" to the formation of "culture" in David Hill Radcliffe, "*Ossian* and the Genres of Culture," *Studies in Romanticism* 31, no. 2 (Summer 1992): 230.

18. See McNally, *Political Economy* 37–40.

19. Norman Maclean, "From Action to Image: Theories of the Lyric in the Eighteenth Century," in *Critics and Criticism*, ed. R. S. Crane, W. R. Keast, Richard McKeon, Norman Maclean, Elder Olson, and Bernard Weinberg (Chicago: University of Chicago Press, 1952) 408–60 and Roger Lonsdale, ed., *The New Oxford Book of Eighteenth Century Verse* (Oxford: Oxford University Press, 1984). "There are many, many lyrics written in the period," observes David Lindley in David Lindley, *Lyric*, ed. John D. Jump, Critical Idiom, vol. 44 (London: Methuen, 1985) 67.

20. Clifford Geertz, *The Interpretation of Cultures* (New York: Basic Books, 1973) 25 and Ralph Cohen, "Introduction," in *The Future of Literary Theory*, ed. Ralph Cohen (New York: Routledge, 1989) xvii–xx.

21. See Howard Caygill, *The Art of Judgement* (New York: Blackwell, 1989); John Guillory, *Cultural Capital: The Problem of Literary Canon Formation* (Chicago: University of Chicago Press, 1993); and Stephen Copley, "Introduction," in *Literature and the Social Order in Eighteenth-Century England*, ed. Stephen Copley, World and Word Series (London: Croom Helm, 1984) 1–21.

22. John Foster, *Class Struggle and the Industrial Revolution: Early Industrial Capitalism in Three English Towns* (New York: St. Martin's Press, 1974) 19.

23. Stephen Marglin, "What Do Bosses Do?: The Origins and Functions of Hierarchy in Capitalist Production," *Review of Radical Political Economics* 6 (1974): 62. See the discussion of this essay in Stewart Clegg and David Dunkerley, *Organization, Class and Control*, ed. John Rex, International Library of Sociology (London: Routledge, 1980) 50–53.

24. Andrew Ure, *The Philosophy of Manufactures; or, An Exposition of the Scientific, Moral, and Commercial Economy of the Factory System of Great Britain* (New York: A. M. Kelley, 1835, 1967) 383.

25. R. A. L. Smith, *Canterbury Cathedral Priory* (Cambridge: Cambridge University Press, 1943) 125.

26. R. E. Pahl, *Divisions of Labour* (Oxford: Basil Blackwell, 1984) 47.

27. See Paul Mantoux, *The Industrial Revolution in the Eighteenth Century: An Outline of the Beginnings of the Modern Factory System in England* (Chicago: University of Chicago Press, 1961, 1983) 451–56 and John Rule, *The Experience of Labour in Eighteenth-Century English Industry* (New York: St. Martin's Press, 1981) 95–123.

28. *Commons Journals* (17 July 1806) Report on Calico Printers' Petition reprinted in *Workers and Employers: Documents on Trade Unions and Industrial Relations in Britain Since the Early Nineteenth Century*, ed. J. T. Ward and W. Hamish Fraser (London: Macmillan, 1980) 12.

29. See *Historicity* 46–56.

30. See Lonsdale, *Woman Poets* 506–7.

31. See *Prose* III.29 and *Historicity* 54–55.

32. "Inscription in a Beautiful Retreat called Fairy Bower," in Lonsdale, *Women Poets* 326–27.

33. For sonnet lovers, by the way, the apostrophe separates an octet of stanzas from a concluding sestet.

34. Rule points out that "at the time of the passing of the General Combination Acts in 1799 and 1800 there were already more than 40 acts prohibiting combinations of workmen to raise wages (*Experience of Labour* 174). Roughly the same material is also available in John Rule, *The Labouring Classes in Early Industrial England, 1750–1850*, ed. J. Stevenson, Themes in British Social History (London: Longmans, 1986) 259–60.

35. See *Workers and Employers* 11 and Malcolm I. Thomis, *The Town Labourer and the Industrial Revolution* (London: B. T. Batsford Ltd., 1974) 139.

36. See Foster's statistics in *Class Struggle* 49–51.

37. Review of *The Excursion* (November 1814) in Francis Jeffrey, *Contributions to the "Edinburgh Review"* (New York: D. Appleton and Company, 1866) 457.

38. Francis Jeffrey, "Combinations of Workmen: Substance of the Speech of Francis Jeffrey, Esq.," in *Repeal of the Combination Acts: Five Pamphlets and One Broadside 1825*, ed. Kenneth E. Carpenter (New York: Arno Press, 1825) 1.

39. William Thompson, *Labor Rewarded: The Claims of Labor and Capital Conciliated or How to Secure to Labor the Whole Products of Its Exertions* (New York: Burt Franklin, 1827, 1971) 1.

40. Thomas Hodgskin, *Labor Defended Against The Claims of Capital or the Unproductiveness of Capital Proved with Reference to the Present Combinations Amongst Journeymen*, Reprints of Economic Classics (New York: A. M. Kelley, 1825, 1922, 1963) 86–87.

41. "To Mr. [S. T.] C[olerid]ge" in Lonsdale, *Women Poets* 310–11.

42. Samuel Johnson, *Lives of the English Poets*, ed. George Birbeck, vol. 1 (Oxford: Clarendon Press, 1905) 194, 171.

43. I am referring to "Ode on the Poetical Character" and *The Prelude*.

Chapter 6. Periodicals, Authorship, and the Romantic Rise of the Novel

Epigraphs: The second quotation is from John Anderson, "A Brutal and Bleak L.A. Story," *Newsday*, 26 May 1993: 63.

1. See James Raven, *Judging New Wealth: Popular Publishing and Responses to Commerce in England 1750–1800* (Oxford: Clarendon Press, 1992) 31–41. Raven emphasizes that "reclaiming the dimensions of this growth in the book trade is a task still embarrassed by the unevenness of late eighteenth-century bibliographical evidence and research" (33), but his compilations of new *English Short Title Catalogue* data, his own research, and other recent bibliographic efforts provide us with our most comprehensive and reliable picture of print production during this period. Two particularly important advantages of his work for my argument are: 1) his data set is far more inclusive than those offered even just a few years earlier (37); and 2) his classifications differentiate among new titles, editions and reprints, and magazine fiction. See also James Raven, *British Fiction, 1750–1770: A Chronological Check-List of Prose Fiction Printed in Britain and Ireland* (Newark: University of Delaware Press, 1987). Cheryl Turner's figures for fiction by women mirror Raven's totals, including "a dramatic, unparalleled surge in the 1780s." See *Living by the Pen: Women Writers in the Eighteenth Century* (London: Routledge, 1992) 39.

2. *The Analytical Review* XXI (February 1795) reprinted in *Novel and Romance 1700–1800: A Documentary Record*, ed. Ioan Williams (New York: Barnes and Noble, 1970) 396.

3. For useful discussions of the thematizing of writing in *Caleb Williams*, see Jacqueline Miller, "The Imperfect Tale: Articulation, Rhetoric, and Self in *Caleb Williams*," *Criticism* 20 (1978): 366–82 and Jerrold E. Hogle, "The Texture of Self in Godwin's *Things as They Are*," *Boundary 2* 7, no. 2 (1979): 261–81. John P. Zomchick makes use of their work to connect the problem of writing the self to "juridical techniques" in *Family and the Law in Eighteenth-Century Fiction: The Public Conscience in the Private Sphere* (Cambridge: Cambridge University Press, 1993) 177–92. B. J. Tysdahl, *William Godwin as Novelist* (London: Athlone, 1981) 28–76 and Pamela Clemit, *The Godwinian Novel: The Rational Fictions of Godwin, Brockden Brown, Mary Shelley* (Oxford: Clarendon Press, 1993) 70–102 focus on the different effects of different kinds of writing in their generic analyses of *Caleb*.

4. David S. Kaufer and Kathleen M. Carley also stress the importance of seeing change as a mixture of continuity and discontinuity:

> Stories of the dominance of new media are simple and elegant but they often leave embarrassing holes (e.g. that newer media often increase the contexts of use for the older media). Writing did not squelch speaking but created new contexts for speech; print created new contexts for writing; electronic communication proliferated the contexts for paper and printing.

See David S. Kaufer and Kathleen M. Carley, *Communication at a Distance: The Influence of Print on Sociocultural Organization and Change*, ed. Dolf Zillmann and Jennings Bryant, Communication (Hillsdale, N.J.: Lawrence Erlbaum Associates, 1993) 6.

5. The speakers, in the order of my description of their papers, were Nancy Armstrong, Margaret Doody, and William Warner. The audience member was John Richetti. My purpose in calling attention to these conferences is not to suggest that they effected a magical transition from "old" work to "new," but to emphasize a *shared* sense of accomplishments and possibilities. I do not, of course, have the space here to list the individual accomplishments in eighteenth-century studies, Romanticism, literary theory, and other disciplines, particularly sociology and anthropology, which set the stage for these conferential moments.

6. In focusing on the desire for fiction, and in turning to places like periodicals to find it, this essay supplements chronologically, and complements conceptually, the efforts of J. Paul Hunter and John Richetti. In *Before Novels: The Cultural Contexts of Eighteenth-Century English Fiction* (New York: Norton, 1990), Hunter taps an extraordinary range of late seventeenth- and early eighteenth-century materials to show, in part, how "all texts—at least all texts that find and create readers—construct a field in which desires and provisions compete" (x). Richetti, in the pioneering *Popular Fiction Before Richardson: Narrative Patterns 1700–1739* (Oxford: Clarendon Press, 1969), reconsiders the rise of the novel in relationship to "popular" literature from the first four decades of the eighteenth century.

7. Anthony J. Little, *Deceleration in the Eighteenth-Century British Economy* (London: Croom Helm, 1976) 5.

8. Phyllis Deane, *The First Industrial Revolution* (Cambridge: Cambridge University Press, 1967) 11. See Little's discussion 99.

9. From Charles Jenner, *The Placid Man: or, Memoirs of Sir Charles Beville*, 1770, reprinted in Barnett, *Eighteenth-Century British Novelists* 128.

10. From the *Edinburgh Review*, November 1783 cited in Alison Adburgham, *Women in Print: Writing Women and Women's Magazines From the Restoration to the Accession of Victoria* (London: Allen and Unwin, 1972) 153.

11. Kernan, *Samuel Johnson and the Impact of Print* (Princeton, Princeton University Press, 1987) 61.

12. "The Editor introduces herself . . . and her 'Associates,'" from vol. I, book I, 1–7, reprinted in Haywood, *The Female Spectator* 17–20.

13. Michel Foucault, "What Is an Author?," in *Language, Counter-Memory, Practice: Selected Essays and Interviews by Michel Foucault* 123.

14. For a fascinating study of earlier conceptions of the author, see A. J. Minnis, *Medieval Theory of Authorship: Scholastic Literary Attitudes in the Later Middle Ages*, 2nd ed. (Aldershot, U.K.: Wildwood House Ltd., 1984, 1988).

15. Robert Mayo, *The English Novel in the Magazines 1740–1815 With a Catalogue of 1375 Magazine Novels and Novelettes* (Evanston, Ill.: Northwestern Uni-

versity Press, 1962) 273–92. Smollett's difficulties with the *British Magazine* (1760–63) occurred despite his reputation being in part the product of his successful launch of the *Critical Review* (1756). Mayo tries to attribute Smollett's problems and those of Lennox to their efforts being "too elevated for the common reader's tastes and interests," but he admits some puzzlement, particularly since the latter's *Lady's Museum* (1760–61) featured works that "were later to enjoy a considerable popularity as repertory pieces" (291).

16. Jurgen Habermas, *The Structural Transformation of the Public Sphere; An Inquiry into a Category of Bourgeois Society*, trans. Thomas Burger and Frederick Lawrence (Cambridge, Mass.: MIT Press, 1989) 30.

17. Anne Dutton, *A Letter to Such of the Servants of Christ, Who May Have Any Scruple about the Lawfulness of PRINTING Any Thing Written by a Woman*, 1743, reprinted in *Women in the Eighteenth Century: Constructions of Femininity*, ed. Vivien Jones (New York: Routledge, 1990) 159.

18. Graham Burchell, "Peculiar Interests: Civil Society and Governing 'The System of Natural Liberty,'" in *The Foucault Effect: Studies in Governmentality With Two Lectures and an Interview with Michel Foucault*, ed. Graham Burchell, Colin Gordon, and Peter Miller (Chicago: University of Chicago Press, 1991) 129.

19. Robert Kiely, *The Romantic Novel in England* (Cambridge, Mass.: Harvard University Press, 1972) 121.

20. See Robert G. Blake, *The Edinburgh Magazine*, in *British Literary Magazines: The Augustan Age and the Age of Johnson, 1698–1788*, ed. Alvin Sullivan (Westport, Conn.: Greenwood Press, 1983) 92.

21. For information about other early women's periodicals, see the essay by Deborah Ayer Sitter and John Sitter, *The Female Spectator* in Sullivan 120–23; Kathryn Shevelow, *Women and Print Culture: The Construction of Femininity in the Early Periodical* (London: Routledge, 1989); and Adburgham, *Women in Print*.

22. Walter Graham, *English Literary Periodicals* (New York: Octagon Books, 1966) 151–71.

23. Mayo estimates that "at least half of the so-called 'original' material printed in the miscellanies from about 1770–1815 was produced by industrious amateurs" (306). For an analysis of earlier instances of the reader-as-writer phenomenon in terms of gender, see Shevelow 58–92.

24. Jon Klancher, *The Making of English Reading Audiences, 1790–1832* (Madison: University of Wisconsin Press, 1987) 20.

25. See the essay by Nathaniel Teich on *The Analytical Review* in Sullivan, *British Literary Magazines: The Augustan Age and the Age of Johnson, 1698–1788* 11–14 and his essay on *The British Critic* in *British Literary Magazines: The Romantic Age, 1789–1836*, ed. Alvin Sullivan (Westport, Conn.: Greenwood Press, 1983) 57–62.

26. For details on the "expansion of the market for feminine reading matter," see Adburgham 142–76.

27. The essay is an appendix to William Godwin, *Things As They Are; or, The Adventures of Caleb Williams*, ed. Maurice Hindle (London: Penguin, 1794, 1988). Godwin refers to "romance or novel" on p. 368.

Chapter 7. The Novel, the Nation, and the Naturalization of Writing

Epigraphs: The first quotation is from Samuel Miller, *A Brief Retrospect of the Eighteenth Century: Part First in Two Volumes Containing a Sketch of the Revolutions and Improvements in Science, Arts, and Literature During that Period*, 2 vols., vol. II (New York: Burt Franklin, 1803; rpt. New York: Lenox Hill, 1970) 172. The second quotation is from Leslie Garis, "Susan Sontag Finds Romance," *New York Times Magazine*, 2 August 1992: 20–23, 31, 43.

1. Williams, *Writing in Society* 7.

2. William Warner, "The Elevation of the Novel in England: Hegemony and Literary History," *ELH* 59 (1992): 577–96.

3. Donna Tartt, *The Secret History* (New York: Random House, 1992).

4. Eliza Haywood, Preface to *The Fair Hebrew: or, a True, but Secret History of Two Jewish Ladies, Who Lately Resided in London*, 1729, reprinted in Williams, *Novel and Romance* 85.

5. Deborah Ross, *Romance, Realism, and Women's Contribution to the Novel* (Lexington: University Press of Kentucky, 1991) 1.

6. Michel de Certeau, *The Practice of Everyday Life*, trans. Steven Rendall (Berkeley: University of California Press, 1984) 134–35.

7. Joseph Bartolomeo argues that "all too routinely, this critical commentary [on the novel] has been consigned to the footnote, the aside—or, occasionally, the chapter—and has been invoked largely for utilitarian purposes in literary histories, surveys of the genre, and critical biographies." He urges that we "mov[e] the discourse to the foreground" to "demonstrate the constitutive cultural role it played, its success in forging a place for the genre in literary and popular culture." I share this desire to "foreground" the critical; for Bartolomeo, however, the concept of *genre* itself remains undisturbed, maintaining the novel's separate stature as a creative generic object whose "rise" his history of criticism helps to explain. I use the term *novelism* in an effort not just to foreground the critical, but—in specific, historical ways—to confound it with the creative and thus denaturalize standard notions of genre and of literature. See Joseph Bartolomeo, *A New Species of Criticism: Eighteenth-Century Discourse on the Novel* (Newark: University of Delaware Press, 1994) 10.

8. Aphra Behn, *Oroonoko, The Rover and Other Works*, ed. Janet Todd (London: Penguin, 1992) 131.

9. Delarivier Manley, *New Atalantis*, ed. Rosalind Ballaster (London: Penguin, 1991) 30.

10. Delarivier Manley, Preface to *The Secret History of Queen Zarah and the Zarazians*, reprinted in Barnett, *Eighteenth-Century British Novelists* 22–27.

11. John Sutton L. Jr., "The Source of Mrs. Manley's Preface to *Queen Zarah*," *Modern Philology* 82 (1984): 167–72.

12. See Shaftesbury's comparisons of the arts, particularly in "Advice to an Author," in Earl of Shaftesbury, *Characteristics of Men, Manners, Opinions, Times, etc.*, ed. John M. Robertson, vol. I (Gloucester, Mass.: P. Smith, 1963) 103–234.

13. Charles Jenner, from *The Placid Man: or, Memoirs of Sir Charles Beville*, 1770, reprinted in Barnett, *Eighteenth-Century British Novelists* 124.

14. Raven, *Judging New Wealth* 13.

15. W. Austin Flanders, *Structures of Experience: History, Society, and Personal Life in the Eighteenth-Century British Novel* (Columbia: University of South Carolina Press, 1984) 180.

16. Wuthnow, *Communities of Discourse* 254–64.

17. The accommodation was also signaled by the redeployment of the critical elements in writing. They were not eliminated, of course, but increasingly partitioned off as a separate discourse: *criticism* came to serve the newly forming discipline of English Literature—a move that amounted, in national terms, to the institutionalization of a now comfortably loyal opposition.

18. Newman, *The Rise of English Nationalism* 240.

19. David Simpson, *Romanticism, Nationalism, and the Revolt Against Theory* (Chicago: University of Chicago Press, 1993).

20. Ernest Gellner, *Nations and Nationalism*, ed. R. I. Moore, New Perspectives on the Past (Oxford: Basil Blackwell, 1983).

21. In looking at earlier periods, Newman does engage the novel through particular novelists, especially Fielding and Smollett, but the sections on the early nineteenth century focus on the poets. Austen and Scott do not appear in the index. Let me emphasize, however, that Newman's forays—as a historian— into Literature were groundbreaking in 1987, particularly his treatment of the late eighteenth century.

22. See my discussion in *Historicity* 127–38.

23. Clara Reeve, "Preface to *The Old English Baron*," reprinted in Barnett, *Eighteenth-Century British Novelists on the Novel* 137.

24. Henry Mackenzie, *The Lounger* 20 (18 June 18 1785) reprinted in Williams, *Novel and Romance* 329.

25. Williams, *Novel and Romance* 22.

26. Marilyn Butler, *Jane Austen and the War of Ideas* (Oxford: Clarendon Press, 1975).

27. The word *new* appears in the review of Austen by Scott cited below. The

other terms are from a review of *Caleb Williams* in The *Analytical Review* XXI (February 1795) reprinted in Williams, *Novel and Romance* 396.

28. These words are Scott's in an unsigned article in the *Quarterly Review* XIV (October 1815) reprinted in *Jane Austen: The Critical Heritage*, ed. B. C. Southam (London: Routledge, 1968) 63. Also see Richard Whately in the *Quarterly Review* XXIV (January 1821) reprinted in Southam.

29. See my discussion of development in relationship to the novel in *Historicity* 125–47.

30. Michel de Certeau, *Heterologies "Discourse on the Other,"* ed. Wlad Godzich and Jochen Schulte-Sasse, trans. Brian Massumi, Theory and History of Literature, vol. 17 (Minneapolis: University of Minnesota Press, 1986) 201–2.

31. John Jeffrey, "Austen on Film," *Sunday Times Culture*, 17 March 1996: 24.

32. Summer 1996, however, saw "a mighty tide of rejected literature known wearily in the trade as returns." See Doreen Carvajal, "The Summer of No Reading," *New York Times*, 1 August 1996: D1, D7.

Chapter 8. What We Remember: The Case of Austen

Epigraphs: The first quotation is from Faye Weldon, "Jane Austen and the Pride of Purists," *New York Times*, 8 October 1995: 15. The second quotation is from an advertisement in the *New York Times*, 28 July 1996: H13.

1. I am referring to the movie *Independence Day*.

2. Anthony Lane, "The Dumbing of Emma," *The New Yorker*, 6 August 1996: 76–77.

3. My thanks to the organizer of this 1993 session, Charles Rzepka.

4. See *Historicity* 125–47.

5. Claudia Johnson, *Jane Austen: Women, Politics, and the Novel* (Chicago: University of Chicago Press, 1988).

6. It is, of course, a device that current critics of the supposed excesses of political correctness still deploy shamelessly in the 1990s.

7. Janet Todd, *The Sign of Angellica: Women, Writing and Fiction, 1660–1800* (New York: Columbia University Press, 1989) 227.

8. By using the term *forgetting*, I am trying to convey a sense of loss and the possibility of recovery. I do not want, however, to naturalize the loss as simply a psychological lapse; in fact, my purpose in this last section is to specify some of the key socioeconomic and institutional ways in which the exclusion worked.

9. Flanders, *Structures of Experience* 172, 180.

10. Peter Danahy, *The Feminization of the Novel* (Gainesville: University of Florida Press, 1991) vii, 47. Pat Spacks's canny arguments for the "essential subversiveness of the eighteenth-century novel" highlight efforts "to reconcile 'masculine' and 'feminine' principles of organization and of action." See Patri-

cia Meyer Spacks, *Desire and Truth: Functions of Plot in Eighteenth-Century English Novels* (Chicago: University of Chicago Press, 1994) 11, 237.

11. Ross, *Romance, Realism* 3–4.

12. See my discussion of Whately in *Historicity* 138–39.

13. Jan Fergus, *Jane Austen: A Literary Life* (London: Macmillan, 1991).

14. See the description of this incident in Deborah Kaplan, *Jane Austen Among Women* (Baltimore: Johns Hopkins University Press, 1992) 100.

15. Fergus argues persuasively against Jane Austen being the author of a letter signed "Sophia Sentiment" published in *Loiterer* 9 (61).

16. Jane Austen, *Northanger Abbey*, ed. R. W. Chapman, 3rd ed., 5 vols., *The Novels of Jane Austen: The Text Based on Collation of the Early Editions* (New York: Oxford University Press, 1817, 1933) 38.

17. Hierarchization was, of course, already taking place earlier in the century but could not fully assume its modern form of high and low culture until the instituting of copyright and the takeoff in publication at the close of the century.

18. Review of *Pride and Prejudice* by William Gifford in *The Quarterly Review*, cited in F. B. Pinion, *A Jane Austen Companion: A Critical Survey and Reference Book* (London: Macmillan, 1973) 181.

19. Klancher, *Making of English Reading Audiences* 20.

20. David Lodge, ed., *Jane Austen, "Emma": A Casebook* (London: Macmillan, 1968, rev. 1991) 14.

21. Scott's review, as I pointed out in the last chapter, was published anonymously in the *Quarterly Review* XIV (1815): 188–201, but it actually appeared in March 1816. It is reprinted in Southam 58–69.

22. These reviews, all published in 1816, are conveniently collected in Lodge 43–45.

23. Introduction, in Jane Austen, *Catherine and Other Writings*, ed. Margaret Anne Doody (Oxford: Oxford University Press, 1993) xxxviii.

24. Let me reemphasize that I use words like "threaten" and "safety" not as aesthetic, but as historical markers—markers that can help me describe the naturalization of writing in the eighteenth century.

25. Samuel Johnson, *"Rambler* 4, 31 March 1750," in *The Yale Edition of the Works of Samuel Johnson*, ed. W. J. Bate, John M. Bullitt, and C. F. Powell, vol. III (New Haven: Yale University Press, 1963) 19–25.

26. The hierarchizing thus transposed socioeconomic difference into aesthetic value.

27. Janet Todd, *Sensibility: An Introduction* (London: Methuen, 1986) 6, 4. Todd points out that, "at the same time" readers are "forced to respond to the emotion conveyed," the "devices" of sentiment—"asterisks, dashes, meandering narrative and fragmentation"—indicate "the inadequacy of the medium—language—in which, despite their intrusive presence, most of the business of the

work is still transacted." In regard to the history of writing, then, the sentimental can be seen as transitional: both enacting (acting out?) writing's power and, by articulating it as inadequate, participating in the taming I am describing (4). For the relationship between Austen's use of language and "real feeling," including the issue of the inadequacy of that language, see James Thompson, *Between Self and World: The Novels of Jane Austen* (University Park: Pennsylvania State University Press, 1988).

28. Richard Simpson, "Jane Austen," *North British Review*, LII (1870) 129–32, reprinted in Lodge 53–57. Lodge cites this essay as "one of the finest studies of Jane Austen ever written" (16).

29. None of these hooks is necessarily unique to Austen, and no single one of them can alone account for her disciplinary fate. Other hooks, as well as the ways they combine, need to be identified and studied.

30. The reference to "Ivory" is in R. W. Chapman, ed., *Jane Austen's Letters: To Her Sister Cassandra and Others*, 2nd ed. (London: Oxford University Press, 1952) 468–69. "Bow-wow" is reprinted in Southam 106. Claudia Johnson notes an increasingly "rigid distinction" by 1815 between "male" and "female" novels (xiv).

31. Scott uses this formula of "more Romantic incident" and "national character" to help to distinguish Edgeworth from Austen, but it certainly applies to his differences with Austen as well. See an enlightening discussion of Scott's efforts to subsume romance in Ian Duncan, *Modern Romance and Transformations of the Novel: The Gothic, Scott, Dickens* (Cambridge: Cambridge University Press, 1992).

32. See, for example, Todd's description of Wollstonecraft's fate in *Angellica* 214–15. The idea of "re-masculinization" is described in Gary Kelly, *Revolutionary Feminism: The Mind and Career of Mary Wollstonecraft* (London: Macmillan, 1992) 227.

33. See, for example, Susan Faludi, *Backlash: The Undeclared War Against American Women* (New York: Crown Publishers, 1991). Also, Susan Jeffords, *The Remasculinization of America: Gender and the Vietnam War* (Bloomington: Indiana University Press, 1989).

Chapter 9. How We Forgot: Reproduction and Reverse Vicariousness

Epigraph: Kennedy Fraser, "Piper Pipe That Song Again," *New Yorker*, 27 May 1996: 130.

1. I present this chapter as a mixing of kinds in order both to highlight the use of numbers as evidence and to stress that they must be handled with care—particularly in regard to issues in which they have been historically misused, such as those involving women. Like other kinds of evidence, quantitative data are subject to manipulation and misinterpretation. I deploy them here not as

superior or unilaterally conclusive, but, in combination with other kinds, as a useful means of rethinking questions and answers posed by standard literary histories.

2. Anthony Lane, "Smack in the Face," *New Yorker*, 22 July 1996: 78.

3. "The Introduction" in Anne Finch, *The Poems of Anne Countess of Winchilsea*, ed. Myra Reynolds (Chicago: University of Chicago Press, 1903) 4.

4. Part II of *A Serious Proposal to the Ladies* 159.

5. Stephen Copley, "Commerce, Conversation and Politeness in the Early Eighteenth-Century Periodical," *British Journal for Eighteenth-Century Studies* 18, no. 1 (Spring 1995): 72.

6. Charles McGrath, "Loose Canon," *New Yorker*, 26 September 1994: 106.

7. Neither is this notion condescending to any particular group, for Kaufer and Carley posit it as common to everyone experiencing the communicative distance of print.

8. Roger Schofield, "British Population Change, 1700–1830," in *The Economic History of Britain Since 1700*, ed. Roderick Floud and Donald McCloskey, vol. I (Cambridge: Cambridge University Press, 1994) 72.

9. Colley, *Britons* 237–81.

10. R. E. Pahl, *Divisions of Labour* 36.

11. See Duncan Bythell, "Women in the Workforce," in *The Industrial Revolution and British Society*, ed. Patrick K. O'Brien and Roland Quinault (Cambridge: Cambridge University Press, 1993) 39–40. For further information on changes in women's work during the late eighteenth century, see Deborah Valenze, *The First Industrial Woman* (New York: Oxford University Press, 1995); Ann Kussmaul, *A General View of the Rural Economy of England, 1538–1840*, ed. Peter Laslett, Roger Schofield, E. A. Shofield, and Daniel Scott Smith Cambridge Studies in Population, Economy and Society in Past Time (Cambridge: Cambridge University Press, 1990); Harriet Bradley, *Men's Work, Women's Work: A Sociological History of the Sexual Division of Labour in Employment*, ed. Michelle Stanworth, Feminist Perspectives (Minneapolis: University of Minnesota Press, 1989) 27–49; Louise A. Tilly and Joan W. Scott, *Women, Work, and Family* (New York: Methuen, 1978, 1987) 11–60; Maxine Berg, *The Age of Manufactures: Industry, Innovation and Work in Britain 1700–1820* (New York: Oxford University Press, 1986) 15–178; and Ivy Pinchbeck, *Women Workers and the Industrial Revolution 1750–1850* (London: Virago, 1930, 1969) 7–66.

12. See Todd, *Angellica* 135 and Lonsdale, *Women Poets* xxxvii.

13. Lonsdale, *Women Poets* 427–29.

14. Mary Wollstonecraft, *A Vindication of the Rights of Woman*, ed. Carol H. Poston (New York: Norton, 1792, 1975) 9.

15. Lonsdale, *Women Poets* xxxviii.

16. See Prest, *The Professions in Early Modern England* 14.

17. John O. Hayden, "Introduction" in Sullivan, *Magazines: The Romantic Age* xvii.

18. John O. Hayden, essay on the *Edinburgh Review* in Sullivan, *Magazines: The Romantic Age* 139, 141.

19. Michael, *The Teaching of English* 377.

20. See a shrewd analysis of how late eighteenth-century anthologizing worked against women in *Romantic Women Poets 1770–1838*, ed. Andrew Ashfield (Manchester: Manchester University Press, 1995) xi–xviii.

21. Simpson made this point at a session called "Romanticism Without Literature: Parallel Universes" held at the 1996 Conference of the North American Society for the Study of Romanticism, in Boston.

22. Ken Auletta, "Behind the Times," *The New Yorker*, 10 June 1996: 48.

INDEX

LIBRARY OF CONGRESS CATALOGING-IN-PUBLICATION DATA

Siskin, Clifford.
    The work of writing : literature and social change in Britain, 1700–1830 /
Clifford Siskin.
        p.   cm.
Includes bibliographical references (p.   ) and index.
ISBN 0-8018-5696-5 (alk. paper)
    1. English literature—18th century—History and criticism.   2. Author-
ship—Social aspects—Great Britain—History—18th century.   3. Authorship—Social aspects—Great Britain—History—19th century.   4. Literature
and society—Great Britain—History—18th century.   5. Literature and society—Great Britain—History—19th century.   6. English literature—19th century—History and criticism.   7. Social change—Great Britain—History—
18th century.   8. Social change—Great Britain—History—19th century.
I. Title.
PR448.S64S57   1998
820.9′005—dc21   97-20656
                                                               CIP